Collecting Colonialism

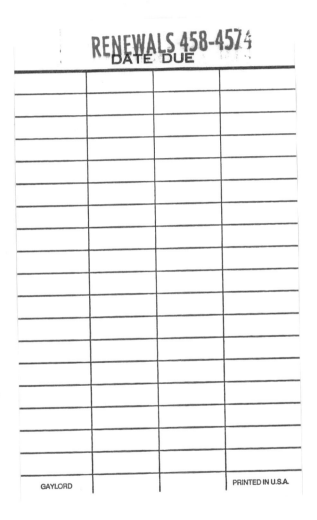

RENEWALS 458-4574

DATE DUE

Collecting Colonialism

Material Culture and Colonial Change

Chris Gosden and Chantal Knowles

BERG

Oxford • New York

First published in 2001 by
Berg
Editorial offices:
150 Cowley Road, Oxford, OX4 1JJ, UK
838 Broadway, Third Floor, New York, NY 10003-4812, USA

Berg is an imprint of Oxford International Publishers Ltd.

Library of Congress Cataloging-in-Publication Data
A catalogue record for this book is available from the Library of Congress.

British Library Cataloguing-in-Publication Data
A catalogue record for this book is available from the British Library.

ISBN 1 85973 403 0 (Cloth)
1 85973 408 1 (Paper)

Typeset by JS Typesetting, Wellingborough, Northants
Printed in the United Kingdom by Biddles Ltd, Guildford and King's Lynn

To Alexander (Sandy) Forrester and Jean Weddell (C.G.)
To Ian and Wendy Knowles (C.K.)

Contents

List of Figures

Maps

Tables

Acknowledgements

This project represents a form of multi-sited ethnography, as it was carried out in four museums and various archives. We have been amazed at the generosity with which our requests to work on collections for several weeks at a time were received. The project was funded by the Leverhulme Trust (F/756/A) to whom we are extremely grateful as this enabled both of us to visit all the collections described and analysed here and to carry out the writing up. In addition the British Academy (SS-2043/APN7292) gave Chris Gosden a personal grant which enabled us to follow up J.A. Todd's collection once it came to light after the project was underway.

In many ways this project has derived out of two different areas of work and inspiration. The first is the Pitt Rivers Museum, where there is so much new thought about approaching museum collections and material culture in general. This project is one outcome of these conversations. The second is the informal network of New Britain scholars who have such a depth of knowledge and abiding interest in the area: Jim Specht, Glenn Summerhayes, Christina Pavlides and Robin Torrence have all influenced our work in fundamental ways.

In each of the four museums in which we worked we were made welcome and were given constant attention and help from all members of staff, making our stays enjoyable and the work very productive. At the Pitt Rivers Museum we would particularly like to thank, Jeremy Coote, Marina de Alarcon, Julia Nicholson and Alison Petch for their help and guidance with the object collections and documentation, Elizabeth Edwards, Emma Dean, Chris Morton, and Gwyneira Isaac for their help with the Manuscript and Photograph collections. In the Field Museum, Chicago we particularly thank John Terrell, Janice Klein and Wil Grewe-Mullins as well as the rest of the Curatorial and administrative staff. A particular thanks must go to Rob Welsch, now based at Dartmouth University, whose work on Lewis made our task so much easier. In Basel Museum der Kulturen, particular thanks are due to Christian Kaufmann, Antje Denner, and Sylvia Ohnemus. In Sydney at the Australian Museum expert assistance and guidance was received from Jim Specht, Liz Bonshek and Nan Goodsell.

Much of the background detail to the collectors and the region's colonial history was gathered in archives across the globe. In addition, information on small West New Britain collections was received from many museums. Anita Herle and Gillian Crowther at the Cambridge University Museum of Archaeology and Anthropology, Godfrey Waller at Cambridge University Library Archives. Dorota Starzecka and

Acknowledgements

Jill Hassell at the British Museum Department of Ethnography, formerly the Museum of Mankind. Nynke Dorhout, and Barbara Isaac at the Peabody Museum, Harvard University. Tom Harding for his researches into the life and career of J. A. Todd, now deposited with the Australian Museum. The staff at SOAS who gave us access to the London Missionary Society archives. Tom Maschio for discussing contemporary material culture from the region. Alan Davies at the State Library of New South Wales for giving us access to and assistance with the H.L. Downing collection of photographs held there and for putting us in touch with his daughter, Mrs Diana McLeish who looked after Jim Specht and the two of us for lunch one day as we pored over her father's diaries, notebooks and photographs.

While in Australia we visited many archives and met many people who were willing to share their expertise and knowledge with us. Monica Wehner and Euan Maidment at the Pacific Manuscripts Bureau, Research School of Pacific and Asian Studies, Australian National University. We are also grateful to the Division of Archaeology and Natural History, Research School of Pacific and Asian Studies who awarded us visiting fellowships and we thank Atholl Anderson for arranging these. Hank Nelson provided us with expert advice on how to approach the documentary evidence on New Guinea between the wars. Merilyn Minnell gave us great help with trawling through colonial records at the National Archives of Australia. Staff at the Australian War Memorial, the National Library of Australia and the library at ANU all gave kind support.

In Canberra and Sydney the hospitality of Jim and Jill Allen, Howard Morphy, Glen Summerhayes, Jim Specht, and Katie and Bryan Roach who looked after us, but also contributed much through conversation and advice. In West New Britain John Namuno, at the West New Britain Cultural Centre supported and encouraged us. We also thank Anne Chowning, Philip Dark, Dorothy and David Counts, Tristan Arbousse-Bastide, Christin Kocher-Schmid, Max Quanchi and Tobias Sperlich.

This project involved a lot of administration and would not have been possible without the support and help of all the staff at the Pitt Rivers Museum, not least Sue Brooks and Julia Cousins for helping to administer the grant. Schuyler Jones and Mike O'Hanlon, the former and current directors, the conservation department Birgitte Speake, Lorraine Rostant and Emma Hook and the technical services Bob Rivers, John Simmons, and Andy Munsch. Maria Economou, Sandra Dudley and Haas Ezzet for their IT support. Malcolm Osman for his continuing work on the archival photographic material and for producing new images relating to the collections, Mark Dickerson for his ability to discover copies of books and papers relating to our work, and Norman Weller who helped in numerous ways. The Friends of the Pitt Rivers Museum, were enthusiastic in their support of the aims of the project.

The various drafts of this manuscript were read by and commented on by the following people and we are grateful for the improvements that were made due to their advice, those faults that remain being entirely our own. Thanks are due to Jeremy Coote, Elizabeth Edwards, Mike O'Hanlon, Christina Pavlides, Alison Petch, Gwyneira Isaac, Glenn Summerhayes, Ian Knowles, Rob Welsch, Ian Lilley, Robin Torrence and Peter White. Special thanks go to Jim Specht who read so much of the manuscript in its final stages and made a crucial set of comments on both facts and theory. We are very grateful to Sven Wair for copy editing and Fran Knight for compiling the index. Kathryn Earle at Berg Press has been encouraging and supportive throughout.

Our understanding of the broader history of colonialism in New Britain has been enhanced by the work we are currently carrying out on the collections in the museums of Germany from this region, the results of which will be published as a second volume. We thank all those in Germany who have helped, although they are too numerous to mention here by name.

Last and certainly not least, our family and friends have supported us throughout in particular Jane Kaye, Emily and Jack and Sam Anwar.

Preface

Colonialism was made up of a mass of small processes with global effects. In thinking about colonialism we are still happier with Wallerstein's (1974, 1980) core/periphery theory or thought about present globalism (Hannerz 1996) than with detailed, local understandings of colonial times and places (Thomas 1994). Smaller scale events are not purely contingent on local circumstances, but provide a scale of analysis focusing on the points at which the strategies and histories of individuals meet broader economic and cultural forces. Broader processes would not exist without local forces and events, so that the study of the local can provide us with new insights into broader forces. Our aim here is to develop a series of detailed case studies from Papua New Guinea to throw light on broader historical and intellectual developments.

Our raw material for this study is provided by museum collections and their attendant documentation. One of our main arguments is that colonial New Guinea was not made up of two separate societies, New Guineans and colonials in collision and confrontation, but rather came to be a single social and cultural field of mutual influence, in which all people, black and white, were linked through the movement of goods and the definition of roles, statuses and forms of morality. Chemists make a distinction between a mixture and a reaction. A mixture is a solution in which different chemicals combine, but retain their original form, whereas a reaction creates something new out of its original constituent parts. Colonial New Guinea was a reaction to which all parties contributed, so that there can be no question that all had influence and agency. Anthropologists have tried to undo or ignore the reaction and focus upon one part, New Guineans, creating a partial and static picture in the process. Museum collections made in New Guinea were created through flows of goods between various parties within this colonial society and museum collectors were part of a much broader and bigger set of collecting activities by many of the whites in New Guinea. Collections were part of a broader flow of payments made in cash and trade items by Europeans for labour, food, cash crops or sex. These museum collections are not what their collectors took them to be: partial, but well-documented records of New Guinean societies. Rather they are complete, although particular, outcomes of individual sets of colonial practices. The study of collections necessitates consideration of all the parties contributing to them, their interests, ambitions and failures. The collectors themselves are documented through their own recording activity and we need to take their intellectual interests, institutional histories, economic resources and social skills into account in understanding what they collected and why. For New Guineans the sale of objects to whites was an important opportunity to develop personal strategies or for the group as a whole to seek to address the moral and cosmological issues facing them through the disruptions of colonialism.

Papua New Guinea had a relatively late history of direct colonial rule, starting in 1884 and ending in 1975. The area we are interested in here, the large island of New Britain, has a rather longer history of European influence dating back to the eighteenth century, although we shall focus on the period between 1910 and 1937. The collections we are focusing on were made by A. B. Lewis who did fieldwork in the area in 1910. As the first curator of anthropology at the Field Museum in Chicago, a major part of his interest was in collecting artefacts which were well documented in terms of their production, use and exchange, so as to show interconnections within New Guinea. He made extensive field notes which go together with the hundreds of objects he collected (the exact number is not known at present), plus some 250 photographs of the area and of items in use. Beatrice Blackwood of the Pitt Rivers Museum was also a curator and made an extensive collection of artefacts from the south coast of New Britain during a seven month stay in 1937, together with meticulous documentation of many aspects of life, plus genealogies, word lists and some 350 photographs. She also made a short movie film. Speiser was in the area during 1929-30 as part of a larger trip to different parts of Melanesia in search of comparative material designed to throw light on Melanesian unity and origins. He collected artefacts, well documented as to provenance, plus photographs and a short film of initiation rites, in which he had a special interest. All his material is held in the Museum der Kulturen, Basel. Our fourth collector is J. A. Todd, a Ph. D. student in Sydney University during the 1930s. Between 1933–4 Todd spent a year near Kandrian, a small government post on the south coast of New Britain. Todd made a collection of artefacts on this trip and took over 1000 photographs, plus an unknown number of sound recordings. The artefact collection is now in the Australian Museum, Sydney but the photographs, sound recordings and all his field notes are missing. As well as analysing the collections themselves, we have put considerable effort into reconstructing the intellectual and institutional histories of these individual collectors as these histories had important effects on their collections. We have also worked with the extensive archival materials deriving from patrol reports, government and mission records and published accounts. Collections represent not just the colonial reaction of white and New Guinean within New Guinea itself, but also a broader set of interests and influences the collectors brought in from elsewhere.

A final theme of our work is provided by recent renewed interest in material culture studies and we seek to answer the broad question of what difference objects made to people's lives. These differences were a mixture of the moral and the physical. We seek to answer how human relations were realised, in the sense of being made real, by producing, exchanging and using objects. The nature of reality was a very definite question for all those involved in creating the novel social world that was colonial New Guinea.

We believe that this is a project of a unique type in its detailed consideration of different collections made at different times in a single area in order to understand change. This book will be a success not only if people read and enjoy it, but also if we can convince others of the vast research potential held in the museums of the world for understanding colonial histories.

People, Objects and Colonial Relations

Let us start by considering an object, since objects are the subject of this book. The focus of our attention is a small brown strip of material, presently housed in the Pitt Rivers Museum, University of Oxford (1938.36.1301). In itself this is an unprepossessing object. The material, which is probably difficult for many to identify, would be immediately recognized by people throughout the Pacific: it is barkcloth. Barkcloth is produced by removing a long strip of bark from the tree of a suitable species, pounding it flat with a wooden or stone beater on some sort of anvil and then leaving it to dry. Barkcloth can be used in a single strip, as is the case here, or combined into larger pieces. In either case, barkcloth is frequently decorated using local pigments or store-bought paints.

The small strip of barkcloth we are considering was collected by Beatrice Blackwood of the Pitt Rivers Museum on the 30 July 1937 from Möwehafen in the Arawe region of the south coast of New Britain, a large island then part of the Australian colony of New Guinea. The Pitt Rivers' accession book entry for this object (written by Blackwood) reads 'First head-binding of new-born child, *ewep*, bandage of bark-cloth, *talis*, fastening made from split stem of *alikuiyi* bush-creeper; Moewehafen, July 1937'. Much the same information was repeated on a metal tag attached to the object. Blackwood also noted in her diary '30th July: *ewep*: Baby's first head bandage: Alola: beads'. This was her short-hand way of saying that she paid the mother, Alola, in beads for the head-binding cloth; just one of 275 transactions made with money or trade goods to make a collection of local artefacts. Blackwood also took photographs of Alola and her little baby, Awadingme (Fig. 1.1) and took cine film of the process of head binding. Surrounding this one object there is a mass of recording and documentation, all of which is held in the Pitt Rivers today and provides insight into life in the Arawe region at the time, but also into Blackwood's interests and field practices.

When collected the strip of barkcloth was already a recycled object and was being used for a purpose other than that for which it was originally produced. In this part of the Pacific, barkcloth was (and sometimes still is) used as male clothing. A strip of barkcloth, decorated with designs using pigments obtained from elsewhere in New Britain through trade, was wrapped around a man's waist and between his legs (Fig. 1.2). When Beatrice Blackwood was in New Britain the

Figure 1.1. Alola, binding the head of her daughter Awadingme. Passismanua village, Kandrian (Pitt Rivers Museum, University of Oxford)

barkcloth was made in a number of inland villages and traded throughout the region (Fig. 7.5). The barkcloth had been a vital part of male regalia when the Germans set up their colony in 1884, and was still commonly worn by men when Blackwood did her fieldwork over fifty years later. However, Blackwood's fieldwork coincided with the coming of the missions which presaged considerable changes, one of which was a change from the relatively scant clothing of both men and women, shocking to the missionaries, to more modest forms of store-bought dress.

The barkcloth Blackwood collected was no longer a men's *malu* (belt), but had been re-used for a second, but vital, cultural purpose. A part of the original belt had been cut off and used to bind the head of a new-born baby. Central to the local bodily aesthetic is the shape of the head, which is in its most pleasing state when elongated, not round, with the elongation of the skull emphasized by hair

Figure 1.2. Man kneeling on ground beating barkcloth with stone barkcloth beater over wooden block (Pitt Rivers Museum, University of Oxford)

short on the sides and longer on the top. Blackwood had originally been instructed to carry out fieldwork in New Britain by Balfour (Curator of the Pitt Rivers Museum) because of two local practices: the use of blow pipes and the existence of head binding. It was unusual to find either of these features in the western Pacific, the nearest parallel to the blow pipes being in Borneo to the west and head binding being found in what was then the New Hebrides (now Vanuatu) to the east. The relations of the Arawe people of New Britain to those elsewhere in the region was of considerable culture historical interest, as head binding and blow pipes might represent a substrate of ancient customs, once widespread, but now submerged beneath later migrations and developments. Part of the impetus to the New Britain fieldwork was culture historical. But there was also a museological dimension. Balfour, then Curator at the Pitt Rivers Museum, was anxious to obtain head-bound skulls for the collections, and so Blackwood went not just to document the practice, but to bring back tangible evidence of how head binding was carried out and what effects it had (Blackwood and Danby 1955: 174–95).

There were also concerns of the missionaries and colonial administrators surrounding the practice. Chinnery, the New Guinea government anthropologist, comments often on head binding in his notes on the south coast of New Britain.[1] There was considerable debate as to whether head binding affected the intelligence of those on whom it was practised, and although the general conclusion was that it did not, many in the administration were probably happy to see the custom cease. The missionaries were also unhappy with such an idolatrous practice, which might be seen as tampering with god's prime creation – the human body. Once the Catholic and Anglican missions established themselves on the south coast of New Britain after 1935, they put pressure on local people to abandon the practice, which they did in part and only started to revive it again in the 1980s.

The head-binding cloth, which is not a striking object in anybody's eyes, can be seen as the centre of a mass of historical connections and debates, some of which are ongoing. For the baby whose head it bound, the cloth is crucial to her personal identity, with the elongation of the skull carried out in the first few weeks of life having a lasting effect throughout the whole of her life. The effect might have had extra piquancy in the time Blackwood was collecting, as an individual then would have been one of the last generation to have a long head. For Beatrice Blackwood the barkcloth would have been amongst one of the most tangible results of her work, and the cloth, whilst not attractive as an item for museum display, was an important piece of culture-historical documentation and thus vital to the teaching and research aspects of a university museum. To the colonial administrator and the missionary, getting rid of head-binding cloths was a sign of progress for many, although for some it might have seemed a dangerous erosion of a harmless local custom. For us, looking back over sixty years after the item was collected, the barkcloth has all these connotations. It was, and is, an important element of an Arawe aesthetic; it is a tangible mark of Beatrice Blackwood's interest at a particular stage in the history of anthropology and museology, and can be connected to the other 274 items she collected, plus her photographs, diaries and notebooks. It can also be linked to other collections made in the area at different times, and other forms of fieldwork, as we shall see.

The apparent singularity of objects when sitting in a glass case or museum store room should not mislead us. Their complexity derives from the fact that objects such as the barkcloth are always in a state of becoming, and this is true not just when produced and used in their original cultural context, but once collected and housed in the museum. The physical circumstances of the object change continuously, but so also do its sets of significances as it accumulates a history. It is possible, when records are made, to reconstruct this history, which carries with it the lives of those involved with the object. An object is best viewed as indicative of process, rather than static relations, and this process is ongoing in the museum as elsewhere, so that there is a series of continuous social relations surrounding the object connecting 'field' and 'museum'.

Barkcloth used for head binding, as other collected objects, contains information on a range of histories. In addition to our main focus, the historical processes of colonialism, there are also the histories of the individuals involved with collecting these objects, their position within the history of anthropology and of museology. This last history leads us to consider what the role of museum objects is and what constructions of past and present we can place upon them. We will look at all these issues in an introductory manner in the present chapter, but need to start by considering the huge and difficult issue of colonialism and its histories.

New Guinean Colonialism

Understanding colonialism is no easy task, especially once one focuses on historical change. There are three basic models of historical change employed to understand the meeting of initially different cultures through colonial relations. Acculturation sees the local culture as being taken over and submerged by the culture of the incoming group, and this may be seen either as a benign change in which case it is labelled 'development' or as less positive in which case it is seen as cultural loss. The second possibility sees a lack of change and the maintenance of tradition, which was the main model for many anthropologists who emphasized the ethnographic present. The third, most subtle, view of change stresses hybridity as an outcome whereby new cultural forms arise out of the meeting of existing cultural logics (Rowlands 1998). In Melanesia there has been a debate between proponents of a model of little change and those who emphasize the changes brought about by colonialism. The nub of the disagreement is about whether Melanesian forms of sociability and of representing the world are utterly different from those of the Western intellectual and social tradition, or whether the last several centuries of colonial involvement in the region have created social forms influenced at quite a deep level by the economic, social and philosophical practices of the West. Foster (1995) has crystallized this difference by distinguishing between what he calls New Melanesia Ethnography and New Melanesian History. The former, associated most obviously with Marilyn Strathern (1988), highlights the fundamental difference between Western and the Melanesian presuppositions about social reality, and uses these differences to highlight the manner in which anthropology has approached Melanesia within a Western mindset. New Melanesian History, by contrast, associated with the work of Thomas (1991), stresses the similarities created by shared histories of colonialism and exchange. Foster also calls for a joining of the two approaches in the New Melanesian Anthropology (Foster 1995: 5). Our view is different to any of these. Europeans and Melanesians have been part of a field of social relations since the middle of the nineteenth century in coastal areas, relations constructed through the movement of goods, gifts and ideas. This has not left either party untouched, but has added to social and cultural change. However, such change has not brought convergence or acculturation but has created new forms of difference, so that Melanesian and Euro-Asian cultures have maintained themselves as different, but the nature of this difference has changed continually.

Melanesian society and culture in New Britain has changed over the last 150 years, but this has not made New Guineans more like Europeans than they were (nor has it made them less like Europeans), they are merely different in novel ways. Similarly, long-term white residents of New Guinea before the Second World War participated in a colonial culture quite different from the form of life they had left in Australia or Europe. But this must not involve 'going native', a constant fear of all and an encouragement to keep up standards. At the risk of over-simplification, we can outline three fields of social interaction (at least) within colonial New Guinea: that provided by indigenous Melanesian society, whether this was found in plantations, towns or villages; that provided by long-term settlers (our focus here is on Europeans); areas of interaction between these two. Looked at temporally, these form three linked arenas of change, with interactions between whites and Melanesians a constant feature, but one which helped create difference between Melanesian or white society, rather than engendering more similarity. In constructing this model we are attempting to provide a general set of ideas which is in tune with, and does justice to, the complex and contradictory nature of change within New Guinean colonial society.

Objects were crucial to the maintenance of an arena holding together the various parties in New Guinea. Blackwood's acquisition of the head-binding cloth was a tiny instance of the sort of exchanges which were constant in New Guinea. Paradoxically the constant movement of objects helped reinforce difference rather than break it down. We shall now turn to the consideration of the movement of objects and the intellectual and social values attached to them.

Cargo Cults

Colonial relations always involved material culture. The main motive for Europeans going to New Guinea was material: to extract copra, rubber, gold or oil, hunt whales or human labour, and make a profit in so doing. Such pursuits necessitated the payment of local people in cash and/or material things, and many relationships of planters and business people were constructed through the flows of materials. Melanesians desired Western objects, but did not want to become Westerners themselves. Rather they attempted to use objects to track down the sources of spiritual power it was thought that whites possessed.

For many Melanesians the coming of whites and colonialism posed a series of intellectual and cosmological puzzles. Puzzlement revolved around the origins of the large amounts of material things Westerners possessed. Cargo cults have been common in New Britain over the last century (Lattas 1998), but are also found in many other parts of Papua New Guinea (Lawrence 1964; Williams 1976). In all areas there are commonalities, as well as differences, in the nature of these cults. Cargo cults derive from the belief that cargo, in the form of Western goods, derives from a non-human, divine source and that Westerners have privileged access to this, an access wrested from Melanesians. Lattas (1998: xi) reports that many in the Kaliai area of West New Britain are convinced that imported cargo is secretly produced by their ancestors, over whom whites have gained control, and that similar beliefs are found widely throughout New Britain. Lawrence (1964) for the southern Madang District records how the local god Manup went to Australia and found white natives there for whom he built the city of Sydney. He then wished to return to his original followers in New Guinea and to do this he turned himself into the Holy Ghost, entered the womb of the Virgin Mary and was reborn as Jesus. When he tried to return to New Guinea, the Jews turned against him, as they did not want to share their wealth with New Guineans and crucified him. The missionaries were told to keep all this secret once they got to New Guinea as no whites wanted New Guineans to know the source of their wealth. The killing of a black Christ by whites, as told in this myth, was the basis for the present colonial order. As well as praying in church for the return of Jesus–Manup, a set of rituals was developed to awaken the consciences of their ancestors and cargo deities and alert them to their plight. Some people destroyed gardens, pigs and other forms of property, and in village cemeteries people set up European-style tables that they decorated with cotton cloth, flowers in bottles, food and tobacco. These acts and rituals, plus the revival of old dances, were designed to create new relationships with the ancestors through which material wealth would flow, and to prevent Europeans stealing cargo from the ancestors before it could reach the villagers (Lawrence 1964: 94–5). Lattas (1998: chap. 2) documents similar beliefs and activities existing in New Britain from the German period onwards.

Cargo cults were not primarily about the desire for objects, but were rather a search for access to the power which is the source of objects and material wealth. Objects were at the centre of Melanesian views of their relationships with whites, relationships which had a series of moral and political aspects to them, aspects which many whites would not have readily grasped in their dealings with the local inhabitants of New Britain. Whites were seen variously as the spirits of the dead or as blocking access to mass-produced goods. Melanesian desires for Western goods were not spurred by a yen for assimilation or basic cultural change, but rather people saw Western goods as posing a series of questions about their standing with ancestral powers and other spiritual forces, causing them to search for reasons why they were less well favoured by the powers of the universe than whites appeared to be. Given this general atmosphere of feeling about mass-produced goods, many relationships with whites which involved transactions would have been attempts by local people to create better relations with their ancestors. These were far from commercial transactions, and although steel axes were better at chopping down trees than stone ones, the acquisition of an axe might not have been primarily the purchase of a utilitarian object.

However, we should also stress that cargo beliefs were a subject of intense debate and by no means everyone felt the same or held identical views over a period of time. Relationships with whites were partly in the nature of experiments to find out what sorts of people they were, what moral values they held and to determine how they could be most advantageously approached. Contacts in colonial culture between whites and locals were frequent and varied. They did not result in one side becoming more like the other, but generated new forms of difference resulting from local cultural logics and forms of colonial contact, as the syncretic nature of cargo cults shows.

Europeans also engaged in a form of cargo cult. Many were obsessed with Melanesian material culture, so that most, if not all, Europeans collected local items in New Guinea, and this included government administrators, missionaries and plantation owners, as well as anthropologists. Collection took place for a range of motives, with many objects representing a set of memories and mnemonics for people's time in New Guinea and the experiences they had there. New Guineans were inclined to see Europeans as their ancestors, especially on first meeting. Europeans saw New Guineans as their ancestors, in a more generalized sense. At the beginning of her monograph on the technology of the Kukuku (entitled *The Technology of a Modern Stone Age People in New Guinea*) Blackwood wrote 'the main aim of my expedition, undertaken on behalf of the Pitt Rivers Museum, was to study the technique of a modern Stone-Age people before it follows that of our own Neolithic forefathers into the realm of archaeology. I was only just in time' (Blackwood 1950: 12). To live and work amongst a 'modern Stone Age' people had a profound effect on many and influenced their dealings with New Guineans. The prevalence of these views is shown in the titles of popular accounts of New Guinea (*Patrol into Yesterday* [McCarthy 1963] or *Adam with Arrows* [Simpson 1954]). No one expected to meet Adam, but contact with New Guineans by academics and others was tinged with a feeling of living within a stage of the world that had vanished elsewhere. Objects collected in New Guinea came not just from another place, but also another time, and this was part of their attraction. The difference between New Guinean views of whites and white views of locals was that whites were more inclined to pigeon-hole New Guineans into categories such as 'native', 'savage' or 'Stone Age', whereas New Guineans felt impelled to learn, so as to discover what sorts of beings these were and how these incomers had such access to objects, an access denied to them. Anthropologists went to learn and so did some others (Gammage's [1998] account of John Black's changing views of the people he met on the Sepik-Hagen patrol demonstrates beautifully that changes of view did occur), but all too often objects were used to sustain an existing European intellectual edifice rather than change it.

In the early part of the century there was a range of German scientific expeditions in New Britain, all of which collected. There were plantation owners like Richard Parkinson who made collections of thousands of items for their personal interest and for sale (Specht in press). It is certain that Parkinson was at one end of a spectrum of amateur collectors who wanted local objects for sale to supplement their earnings or as mementoes of their time in New Guinea. There were also private professional collectors, such as Schoede, who was based in Hamburg and sold items to museums and private individuals around the world. Schoede had his own boat and finances and certainly collected in large amounts (Knowles, Gosden and Leinnert-Emmerlich in press). Last and perhaps least in terms of their impact on the region were the museum collectors, such as Lewis, Speiser, Blackwood and Todd, our subjects here. The important aspect of museum collections is that they are generally well-documented examples of broader collecting practice, and help reveal the sorts of relations involved in collecting and the values, monetary or otherwise, attached to it. Collecting cannot be understood as an isolated activity, but one which was deeply embedded in the overall set of colonial relations pertaining at the time. For instance, Marcus Schindelbeck has discussed Lewis's collecting on the Sepik in 1910, when the captain of the *Siar* on which he was travelling would not allow him to collect on the way up the river, as this would make his recruitment of labourers, to be paid in trade goods, much more difficult. On the way down river, the captain who had been unsuccessful in his attempts to recruit, collected 2,000 artefacts for sale in order to turn the trip to profit (Schindelbeck 1997: 35–6).

One effect of collection may well have been to raise the levels of production of some local artefacts to meet the needs of Westerners. Many thousands and probably tens of thousands of objects were removed from the south coast of New Britain between the 1880s and the Second World War. This would have had an enormous impact on the levels of production by local people, and possibly also an impact on the type of object produced. In addition to production, the sale of objects would have set up a mass of relationships between local people and Europeans, plus non-local New Guineans, which would have been important in shaping peoples lives. From the point of view of local people, when either producing or owning an object, they would have had an extra realm of choice to that which existed previously, having to decide whether to dedicate their objects to discharging obligations to exchange partners or contributions to bride price or mortuary rituals, or whether to sell objects to Europeans and their New Guinean representatives.

New Guineans were interested in Western mass-produced goods, but were encouraged towards mass-production themselves by white demand.

The exchange of objects in New Guinea was a trans-cultural phenomenon, not deriving from the norms of exchange of either party. Whites did buy local objects for commercial re-sale for profit and for academic interest; Melanesians did acquire useful objects but always through sets of relationships with whites which were exploratory. Individuals did create stable relationships: the long-serving plantation owner had well-understood relationships with some of his workers, as we shall see. But many transactions occurred between people who did not know each other, or who had only temporary relationships, as is the case with the collectors we look at here. The lack of norms gave an irregular feel to transactions of all kinds, and uncertainties about forms of relationships were increased by the lack of recognition on the part of many of the full depth of colonial relations.

Melanesia: Colonial Culture in Denial

Our basic model of colonial New Guinea is that all members of society were linked by continuous social relations, many of which involved objects. Melanesians, Europeans and Asians met constantly on plantations, in villages, mission stations, towns and in the bush, and this resulted in the exchange of information, objects and money. But at the level of cultural representations, the constancy of these social links, the dependencies they set up for all the parties involved, and the true nature of power within these relationships was not acknowledged. We would see colonial culture in New Guinea as being in a state of denial, especially on the part of whites, so that forms of representation contained no recognition at all of the depth of mutual implication of blacks, whites and Asians. The dissonance between the multiplicity of social links and the lack of an adequate scheme to represent and understand these links deepened uncertainties felt by all parties and led to meetings between different parties being uneasy and often staged. Objects are important in a number of ways here. First, the quantity of objects exchanged between whites and Melanesians allows us to document the links between people. Secondly, objects had a lot of work to do in representing one group to another, and this representational role was a major reason why they were collected by museum professionals and many others. The interests of museology link into the basic structures and neuroses of colonial culture, making a direct connection between the academic study and lived experience of the colony.

At the level of perceived custom and forms of representation, the different groups had no means of conceiving of, or thinking about, the ties that bound them. Each side thought about the other, but mainly in terms of difference and Otherness. The white community in New Guinea was a literate one; many accounts of people's time in the colony survive, and it is possible to pick out recurring themes in people's writings. Most whites stressed their separateness from Melanesian society. All the patrol officers write of being alone in the bush, even when surrounded by dense populations of locals, so that cultural isolation was transmuted into physical isolation. 'Ambunti had the reputation of being the loneliest station in New Guinea but as I had two years of solitude in Nakanai behind me, a four-man posting seemed very like overcrowding' (McCarthy 1963: 49). The estimated 4,000 people in the Nakanai district vanish from this account, with solitude being a condition of isolation from other whites, rather than from all human contact. The anthropologists did the opposite, making the white community disappear from view and stressing the immediacy of their links with relatively pristine locals. Todd wrote of the south coast of New Britain that 'From the sociological point of view, these people are in excellent condition for investigation. They have been subjected to that slight contact with European culture which is a prerequisite for successful fieldwork. On the other hand, however, their culture is, as yet, practically unimpaired.'[2] The plantation in the area that he worked in disappeared from his account, as did the regular visits by schooners on trading and recruiting voyages; although it must be said that it might well have been unwise to stress the impact of non-Melanesians in a grant application at the time.

Anthropologists were not isolated in villages in New Guinea, but rather were temporary members of a broader colonial society, of which they studied only a part. In fact, in order to operate in New Guinea they had to be inducted into life in Rabaul or the government station, and here people like Chinnery, the government anthropologist and administrator, were vital in explaining the customs of the locals, who included the Government Secretary or the manager of the local Burns Philp store, in addition to the indigenous inhabitants. To stress the temporary nature of anthropologists' participation in colonial New Guinea society is to ignore the fact that there were a series of values and roles set aside for them. McCarthy (1963: 9) discussing old (white) New Guinea hands' attitudes to the 'mollycoddling' regime in Papua quotes some as saying that Hubert Murray, Papua's governor 'was encouraging nothing more than an anthropologists' zoo on his side of the border'. A new anthropologist in New Guinea may have been innocent, but the society which greeted them was not, having a range of defined views as to their likely disruptive or beneficial effects, and this was as true of their informants as the white element of the community. Our anthropologists also operated through networks of dependency on New Guineans, and, just as did patrol officers or plantation owners, many structured their activities through their close personal links with servants, key informants and others, all of whom knew how to deal with white people.

There is quite a considerable first-contact literature, which gives the initial impressions of Papua New Guineans to seeing white patrols (Connolly and Anderson 1987; Schieffelin and Crittenden 1991), but far fewer accounts of what colonial relations were like once they were established. One hint that whites were not always central to New Guinean's perceptions of colonial relations is given by Gammage's account (1998) of the Sepik-Hagen patrol, in which some local people who talked about the patrol later were unaware that it was led by white people, as they only noticed the mass of Melanesian carriers, soldiers and police who made up the bulk the of the patrol. Most of the interactions on that patrol were between patrolling New Guineans and local New Guineans. The patrol itself brought about a whole series of initially unlikely alliances between police and carriers from different groups, who were attempting to make their name and fortune through exploration, trade and robbery. Whites always saw themselves as the centre of things, and were rarely aware of the mass of interactions around them and the fact that they could only accomplish what they did through the help and thought of local people.

Colonial society in New Guinea had a very partial sense of itself, and this comes out in the contradictions inherent in the social ties which held people together and the lack of joint representation which kept them apart. Particular sets of relationships were not highlighted by the participants in colonial culture: whites did not emphasize any form of dependency on local people or situations in which New Guineans had power over them (or could only conceive of such situations in terms of extreme danger). McCarthy's statement is comparatively rare – 'Boko was not only my cook. After twelve months with me he had developed into a travelling companion, general adviser and interpreter' (McCarthy 1963: 31). Many of the wiser patrol officers would have had an equivalent to Boko, someone to whom they could turn for advice in a range of situations, and, as we shall see, many anthropologists had similar relationships. We should not forget, however, McCarthy's emphasis of solitude in Nakanai, something he might not have emphasized had he enjoyed a close working relationship with another white. Many forms of mutuality were never a real part of the sense that white people had of the culture in which they lived. This fractured people's basic scheme of representation, only allowing each side to think about the other in those distanced terms and not to see mutualities of power and dependence.

New Guineans were more aware of the complexity of any relationship with whites, and were inclined to see whites as somehow related to them. A striking instance of this is Batari's claim to be McCarthy. Batari was a Nakanai, who became a cargo-cult leader, who came to see McCarthy at the government station, accompanied by Boko, McCarthy's old adviser and cook, among others. Batari said he had been visited by spirits who told him

> Makati is our friend but he is now dead – and you, Batari, are also dead. The spirit of Makati has now entered your body while Makati's body now contains your spirit. So you must go and tell Makati this, our message . . . In a short time all the white men and all the Chinese will leave New Guinea. The goods that the white men have prevented

the New Guinea people from having will then be distributed to the New Guinea people. (McCarthy 1963: 189)

There is conflict as well as closeness in Batari's views, which in many ways reflects quite accurately the contradictory nature of colonial culture. It is certainly no less realistic than the denial of mutuality on the part of many whites.

The main gap in whites' discourse and knowledge of their own situation was of the ties that bound people together across racial and cultural differences. The absence of a discourse of mutuality made the basis of their power seem uncertain and shifting. As a result there were constant attempts by whites to conjure up a feeling of being in control through a series of performances and negotiations. Objects were central to both negotiation and performativity.

A Radically Performative Culture

White colonial cultural had a theatrical element to it, being based around correct forms of dress, housing, comportment and well-staged ways of doing things. It held this in common with colonial cultures in many other parts of the world. New Guineans copied elements of white colonial culture, in ways which was not always to the liking of whites. In both cases material culture was central to the performances and appearances of colonialism.

Roles and statuses were marked in material terms in a rigidly defined manner. An extract from a New Guinea government handbook from 1936 gives some idea of the distinctions which were applied.

> The standard attire for white men is the white duck coat and trousers, with shirt of white or cream silk ... the white solar topee is the customary headgear ... evening wear for men comprises black dress trousers, white starched dress shirt, cummerbund and short white mess jacket ... fashions may be varied in the bush, or where it is not possible to conform to the convention of an entire change of clothes at least daily. (quoted in Downs 1986: 51–2)

New patrol officers arriving in Rabaul were told to visit a Chinese tailor to kit themselves out with the requisite clothing. Nor did dress regulations apply only to whites. Forms of dress were laid down for indigenous government employees, who had to wear short *lavalava*, which by official order should come to just above the knee. Downs, a patrol officer who arrived in Rabaul in early 1936, noted that 'There was an irrational belief among Europeans that long *lavalava* were an expression of insolence and worn by people of insubordinate or even rebellious nature', whereas local people in fact preferred them due to their comfort and elegance (Downs 1986: 53). Village officials all had caps and canes, which were

Figure 1.3. Three police 'boys' in uniform (Pitt Rivers Museum, University of Oxford)

their emblems of office, and were expected to wear store-bought dress, and the short *lavalava*, when greeting patrol officers in their area; soldiers and police also had their own uniforms (Fig. 1.3). The marking of statuses and roles in colonial culture was to provide a regularity and predictability that the culture otherwise lacked. However, these material markings were more than that, they were performative.

The lack of a means of imagining links between black and white gave New Guinean culture a radically performative aspect. We use the term 'performative' in a manner which follows Judith Butler's (1993, 1997) usage. She, in turn, follows speech-act theorists, who have concentrated on the class of acts of speech which can actually make a difference to states of affairs in the world. (For example, a vicar saying 'I pronounce you man and wife' helps join single people in marriage and brings about a new state of affairs). Butler looks at a range of acts (not just of speech) which realize things, in the sense of making them real. Dress and bodily comportment realize gender differences, and these differences could not exist in the same form without the acts and objects connected to them. For Butler, all cultures are performative: sex, gender and class, for instance, are names given to differences and mutualities which exist through both schemes of representation and the acts which bring them to life. Colonial societies have both differences and similarities with other social forms in this respect. Because the social relations that bind colonial societies together were not sufficiently recognized at the level of representation, these relations only existed insofar as they were performed: performances brought them to life and they then sunk out of sight, below the level of consciousness. Colonial New Guinea was only held together through acts, because representations were too partial to encompass all social relations. The radical performativity of these social forms led to a stress on both formalization of clothing and comportment, but also of constant negotiation of roles and relations. The experimental nature of colonial culture meant that there was no sense of a centre to the culture, with the outcomes of many encounters being unknown. Most cultural forms tend to reify themselves, to imagine that social life is more real, or has more essence, than it does. New Guinean colonial culture did the opposite, so that performances were attempting to make real something no one was sure existed.

Many of the encounters between whites and New Guineans were staged. Patrols through rural areas created a whole series of mini performances as people in villages lined up to have a census taken, medical treatment administered and head taxes collected. During all of this, villagers often wore store-bought clothing and certainly the *luluai* and *tultuls* would have been dressed in their caps, short *lavalava* and carrying their badges of office. Each person stepped up to the table to be registered and to pay their tax, and not only are the physical symbols of power evident (Fig. 1.4), but also the physical stances of people indicates a variety of attitudes to the whole performance. The setting up of camp on patrol was a highly stylized affair. A flag was a compulsory item of patrol equipment, and District Standing instructions stated

> Immediately a police patrol enters a village, the Australian flag will be hoisted outside the quarters of the senior European officer of the patrol. It will be lowered on his departure. During the stay of the patrol, it will be hoisted at sunrise and lowered at sunset. On all occasions when the flag is hoisted or lowered the compliments [presenting arms] will be paid. (*Official Handbook of the Territory of New Guinea* 1937: 296)

Cargo rituals and activities often played on the more formalized aspects of white colonial culture. F.E. Williams (1976: 348) noted that flag poles were a constant

Figure 1.4. Government officials carrying out a census (Pitt Rivers Museum, University of Oxford)

and important element of cargo-cult activities in the Gulf area and were seen as means by which certain individuals could receive messages from spirits in the sky. In the Nakanai area, Batari created a militia of 600 men who marched in European style and carried sticks which were seen to act as rifles; these men acted with military discipline themselves and also disciplined villagers, in much the same manner as colonial administrators did, through fines and punishments (Lattas 1998: 37–48). These military forms were seen as both means of driving whites out, but also as a way of communicating with the dead to ensure the arrival of larger amounts of cargo. Whilst generally desiring New Guinean assimilation, whites found these parodies of themselves extremely disturbing (Lattas 1998: 45), as it turned the colonial acts intended to create a sense of power back on themselves, using the outward forms of marching and flag waving to subvert white colonial power.

In a radically performative culture, objects will be crucially important because social effects can only be realized through practical and material means. We will focus on objects collected by whites, as we have most information on that, but we also need to recognize that collection was part of much more complex movements of materials, and short *lavalava* had a strong performative aspect when worn by a New Guinean, creating and reinforcing values which might not have existed in the quite the same way without it. In looking at collections we need to recognize that the motives of the makers and transactors of objects were crucial. Were New Guineans trying to set up lasting relations with whites through objects, to incorporate white people into a network of reciprocities from which they could not then escape? For whites, there was certainly a salvage paradigm at work: they were collecting vanishing examples of dying cultures, as well as memory prompts for their time in the tropics. There is a considerable irony here as the demands of white collectors may well have led to the increased production of objects, so that 'traditional' cultural forms were reinforced through the new sets of social connections and performative roles created through colonialism.

European interests were not static or all the same. Our analysis of the different collection practices of Lewis, Speiser and Blackwood shows that these reflect varying intellectual interests. Commercial traders, of course, had different sets of agendas again, mainly deriving from the demand for different objects in the market place. In short, the interest and actions of whites were hybrid. They derived partly from influences from outside New Guinea, but also from what was possible and appropriate within New Guinea and the myriad forms of negotiation that surrounded the acquisition of objects. For us, there is a continuous field of social and intellectual relations linking objects in the 'field' to their present resting places in museums, and the nature and significance of objects derives from the sum total of these relations. Obviously, objects in museums are no more divorced from social relations than they are whilst still in New Guinea. It is just that the nature of the relations has changed. Objects partake of continuous fields of relations linking New Guinea and museums, but these are relations of transformation and are not the same, with identical effects everywhere.

Objects as Process

In attempting to understand historical change through the analysis of objects we need a theory of objects which allows us to think about how new forms of objects and novel sets of social relations are linked. Gell (1998) stressed that the formal analysis of objects should start from the effect objects have in creating and maintaining social relations of particular types. The effects of objects are vital to the social process, but the effects of finished objects give us only part of the story. By definition all artefacts have to be created by people, often in combination with each other, and on many occasions artefacts are also exchanged between their makers and subsequent users. In producing artefacts, as well as in exchanging them, a whole series of social relations is set up. However, the production process is never one-way: people are produced through interaction with the material world as well as things. There have been many critiques of the western division between subject and object. Marx in the nineteenth century and Heidegger in the twentieth both felt that Western views of technology see the production of objects as a technical and economic matter, whereas the production of people is seen as a psychological or social one. To separate the technical from the existential was typical of the alienating powers of capitalism and modernity in not allowing a rounded grasp of people in the world. As the Kellers put it in their study of blacksmiths, 'The mind–body dualism typical of western science and philosophy has failed to account for the subjective experience of unity in productive activity. The separation of mind and body in research and the dissolution of activity systems in scholarly investigation also fails to provide accounts of the human realization of fulfillment in accomplishment' (Keller and Keller 1996: 174). A counter-view is that people produce objects, but are produced by this process as socially and physically skilled beings, with senses attuned in manners that derive from the exercise of their productive faculties (Gosden 1994a, 1999; Dobres 2000). Similar ideas have come into anthropology through a rather different intellectual tradition than either that of Marx or Heidegger, through the work of Marcel Mauss (James and Allen 1998). Mauss saw the body as a social and technical product, as much as any other object, and much of the most currently influential areas of his thought concern the body.

Mauss felt that we all carry out what he called *actes traditionnels efficaces* (traditionally efficacious actions) which are taken-for-granted acts of daily life which are known to have the desired effect (Mauss 1979; Schlanger 1998). In learning how to effect the world physically, people learn how to become members of society. Mauss coined the term *habitus* for habitual actions which are socially learned but unconsciously deployed. Simple activities such as walking or swimming differ from one part of the world to another and reflect unconscious forms of socialization. Such acts are often sequential, forming chains of bodily actions (*enchaînment organiques*) and their constant repetition not only effects the physical world, but gives members of a community a sense of togetherness. Mauss made a punning, but still serious, link between the body and the body politic, seeing that the routines of daily life committed people through the details of their own lives to communal life as a whole. Technology and techniques represent something of a total social fact, deriving from and illuminating most areas of people's lives, many of which would remain otherwise hidden.

A number of these ideas have been very influential, initially within the French tradition and then beyond. The work of Leroi-Gourhan (1943, 1945) featured the idea of *chaîne opératoire*, developed to look at how the sequences of operations necessary for making artefacts are also socially learnt and socially efficacious.

The production of stone tools, for instance, is a sequential business starting off with large blocks of stone and reducing these down to many smaller ones following a set sequence of stages. There is physical skill involved in following the sequence, but also being able to adapt to the exact nature of the raw material, so that sequences of action always involve the intelligent deployment of skill, not purely routinized action. The desired products are another important influence on what is produced, and because artefacts produce social relations, then the production of the artefacts and the skills necessary for this are also tied into the network of social relations and obligations. One of us (Gosden 1994a) developed the idea of a framework of reference to highlight the fact that the production of an artefact in one place has implicit within it a series of spatial and temporal dimensions, because the artefact will often be used at times and places distant from its point of production and by people other than the maker. *Chaînes opératoires* are not singular sequences of actions unfolding in one place, but connect into many times and places in a manner determined by the nature of their social embeddedness. For a more extended discussion of *chaîne opératoire* and a case-study of how this concept might be used in a rounded manner, see Dobres (2000) and also Lemonnier (1993) for its application to a New Guinean context.

Such abstract points are probably best approached through an example, which can give some sense of what we mean and can be amplified later. On the south coast of New Britain through the last century and still today, women wear shell armbands for both everyday and ceremonial occasions. These armbands are found in many museum collections, although they are rarely displayed, as they are not especially striking objects. Today such armbands are made in many places along the south coast, but early last century they were all made in the Siassi Islands and traded to New Britain, often to be exchanged for food, and the best armbands are still thought to be those made in Siassi. Armbands are made from large specimens of *Trochus niloticus*, a reef shell relatively common on the extensive reefs surrounding the Siassi Islands. These are gathered by women and generally also worked by women. Armbands are made through a particular reduction sequence through which the top, conical part of the shell is cut off, leaving only the base, which may be up to 130 mm across, and the centre of the base is then removed through flaking or cutting, leaving the outer portion of the base as a continuous circle. This is then rubbed down until it is smooth and rounded and then designs of diagonal or vertical lines are cut into the outer surface and stained with soot from lamps or ochre. Even today with relatively abundant metal knives and files, this is a skilled and time-consuming process, and much more so a century ago when metal was only starting to be introduced. A single woman might have gathered the shells and worked them, or this might have involved a number of people. Some of the armbands would have been bound together in groups of six or more and sent off on trading expeditions to New Britain and elsewhere, which were mainly (although not exclusively) run by men. The armbands were exchanged often for food, or these days for money, which would have been returned by the male relative to the woman producing the armbands. This involved negotiation between the female producers and the man doing the exchanging and this man and the woman buying the armbands. Armbands became the personal property of the woman who bought them; less good examples may have been used everyday, with more attractive objects being reserved for special occasions, and such armbands may also be passed from mother to daughter. If looked after, armbands could last for decades, if not longer, and pass between a number of human generations. Armbands were also sought by collectors as evidence of native ornament and as relatively cheap items that people were often quite happy to part with for the right exchange item, and this accounts for their presence in many museum store rooms around the world.

Armbands are relatively ordinary items, not especially valued or creative of relationships, although a woman may get very attached to old armbands that have special memories and personal significance. Nevertheless, their creation, exchange and use involves a number of people and relationships, and as items which are constantly produced and traded they help maintain the overall fabric of social relations in a manner all the more important for the fact that they are aspects of life which are taken for granted. Like any object, armbands are always in motion, from the moment a trochus shell is gathered from the reef with the intention to make something from it. They are either transformed physically or spatially through production and exchange, or in terms of their significance through decades of ownership or use they become a part of a woman's biography or of the female line more generally, once passed down from one generation to the next.

If confronted with a collector like Beatrice Blackwood, the degree of attachment to a set of armbands would determine the reaction to an offer to buy. The decision whether to sell would also have been influenced by the nature of the relationship which was desired with Blackwood. As a visitor who had stayed for sometime, Blackwood might be seen as a part of the social landscape who might become a longer-term or recurrent presence and thus well worth cultivating a relationship with through the gift of an armband. On the other hand, Blackwood as an individual may have been less important than someone who would convey the objects to a *haus tambuna* (house of the ancestors, i.e. a museum) in England with beneficial spiritual effects. Or Blackwood might have been seen purely as a useful source of money and tobacco with whom it was expedient to engage in exchanges for items of more immediate attraction than the armband. Transactions with outsiders were thus influenced by a range of complex considerations covering attachment to the item to be given up, the nature of the relationship desired with the transactor, and the lure of the items to be obtained through exchange.

But there is also an important phenomenological perspective to all this, concerning embodied skills and meanings through the production and exchange of things. The woman making the armbands had to acquire the necessary physical skills to make a good armband, which would have become part of her sense of self, as well as an element of her identity within the group. She also needed the right set of social skills and contacts through which to exchange the things she made, and all the armbands she had transacted helped define her social universe and feeling of herself – a set of feelings reciprocated by those receiving armbands, who maintained some sort of link through the paths of gift exchange, which had also been mediated and partly transformed through the men facilitating the exchanges. Personal identity, time and space were all partly shaped by the armbands made and transacted, and the relatively humble nature of items makes the point that people's lives were constructed through a series of taken-for-granted forms of action and objects which made up the fabric of life.

Nor were the production and exchange of armbands a purely linear matter of production, exchange and use, but were embedded in a mass of other actions and relationships. Rights to particular areas of reef were as closely guarded as rights to land, so that where a woman gathered was influenced by kinship relations. To produce shell armbands, knives and files are needed in the present, and these must be bought with money or produce which must be obtained somehow. The exchange expeditions from Siassi to New Britain are influenced by a mass of considerations from having enough exchange items to make an expedition worthwhile to knowledge that one's kin in New Britain had the desire and the materials to engage in exchanges. The exact transactions of armshells will be influenced by various women's desire, the strength of the kinship tie with the woman who produced them, and the objects to use in exchange.

A change in any one aspect of these networks of relationships between people and things can bring about multiple alterations of relationships. The over-exploitation of a reef or death of trochus through disease will affect all the women producing armbands and all those wanting to exchange or buy them. In colonial New Guinea trochus were also sought by traders who supplied button makers in Australia and Europe. Ian Mack, a patrol officer noted that after the introduction of the head tax of 10s per adult, the reefs in Kombe on the north coast of New Britain had been denuded of trochus by people selling these to traders to make money.[3] Such extra pressures on the reefs would have had an impact on the production of shell armbands. In this chapter we are looking at much more major effects through the impact of colonialism, which brought about such changes as new exchange relations, new forms of technology, labour recruitment and the need to garden in order to supply plantations with food. These together brought about a major reorientation of society's productive effort and all their relationships of exchange and use of objects. The effects are subtle and cannot be charted in detail, but a processual view of objects whereby they go through a series of changes in production, exchange and use is essential in trying to tie down some of the complexity of the changes.

As we have stressed above, the sets of connection that bound people together in colonial New Guinea included all the main players, of all races and types. Colonial relations involve new forms of *enchaînement organique* and novel aspects of physical and social action. Colonial relations operated at a physical level to join people together, often through the movement of objects, even if this was not explicitly recognized within the discourses of colonialism. We shall show how chains of action involving production, exchange and use linked together objects and people stretching from New Guinea to museums. Which objects were collected, their processes of collection and their subsequent use in a museum context can only be understood against the background of the originating set of relations in New Guinea. Looking back in time, we can now use museum objects, shaped as they were by the sets of aesthetic and social relations in New Guinea to reflect back on those relations and their changes through time.

Colonial relations gave objects new sets of contexts and effects. To produce an object for someone known to you using one's personal labour, skill and care is quite a different thing from making an identical object which may well fall into the hands of a total stranger. In this latter case the consequences of such a transaction would not be easy to know or predict and these transactions had an experimental aspect to them. Colonial relations might be best be seen as a series of experiments, no two of which ever had quite the same outcome, as the conditions under which they were conducted continuously varied.

Metaphors

There are many metaphors used in writing about objects. Things are said to have biographies (Kopytoff 1986; Gosden and Marshall 1999) or to help tell people's biographies (Hoskins 1998); they might also be seen to have agency (Gell 1998) or to be processual (see above). And Strathern (1993, 1999) has alerted us to the fact that terms like object (which presupposes some sort of opposing subject) and property are loaded with Western intellectual baggage, making them doubtful tools in understanding the relationship of people and things within other cultural forms. We need to be aware of the metaphors we use and the channels down which they send our thoughts. We have not quite found the right language to express the mutual implication of people and things. On the one hand we are wary of making things too active: things are not agents in their own right, and the material world is only given force and significance through human activity. On the other hand, things are not a passive stage setting to human action. We are all socialized within particular material settings, which are in some sense internal to us and our sense of physical possibility. The deep mutual involvement of people and things means that much social life is achieved through objects and is influenced by the qualities and properties of those objects. We want to include things as a central element in our social analysis, but any use of the active voice when describing objects must be suspect.

Let us return to our crumpled piece of barkcloth with a new appreciation of the complexities surrounding its production, and focus on the complexities of writing about it. Our writing now is one stratum of a series of layered accounts about these objects. The first layers were produced by their collectors. An assiduous fieldworker such as Beatrice Blackwood produced a mass of documentation, as did Felix Speiser, as we outlined at the beginning of this chapter. One peculiarity of the four collectors we have looked at is that they published almost nothing from their mass of observations in the field. This is a major possible stratum of record and thought which is missing. However, Blackwood and others lectured on their collections and wrote about them in letters and papers delivered at conferences.

Our work is part of a resurgence of interest in material culture, but also in the histories of colonialism and the discipline of anthropology. We are part of a wave of interest in museum collections as historical sources of documentation and of objects preserved to some extent from the threat of decay. We have employed terms in common use, such as the biography of objects, to start to chart the accumulating history of objects. But we have to be aware that we must not give objects too many human properties: objects cannot tell their own biographies – we have to construct them from the materials available to us. Different people, such as those presently living in New Britain, would tell varying tales about exactly the same things. The physical presence of objects makes them appear direct representatives of the past in the present, but existing now in new contexts they are objects with new significances. These significant others are significant in ways we make them to a large extent.

Barkcloth for head binding looks to be an indigenous object, in an indigenous context, used in tune with a local aesthetic, and it is partly all of those things. But only partly. The fact of its presence in Oxford makes it a transformed object, not just in terms of its physical location but also in its significances. For Blackwood it was the tangible marker of an unusual custom, head binding, which might have historical and cultural significance. For the museum visitor it promotes the frisson of real difference: people who bind their heads are willing and able to transform their bodies to meet aesthetic standards at odds with our own. For the museum today it is a node in a set of connections, informing us of the history of this corner of Papua New Guinea and of customs then about to be suppressed by the new missionaries, but now reviving. It also acts as a nexus of information on the history of anthropology and the interests of the collectors. As museum curators we also ponder, and sometimes act, on the links this object and the others in our care have with local people, and whether they should stay or be returned. For a museum, or at least an ethnographic museum, the biography of an object is vital, and the more complex and rich that biography is, the better museum curators are pleased.

Colonialism in New Guinea created a new culture which joined all parties through continual social relations. Objects were crucial to these relations. But the linking of white, black and Asian did not make for acculturation, or even hybridity, but rather produced novel forms of difference. These forms of difference were constantly novel due to the experimental nature of social relations, especially on the part of New Guineans. Performances, such as those set up by whites, were an attempt to stabilize relations, make New Guineans true subjects of European power, and to internalize new norms of discipline and comportment. The use made of flag poles and marching in cargo cults, which so disturbed Europeans, shows how important the performative aspects of material culture were in realizing the relations desired by Europeans. Experiment was not just found at the point of exchange of objects, but reached deep into local peoples lives through the processes of production and use of objects within a colonial context. Colonial culture was the product of all parties involved in it, and cannot be understood in terms of the top-down imposition of power and the bottom-up resistance to it. Experiment, instability and novelty were the key elements of colonial culture, which constantly shifted the dimensions of the world in which people lived. Many of these shifts were caused by objects and the relations which surrounded them.

Objects are simple, but in complex ways, and this complexity derives partly from the multi-stranded nature of the colonial society with its mass of motives and influences from within New Guinea and outside. We are hoping to demonstrate that objects represent a barium meal, making apparent many of the connections of colonialism that would otherwise remain invisible. It is to the nature of colonial society in New Britain and its changes over time that we now turn.

Notes

1. Chinnery Papers, National Library of Australia, MS 766/20/23.
2. J.A. Todd's research proposal. Elkin Papers, Series 40, Item 77, Box 160, Sydney University.

3. Patrol Report written by Ian McCallum Mack for 14 October – 3 November 1927. Microfilm of patrol reports (PMB 1036) held in Pacific Manuscripts Bureau, Australian National University. Original held in National Library of Australia.

–2–

Colonial Culture and History in West New Britain

New Britain is a large, sparsely populated island. It has one of the longest colonial histories in New Guinea, most notably at its eastern end, the Gazelle Peninsula. Our aim here is to provide a bridge between the general notions of colonial relations provided in the last chapter and a more detailed history of the region during the earlier colonial period. In order to give some structure to our discussion of history we have divided the last 130 years into two time periods. Periodization is always difficult and arbitrary, but the timespan 1884–1914 covers the German colonial period, which sees a shift from labour recruitment and trade to a plantation economy and from a random and violent set of colonial relations to more regularized and less chaotic interactions from the start of the twentieth century. Between 1900 and 1914 is when the structures of administration were set up. Our second period 1914–42 is a period of Australian Administration, first under a military regime and then a civil administration from 1921 when New Guinea became a Territory Mandated to Australia under the League of Nations. For local people this period saw a massive change in settlement patterns, subsistence, forms of trade and ritual, which are the focus of our analysis in the book as a whole. Structures of administration show considerable continuity with the German regime in type and culture, and after the First World War there was continued growth of plantation economy; this is the time at which the colonial process comes into greater focus through a larger number of documents and books

Initial Histories: Pre-contact Societies in New Britain and Subsequent Changes

People have lived in New Britain for the last 35,000 years, and ways of life have changed continually during that time, as we shall see in Chapter Nine. Forms of settlement and kinship found at the beginning of the colonial period have an antiquity of 1,000 years or less. Western New Britain was linked to the mainland of New Guinea through the specialist traders on the Siassi Islands, and this trading system grew up 500 years ago or less (Lilley 1986). The Siassi trading system not only facilitated the movement of items in exchange, but also provided the conduit for movements of language and ceremony, as we shall see (Map 1). Colonial culture grew up in a social world which was relatively recent and was in the throes of further change.

Linguistic divisions and histories provide a means of understanding some of the diversity and unity of the society in western New Britain prior to colonialism. As Ross writes (1988: 160) no published descriptions exist for most of the languages of this area. Nevertheless, some tentative groupings can be made. The Lamogai chain (also known as Bibling [Chowning 1996]) is made up of the Mouk, Aria and Lamogai languages (Gimi, Ivanga and Lamogai); the Passismanua chain contains Miu, Kaulong and Sengseng with Psohoh at a slightly further remove; the West Arawe chain is composed of Arove (Arawe), Aiklep (Agerlep) and Apalik (Palik); the East Arawe chain is made up of Akolet, Avau, Atiu and Bebeli (Kapore); with Mangseng being an outlier of the larger Arawe chain (Ross 1988: Fig. 5). The groups that we are particularly concerned with here are the Passismanua and the East and West Arawe chains (Map 2). Ross (1988: 160) feels that much of the differentiation of these groups might be recent, and it is also worth noting that some of the languages most closely related are not contiguous with each other. There has thus been some recent movement of people and linguistic change in the area. At a slightly deeper historical level, all these languages are part of the north New Guinea group which includes all the Austronesian languages of West New Britain (except for those of the Willaumez Peninsula, the Nakanai and Bali-Witu), plus groups of languages along the north New Guinea coast, as far as the Schouten Islands (Ross 1989: 137). This linguistic history derives from the close links between western New Britain and the north New Guinea coast in trade, and the fact that there might have been movements of people from the New Guinea coast over the last few centuries. It is quite likely that some of the languages and their speakers have only entered western New Britain since the trade links with New Guinea became more regular over the last five hundred years.

Linguistic history is only one element of complex historical change within the area. Links set up through material culture cross-cut linguistic similarities and differences. Chowning (1978) has discerned three main 'culture areas' within West New Britain, each with its own set of material culture. The first of these is covered by Arawe, Bibling and Passismanua (Chowning's Whiteman) speakers on the south coast and adjacent inland areas. This area is the one in which we are focusing on in this book and which we shall call Arawe as a shorthand designation This area is characterized by skull deformation, blow pipes, *mokmok* and *singa* stones (used as wealth and for sorcery), pearl shells, three-piece shields, barkcloth belts for men, and rounded pig-tusk mouth ornaments (see Chapter Three for a full description of the material culture of the Arawe region). These are all objects which form the focus of our analysis in this book. Most of this material is still in use and is vital for initiations, bride-price and mortuary payments, as well as in exchange.

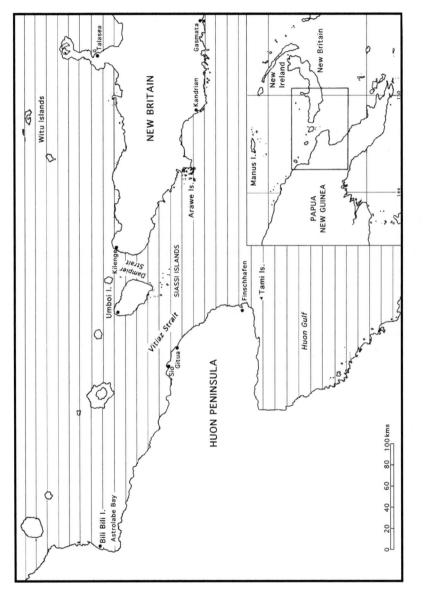

Map 1. West New Britain and part of mainland Papua New Guinea

The second group is made up of the Maleu (Kilenge and Lolo) and Bariai (Kaliai, Bariai and Kove) speakers found at the very western end of New Britain and along the north coast. Life in this area is marked out by ceremonials necessitating the use of masks of different types, highly decorated men's houses and shell money, and particularly elaborate forms of initiation. The third group, found on the north coast has seen most change in the post-war period due to massive oil-palm plantations and settlers from elsewhere, and is thus is less obviously differentiated in the present as older forms of material culture have been given up. But the area from the Willaumez Peninsula to the base of the Gazelle Peninsula, inhabited by the Nakanai, Bakovi and Bulu speakers was characterized by a distinctive male headdress made of rings, spears decorated with nassa shells, and shell money (Chowning 1978: 297). It is likely that these areas of distribution of material culture have some longevity to them, although their exact time depth is unknown.

A more rapidly changing aspect of history is that of ritual and ceremony, some of which is regularly exchanged from one area to another. This has contributed to a complex social landscape with material culture, language and ritual each having slightly different spatial distributions. Much ceremony has been exchanged, dances such as Sia brought by the Siassis from New Guinea and danced amongst the Bariai speakers of the north coast and a number of groups on the south coast, including the Arawe Islanders and the people around Kandrian. There is a complex history of the trade in, and introduction of, rituals, and it is hard to say exactly what the situation was at the start of the colonial period. For example, in Kilenge on the north coast, Zelenietz and Grant (1981: 98–9) note that there were six ceremonial cycles to honour the recently dead and for the initiation of children which went on for two to five years. Two of these cycles (Natavutavu and Bukumu) were autochthonous, Sia came via Siassi from New Guinea, Takiluange from Bali-Witu amd Aiyu from the Kaulong, and in each the songs were performed in their language of origin.

Another obvious element which cross-cut ties of language and bounded areas of material culture is the movement of items by Siassi traders (Harding 1967). Here again there have been historical shifts, with the Tami Islanders more prominent in the trade in the late nineteenth century, trading objects such as wooden bowls, and most of their trade routes being appropriated by the Siassi Islanders early in the twentieth century. The Siassis voyaged directly to the Arawe Islands on the south coast of New Britain, and possibly also to the Kandrian region on occasions, and continue to do so in the present. The Arawe Islanders use their sets of connections to move Siassi trade items and other things to Kandrian (Fig. 2.1 shows a local sailing canoe) and as far as Gasmata, as well as along inland trade routes, chiefly the one from Sara village on the south coast to the Lamogai area and on to the north coast. The Siassis have excellent links with the Maleu and Bariai speakers and the Kove acted as middlemen moving both Siassi items and

Figure 2.1. Outrigger canoe coming towards shore (Pitt Rivers Museum, University of Oxford)

products from the Kilenge area to the Willaumez Peninsula and to Bali-Witu. From there they could make their way to the Nakanai. In short, there would be few communities, either coastal or inland, who did not receive items moved by the Siassis in the whole of West New Britain, although especially in former times there would have been concentrations of material on the coast.

There has been a complex series of movements of languages, rituals and material culture over the last few centuries, which has created a complicated social landscape at the western end of New Britain. Differences between groups are not clear cut, but rather each area has a slightly different mix of customs and material culture. People moving from one community to another within western New Britain and across to the coast of New Guinea would find things local to the area they are visiting, but mixed together with familiar objects and practices. We suspect, but cannot be sure, that various areas were rather more distinct from each other in material culture, customs and probably language at the time of contact with the Germans than they are now. But this is a difference of degree rather than kind, with colonial culture opening up the possibilities for travelling and mixing, and this only accelerated transfers of objects and ceremonies that were happening anyway. This has led to a greater similarity of one group to another, although considerable diversity is still evident in the present. But the process is by no means one-way, as Thurston (1992: 132) has observed for the Anem speakers of the northwest coast (the one Non-Austronesian language in that region) where people are attempting to remove foreign influences (which include both English and Kilenge vocabulary) from their language and culture and to maintain their distinctiveness. There are complex processes at work here, made more complex by the addition of colonial relations. We move now to an outline of the colonial history, combining the formal changes of the administration with some feel for the nature of the human relationships through which the colonial regime was sustained.

Trader to Plantation, Hamlet to Village: German New Guinea 1884–1914

This was the period in which colonial culture was set up and saw a shift from violent and confused relations between local people and recruiters and traders up until 1900, to more regularized and regulated types of colonial interaction from the start of the twentieth century.

The history of German New Guinea can be baldly summarized as a shift from labour recruiting and trading with a relatively small and dispersed non-Melanesian population, to settlers who were found in relatively large numbers on the Gazelle Peninsula and New Ireland who ran plantations and owned businesses of various types. As far as the Melanesian inhabitants of the region were concerned, this saw a shift from sporadic, but often violent, contacts with outsiders, who brought guns and diseases, through a period of open resistance when land was being appropriated, to a more regularized set of relations with outsiders within the major centres of colonial populations and beyond. Although German New Guinea was a period of tense mutual exploration with first contacts between outsiders and locals, there was no frontier that moved in a systematic manner, but rather a series of pockets of influence, which shifted in importance both geographically and socially.

The firm of Godeffroy und Sohn set up their first trading station at Matupi in Blanche Bay near the present-day town of Rabaul in 1874, and were soon followed by the smaller firm of Robertson and Hernsheim in 1875. They found the locals well-accustomed to white traders and already speaking pidgin (Hempenstall 1978: 119), due to the activities of whalers and recruiters (Gray 1999). The missionary George Brown was also in the first trickle of settlement, and he set up mission stations and made converts between 1877 and 1881. These early traders lived very isolated lives, isolated that is from other Europeans, but they were plunged into a mass of relations with local people, which were not always that happy. Ten of Godeffroy's twelve agents died in the late 1870s, and the fire arms which were a part of early trade exacerbated conflicts. There were said to be 700 guns in Tolai hands by 1887 (Hempenstall 1978: 123). Relations were mediated almost entirely through objects, especially in the absence of much mutual language, and at first exchange rates were very beneficial for the traders, so that in 1875 a length of tobacco could buy between twenty-five and forty coconuts, whereas five years later it brought only fifteen, and knives, axes and firearms had replaced the original cheap trade goods of red cloth, glass pearls and empty bottles.

The lack of a long tradition of German colonial rule and the confused pattern of the early administration of German New Guinea meant that there was little consistency in the instruments or policies of government, and the Governor in New Guinea had much freedom, as did individual station officers. This started to change after the government take-over of administration in 1899, and Governor Hahl, who had arrived in 1896, constructed a system of administration which lasted little changed through the period of Australian rule. Hahl was determined to educate people in the service of capitalism and was willing to make an effort to get to grips with local culture in order to learn how this could be done. Hahl was concerned to increase local people's economic dependency on the white community and to make local labour available to the administration. In 1903 a Government Instruction said that all able-bodied men had to work for up to four weeks a year on road construction and maintenance or on the government plantations. A head tax of 5 marks was an alternative, and this provided people with a regular need for money, if they wished to keep their time free. It was levied for the first time in the Gazelle Peninsula in 1906. From 1896 onwards Hahl also appointed a series of village headmen, the *luluai*s (a corruption of a Tolai word for leader) and their deputies, the *tultul*s. Their initial roles were to supervise road construction and adjudicate in local disputes, such that they could impose fines of up to 25 marks (10 fathoms of *tambu* [shell money]). By 1900 there were forty-four luluais on the Gazelle Peninsula and twenty-three in the Duke of Yorks, which were the only areas of Hahl's authority.

Government influence gradually spread over the next fourteen years as new government stations and sub-stations were set up. The administrative structure that the Australians took over in 1914 consisted of district offices in Kavieng, Madang and Rabaul, plus second-class stations at Namatanai, Kieta, Morobe, Aitape and Lorengau (Rowley 1958: 16). The administrative staff was not huge and was mainly concentrated in Rabaul: in 1913 there were eighty-four administrative staff altogether in New Guinea, seventy-two in the Bismarck Archipelago and the Solomons and twelve on mainland New Guinea. Each station had at least one German officer, and these officers laid and maintained roads, levied the head tax, appointed luluais and tultuls, kept law and order, and attempted some mild regulation of recruiting. One feature of the German administration was the lack of regular foot patrols, making this a maritime administration. The effectiveness and influence of local officers depended on the availability of vessels to tour their region and on their own personal characteristics. Some, like the famous Boluminski in Kavieng, had an immediate and lasting influence laying out roads and levying taxes in a manner conducive to the health of the colonial regime, if not that of the local communities. By 1914 the areas of New Britain deemed to be 'within the organization' included the Gazelle Peninsula, the north coast to the Willaumez Peninsula and the south coast to Gasmata, plus Bali-Witu. Hahl had plans to set up third-class stations at Thileniushafen (Gasmata) on the south coast and Komethafen (Eleonora Bay) on the north in 1915 to allow control over the interior of western New Britain, making it possible to recruit there, relieving pressures on the coastal areas (Rowley 1958: 35). The new stations never happened under the Germans, partly because Hahl left New Guinea in 1914 and then because the war intervened.

Between 1900 and 1914 the colonial economy was transformed from that of trade to plantations, which had a series of effects on the local population. New Guinea became 'a copra colony', although trade still supplied more than 50 per cent of the Protectorate's copra exports in 1909 (Firth 1973: 134, 136). The new plantations alienated land and there was a series of wars on the Gazelle over land from the late 1890s to early in the twentieth century. One result of this was the setting up of native reserves of land which could not be further alienated. However, much of this land might have been used for the plantations indirectly. The new plantations had a considerable demand for food. Some of this was imported but a good deal was grown locally. The relatively generous allowances of the Forsayth plantations (it was the Forsayths who set up the first plantation at Ralum in 1886) gave each worker 680 gm of rice per day, plus 2,500 gm of fresh fruit and vegetable per day and 400 gm of fish or meat a week (either fresh or imported) (Firth 1973: 213). All the rice was imported, but most of the fruit and vegetables was local, plus a proportion of the meat and fish. By 1913, at the peak of the plantation economy, 14,990 labourers were employed in the Bismarck Archipelago as a whole (Firth 1977: 15). At a very rough estimate, this would provide a demand for 37,000 kg of fresh fruit and vegetables per day, plus whatever contributions of fish and meat were made from the local economy. This would represent a considerable investment of time and labour, although it is pointless to speculate too far on how much land would have been under cultivation to supply the plantations. However, it was noted that people of the Sulka and Mengen areas were re-settling near the Gazelle Peninsula in order to garden for the plantations (Sack and Clark 1979). Steel axes and bush knives, in demand at this time, would have helped clear larger areas for planting.

Thus when plantations were set up on the south coast of New Britain around the turn of the century, similar sets of relationships would have pertained, and it is no surprise that there were considerable shifts in settlement pattern and of subsistence at about this time. On the Arawe Islands where people were previously spread among a number of small hamlets on the south coast of New Britain and a number of islands, they now cluster in big villages on five islands and one area of

Figure 2.2. Men with spears and shields standing in front of a palisaded village in the Kaulong area (H.L. Downing Collection, State Library of New South Wales)

the mainland (Gosden and Pavlides 1994). In the present, people in many parts of the province and particularly on the coast live in villages of several hundred inhabitants, but these were formed often around the beginning of this century from a number of smaller hamlets, each of which was defended and centred around a men's house (Fig. 2.2) (Counts and Counts 1970: 92; Zelenietz and Grant 1986: 204). Chinnery (1925, 1926) has reported an identical form of organization for the Kaulong and other areas of the south coast.

These small hamlets seem to have been the basic settlement pattern throughout West New Britain and the Siassi Islands (Freedman 1970), being given up on the coast fairly early in the history of European colonialism and later (if at all) in the inland areas. But this was not just a settlement pattern but a form of social organization based on cognatic ties which allowed changing rights to land and other resources. Goodale (1995) provides the best account of the ties between people and people and people and places created by this form of settlement, drawing on accounts provided by inland Kaulong people in the 1960s. In Kaulong *bi* refers to a hamlet with around fifteen men, women and children affiliated to it. The *bi* has a *mang* or house, which all can use, but only men can sleep in it, and the house is surrounded by useful trees and plants. The *bi* was set up by an ancestral figure some generations previously, and deceased affiliates are buried in the dirt floor of the *mang*. All important exchanges and ceremonies take place in the *bi* clearing. Although each individual has one primary affiliation, each can claim links to many hamlets and groups through both their mother's and father's lines.

People are extremely mobile, clearing gardens and sleeping in many different places during their lifetimes, and mobility brings into being complicated personal links. As Goodale (1995: 116) writes, 'men and women establish personal networks by reaffirming relatedness through travel and trade and through permanent or shifting residential cooperation and affiliation. Links in personal networks are created and maintained or broken and dissolved through continued or discontinued personal action.' Each individual has more potential links than they can make use of in their life time, and big men and women are those who can mobilize and extend their personal networks and thus their personal influence.

Among the Kilenge the hamlets, known as *naulum*, were based around men's houses which were also known by the same term. The *naulum* owned land, pig nets, ceremonial designs, areas of reef and the sea inside the reef. The *naulum* existed as a group of people who controlled property and resources, the building of the men's house, and through the use rights alloted to each of the members. It was also the unit of labour for clearing garden land and the body which co-ordinated ceremonial cycles such as the *narogo* (Zelenietz and Grant 1986: 205, 211). From the point of view of the individual, each person had a mass of possible entitlements to group membership, not all of which could possibly be activated through their lifetime. Thus the decisions of grandparents and parents as to which group memberships to take up and which not affected, although did not determine, the decisions of their descendants.

Throughout western New Britain there seems to have been a single form of settlement pattern and social structure, which might be quite ancient (Gosden and Pavlides 1994). It allowed for both mobility of settlement and open links between groups. What happened from the early twentieth century onwards is that the settlement pattern changed from small hamlets to large villages, but the open network of connections continued and expanded. People congregated into larger villages, but were still able to move regularly from one area to another on trading expeditions or to take up gardening land in a new place through kin connections. New larger settlements formed a labour pool for larger gardens to feed the settlements themselves, but also the new needs of plantations and traders for food. The new villages were also focal points in the movement of people through the area utilizing their kin connections to travel far and wide. The large villages at first only existed on the coast, where government influence was greatest, and settlement agglomeration happened later inland; in some areas, such as where Goodale worked, it has never happened. All these changes brought into question the nature of the community. Further change was brought about by the numbers of people (mainly men) leaving villages to work on plantations or in towns, drawn by the activities of labour recruiters, as they were euphemistically called.

Recruiting around New Britain, even at its western end, was intense. Between 1912 and the start of 1914 there was a ban on recruitment in the Sulka and Mengen

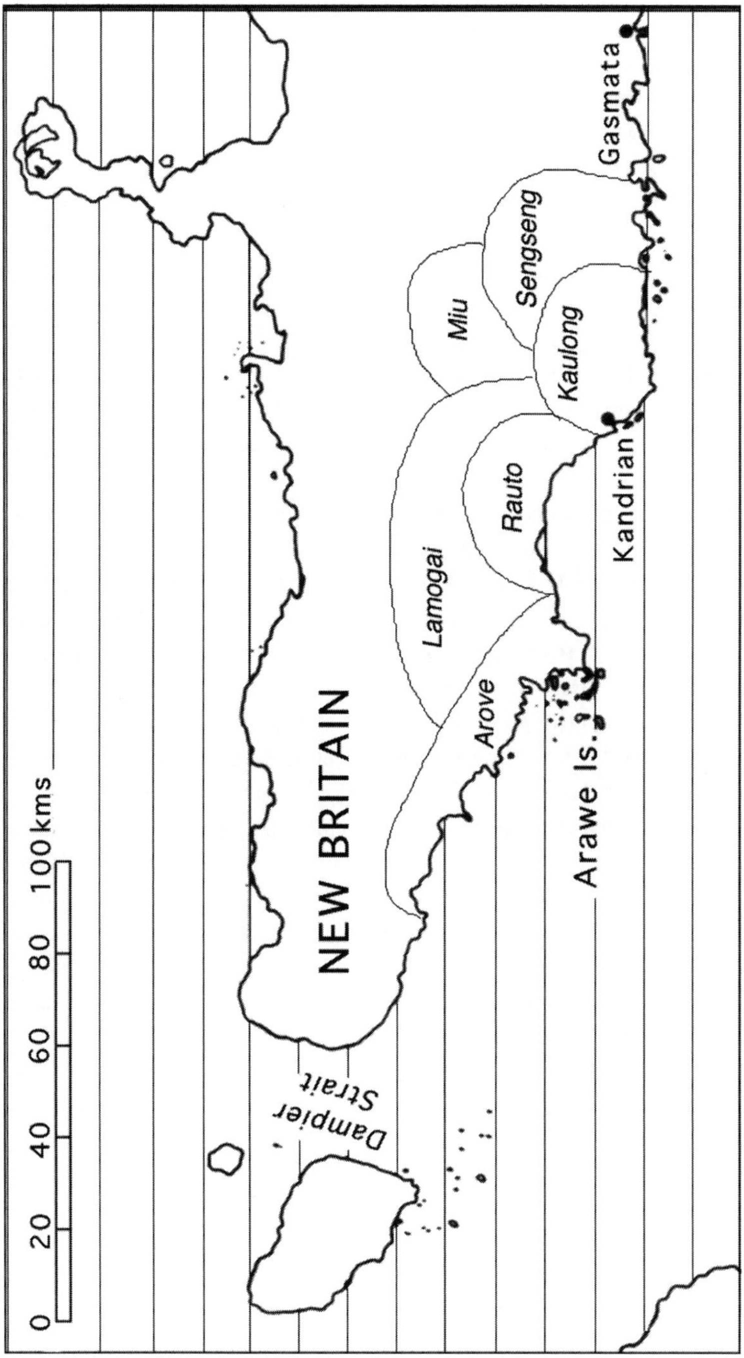

Map 2. The linguistic boundaries in the Arawe region of southwest New Britain

areas and the whole coastline from Cape Gloucester to Montagu Harbour. It was noted that ruthless recruiting by the Forsayths had made villagers flee inland, and one of their recruiters, Karl Münster, was sentenced to three month's jail, which was extremely unusual (Firth 1973: 224, 228). In 1913 a Forsayth recruiter broke the prohibition by recruiting labourers for the company's Arawe plantation from Rauto on the adjacent coast. In 1913 recruitment was reaching its limit in coastal areas: it is estimated that nearly every unmarried man in the villages of the northwest coast of New Britain was a recruit that year or had been one recently (Firth 1973: 173), and much the same might have been true of the south coast.

The process of recruiting was obviously a violent and destructive one, which had multiple effects. Guns, ammunition and other European goods were introduced into the area, and many men, plus some women, would have gone off to work in plantations or as servants. The Germans estimated that there were 152,075 people living on the Bismarck Archipelago in January 1914, and although we should not let the spurious accuracy of this figure mislead us, it does provide an estimate with some factual backing (Firth 1973: 142). Of these 17,529 were working for Europeans or Chinese in some capacity – that is getting on for 12 per cent of the population at one time. Given the turn-over of workers, this meant a considerable percentage of the censused population would have experienced plantation or other work at some point in their lives and had access to European goods. The Gazelle Peninsula and northern New Ireland were both centres of plantations; the latter area was a major source of recruits. However, all the coastal areas would have had their settlement patterns and social structures changed in a major way.

The other set of devastating changes that came about in the German period was epidemics of disease. Smallpox and flu epidemics spread right through New Guinea in 1893–4 and had major effects in the Bismarck Archipelago (Parkinson 1999 [1907]: 90–1). Estimates of how many people died are difficult to come by. In Witu plantations were set up on land left vacant after 50 per cent of the population died from smallpox and the suppression of two uprisings in 1901 and 1903 (Firth 1973: 136). Witu was densely populated so might have suffered worse than some areas from density-dependent diseases. However, the Arawe Islands also represent high levels of population, and according to local testimony many died at this time. A further devastating event which had a major effect on the west end of New Britain and its south coast was the collapse of the Ritter volcano in 1888. Ritter is out in the Vitiaz Strait and its collapse created tidal waves (tsunamis) which wiped out villages in the Cape Gloucester area, along the coast of Umboi and along the south coast, where local people have stories of waves several metres high. Loss of life would have been high on Gloucester and Umboi, but less on the south coast where destruction of villages and gardens would have been the main effects. This geological event, essentially random when viewed in terms of historical process, would have added an extra dimension to the confusion and disruption of the times.

Colonial Culture in New Britain 1914–42

In terms of formal administration, this period takes us from the start of the Australian Military Administration to the Mandated Territory of New Guinea, and from the confused situation of change during the war to a settled white colonial society centred on Rabaul and reaching out into the plantations and missions. For local people this period was one in which populations started to rise after the disease and violence of the nineteenth century, albeit slowly. There was a more obvious government presence in many areas, with patrol officers moving around on foot. There were new forms of leadership in evidence and the expansion of the trading system through utilizing the multiplicity of kin links detailed above, together with links with white traders and collectors.

An Australian Expeditionary force under Colonel W. Holmes took over Rabaul, and with it the effective control of New Guinea, with little bloodshed right at the beginning of the First World War. The move from one administration to another caused considerable disruption. The colony's external contacts were no longer with Germany via Singapore, but now south to Sydney, and the internal shipping and other forms of connection ground to a halt. This meant that plantations had their supplies of rice and other foods disrupted and there was much pillaging of villages and gardens. When order was restored it was on the basis of German law, and many of the German officials remained in place until the end of 1914 and beyond. Certainly the majority of the plantation owners stayed, and investments by Germans in plantations actually went up during the war (Rowley 1958: 60), partly due to the belief many patriots had that Germany would win, but also because copra prices stayed buoyant and the military was concerned that business structures were still able to function effectively. Of the 254 missionaries in New Guinea in 1922, 222 were German. Alongside the existing German community was the military administration which totalled over 600 men, who operated both as soldiers and administrators. The two colonial communities obviously had ambiguous relations, but not necessarily poor ones.

Military authority and hierarchy permeated the whole administration in New Guinea, in contrast to the more relaxed and democratic structures in Papua, but in a manner which chimed well with the feelings of the Germans. This made for a continuity of style between the Germans and the Australian military which had a lasting effect on the approach to administration in New Guinea with its harsher labour ordinances and stricter legal code than that found in Papua. The respect for hierarchy was reinforced by the fact that many of those who became patrol officers and office workers had seen active service during the war and were actively sought as the most fitting members of the service. Mair (1970: 15) notes the gulf of styles and attitudes that yawned between the administrative services of Papua and New Guinea.

Holmes was replaced as Administrator by Pethebridge who in February 1915 created the structure of government departments (Supplies and Ordnance, Treasury and Bank, Works, Native Affairs and Police etc.) which was to remain when New Guinea became a Mandated Territory under the League of Nations in 1921. Successive administrators extended the pattern of stations and sub-stations. In 1918 a sub-station was set up in Talasea, followed by the movement of the station set up at Ablingi in 1917 to Gasmata in 1919. Sub-district officers and deputy district officers were created, and it was felt that no sub-station should ever have just one white officer. A system of training for patrol officers was set up, plus the need for them to patrol on foot was established. Small but significant symbolic changes were made: the German caps and staffs of office used by luluais was replaced with Australian equivalents, although the name was retained. There was concern that in February 1916 the Talasea luluais still had the German badges of office (Rowley 1958:40).

In 1920 an extra element was added to the administrative structure when the Commonwealth Government passed an Expropriation Ordinance to confiscate all German-owned property, which was sold to Australian citizens, many of them ex-servicemen. The body to oversee this, the Expropriation Board, had as its chairman W.H. Lucas, formerly of Burns Philp, who took instructions directly from the Commonwealth Government which gave him a power which sat uneasily with that of the local administration.

After 1921 New Britain became a District, headed by a District Officer and divided into the two sub-districts of Talasea and Gasmata, each in theory with its own Assistant District Officer (although often only manned by patrol officers). These men in the field had a range of powers and duties, including opening up new areas to tax collecting, recruiting and health services, overseeing the law pertaining to labour ordinances, taxes and criminal offences. They were required to send back regular reports, which, where they still exist, form valuable sources of historical data. New Guinea patrol officers were also a literary lot and have produced a number of readable and valuable memoirs of their time in New Guinea; accounts with some mention of New Britain include Downs (1986), McCarthy (1963) and Wright (1966). In New Britain and elsewhere within New Guinea foot patrols were made to a number of barely contacted areas. The watchword of the administration in this regard was control. Areas were divided into three categories: uncontrolled, pacified and controlled. The first two had either no government influence or only enough to prevent warfare, whereas only the third was thought to experience the full benefits of government, which included paying taxes, lining for censuses, having some form of health care and feeling the weight of the law.

The perception of the white population was that government was created and exercised by white people, but this was only partly true. A patrol post in newly opened country (see McCarthy's description of the post at Mulutu in the Nakanai area in 1927) had a (white) patrol officer, half a dozen native police, one native medical orderly and some labourers. They would create luluais and tultuls in the local villages, who in theory provided the presence of the government at the local level.

The majority of the people involved in governing were Melanesians, and many of the decisions of patrol officers and others must have been refracted through Melanesian interactions and forms of understanding. This might have had both positive and negative consequences, as the many stories of police constables taking the law into their own hands testify (see Gammage 1998). Control was not a simple matter of white desires imposed on blacks, but a more complex and messy set of understandings and misunderstandings, depending on the sensitivity of the individuals, their experience in colonial encounters, and the motives of all parties. Nor were the villagers merely recipients of outside influences. As we shall see in more detail below, many a luluai had his own aims in encounters with the government. Chinnery, the government anthropologist, was worried about the growing power of paramount luluais, which could lead to resistance to Europeans.[1]

Along with this form of organization, which allowed much strategic decision making to take place, was an ascribed leadership with particular titles, such as *natavolo* for male leaders and *nagarara* for their female equivalents in Kilenge (Zelenietz 1980: 137). From the German period onward, when the government leadership roles of luluai and tultul were introduced, there has been much confusion over the relationship between pre-contact forms of leadership and those of the later period. This makes it difficult to reconstruct the earlier situation. However, certain features of pre-colonial leadership appear clear. Leadership titles were inherited, and there was some endogamy within this group, with leaders only marrying others of the same rank. Leadership titles were portable, so that if a person moved from one hamlet to another they took their title with them, and there might have been a pattern where people were more likely to be leaders outside their kinship group than inside, a form of stranger king/queen as seen from Polynesia. There might have been different tiers of leadership ranging from the head of a hamlet to the leader of a group of hamlets, and while inheritance was a necessary condition of rank, the exact level of rank might have been determined by achievement in a series of different arenas, such as war, trade, ritual, hunting and fishing. War and trade were often linked, in that a negotiated settlement to a conflict often initiated a cycle of exchange and ritual. With the advent of colonial peace, trade and ritual gained a much greater importance than previously as an avenue to achieved status, and may have lead to a greater prevelance of sorcery, as a more covert means of pursuing conflicts. This account is taken from Zelenietz (1980: chap. 3) on the Kilenge, but a similar structure was reported to us on the Arawe Islands and from elsewhere in the region.

Figure 2.3. M.V. *Siassi* leaving Kandrian (Pitt Rivers Museum, University of Oxford)

Vital to the European community outside the towns was a network of plantations, and by the 1920s there was a number of these along the south coast of New Britain, notably at Lindenhafen, Aliwa plantation at Möwehafen/Kandrian, and the Arawe plantation. These represented points at which ships called (Fig. 2.3) bringing mail and supplies, places of rest and comfort with European food and alcohol, so that they could seem little oases of Western society for the culture-shocked traveller or anthropologist. Many of the plantations had been set up in the German period and went into Australian hands through the activities of the Expropriation Board. They represented small mixed communities living in close proximity. The Expropriation Board's description of Arawe Plantation, published in 1925, gives a total size of 606 ha, carrying 51,070 coconuts and being worked by 170 labourers. They were housed in eight sets of married quarters, plus ten labourers' houses, all made of local materials. It seems that not all labourers could have lived in these houses, and thus quite a number must have commuted from villages within the Arawe Islands. There was one Chinese dwelling and a trade store, plus kerosene, rice and drug stores, and a hospital. The bungalow occupied by the European manager was made of weatherboard and was the one building made of non-local materials, and had a separate bathroom, pantry, kitchen and office. In addition, there were four copra dryers, a wharf and a wharf shed, a 3.5 ton cutter, 5 horses, 50 wild pigs, 78 goats and 17 fowls. *The Military Terrain Handbook* (No. 57, 1943) contains an aerial photograph (1943: Fig. 15) showing the layout and indicating that not much has changed since 1925. We have no details on the community, but presumably it was made up of a European, a Chinese and workers from different parts of New Guinea and Melanesia.

In 1930 patrol officer Horace Niall set up a new patrol post at Kandrian, which had been known to the Germans as Möwehafen. He arrived by sea-going canoe with ten native police and sixteen Sepik prisoners suffering life imprisonment for collecting heads to decorate a new *haus tamboran*.[2] This represented a further extension of government influence and set up the situation in which both Todd and Blackwood were to work in the later 1930s.

The other set of relationships which was vital to colonial society in New Guinea was those surrounding the missions. The history of mission activity on the south coast of New Britain is obscure and difficult to disentangle from the various records which exist. There seems to have been no formal missionary activity on the south coast of New Britain during the German period or in the immediate post-war years. The first missionaries appear to have been Anglicans who visited the area in 1928, following the setting up of the Rabaul Anglican Mission in 1924. In this year Rev. Sherwin, after travelling along the south coast, set up a mission station at Sag Sag at the very western end of New Britain, remaining there until 1935. Around 1928 Rev. Cartridge and the carpenter, Mr Titler, settled on Kauptimete island in the Arawe group. This group saw some success, and when the Archbishop passed through on his annual tour in 1933 he was able to baptize 171 converts. By 1935 there were six mission stations between Sag Sag and Kandrian, some run by white priests and at least two by Solomon Island Brothers. A school had been set up in Kumbun, also in the Arawe Islands, in 1935.[3] By the middle 1930s the Roman Catholic missions had also set up stations along the south coast and this history is even more obscure than for the Anglicans. Father Scharmach might have been resident on the islands off Kandrian from around 1925, although this seems quite uncertain. However, from 1935 onwards a mission station was set up on Pililo, in the Arawe Islands, followed in 1936 by a Mission at Turuk above Kandrian.[4] There was a combination of European (initially German, but later Irish) fathers and Melanesian catechists running the stations.

The missions had a complex set of effects, which, like their history, is hard to sum up succinctly. At a socio-economic level they would have acted like plantations, in that they caused the alienation of small but important areas of land from local hands. They would also have needed locally grown food to supplement foodstuffs coming from Rabaul, and food would have been exchanged for material items or money, introducing an extra source of Western goods. Education was also seen as an important path to understanding god's word, and the missions set up schools where they could, and they not only attempted to change peoples' religious beliefs, but also to inculcate habits of mind, such as reading, writing and arithmetic, which helped change world views in complex ways and which continue to do so down to the present. The social and cultural relations surrounding the missions were also complex. Missionizing was carried out through a combination of local agency, where people asked the church to come to their area, Melanesian and other Pacific Islander missionaries, and European influences. The Europeans were themselves quite a disparate bunch, with the Anglicans being solidly Anglo-Saxon and the early Catholics being German. There was also considerable competition between missions. Blackwood records her frustration at the number of missionaries passing through the Kandrian area in 1937. Todd notes in a letter to Elkin, then Professor of the Anthropology Department, Sydney University, that the new missionaries on the south coast 'spend a lot of time trying to cut each others throats in the christian like manner [sic]. The catechist was through here some weeks ago and got a hot reception from the local tultul who will have nothing to do with catechists. The priest was more or less antagonistic to the anthropologist and insinuated that I chased the catechist.'[5] This is a cameo of relationships engendered by the mission: the tultul was angry at the catechist (both presumably Melanesians), which caused the European priest to berate the anthropologist; all of which occurred within an atmosphere of competition between different missions. One element of history that is not especially well understood is the possible correlation between the coming of the missions and cargo culting. It seems clear that cargo cults date back at least to the German period in New Britain (Lattas 1998: 31) and that the war created a large number of cults, some of which might have their origins in the 1930s with the coming of the missions on the south coast.

We have seen in the previous section how settlement patterns and subsistence changed early in the century on the coast and that population had declined massively due to the impact of smallpox and other diseases. Ian Mack, a patrol officer who left especially detailed patrol reports noted for the Wariai area on the north coast between 14 and 24 December 1931, 'Many indentured labourers wives left in villages, have no children which affects population growth. 17 % of women married for more than one year have no kids. No short cuts to improving birth rate.'[6] Birth rates are a recurring theme in patrol reports of this date. However, low population levels did not effect the expansion of trade.

Many areas saw the introduction of new items of trade, such as Tolai shell money, which might only have reached as far as the Nakanai area before the arrival of the Germans but is now very common in the Bariai speaking areas and is taken by the Siassis to the north coast of New Guinea. There has also been considerable adoption of material culture from other areas. The Kove have borrowed large elements of ceremonial life and the associated artefacts from the Kilenge within this century and this has completely transformed Kove culture (Chowning 1969: 37). Even the Sengseng, who are conservative and nervous of outsiders, have accepted innovations in song, language, story and magic (Chowning 1969: 37).

Chowning (1969: 29) makes the more general points that labour recruiting brought men (and to a lesser extent women) from different groups into close proximity, where they could learn each other's customs; missionaries brought assistants from other parts of the Pacific who had their own effects on local cultures, and pacification made it much safer to travel than before and experience other peoples' ways of life. Also there is a very complex story of the uptake of Western goods, including money, which in some areas such as the Kaliai has been accepted into ceremonial payments (Counts and Counts 1970), but in other areas such as the Arawe Islands is kept rigidly apart from all local exchange media and cannot be used for brideprice or other forms of ceremonial payment.

There was a complex cline of influence from early contact on the coast to some of the latest white contacts anywhere in New Guinea for inland areas. Government patrols into the inland areas coincided with a greater frequency of relations between the inland and coast. For instance, the Sengseng, who were first contacted by white patrols in the late 1950s, received shells, coconuts, lizard skins and salt from the coast and gave shields, barkcloth, minerals, tobacco and betel nut in return (Chowning 1978: 297). Similarly, with the Kaliai: shields, spears and barkcloth came from the Lamogai, to whom coastal products went in return (Counts and Counts 1970: 96). The Kove received barkcloth, shields, shell money, pigs and dogs, from or via the Lamogai, and gave them ochre, obsidian, mats, baskets, betel nut, coconuts, pearl shells, turtle shell, edible shellfish and salt water (Chowning 1978: 298). Over the last few decades, social and physical access to the interior has increased, so that in the pre-contact period there were probably few pearl shells in the interior where now they circulate in enormous numbers (Chowning 1978: 302). Goodale (1995) notes how gold lip shells spread into the interior from the coast from the 1930s onwards. Trade was conducted in all areas through a system of trade friends, who were both inherited and newly made (Harding 1967: 165–9). Trade friends were viewed as kin, and indeed the relationship often led to kinship links, as marriages were arranged through trade friendships. The expansion of trade in the early twentieth century would have occurred partly through expanding the number of trade friends in existence, which in turn would have created more wide-ranging kinship links. We cannot help but wonder whether white traders, especially those who were long-term residents in New Britain, were conceived within the idiom of trade friendship and what difference this might have made to their ability to trade.

The end of the period we are looking at here saw the start of the Second World War which brought about the largest number of outsiders, with first the Japanese invasion in 1942 and then the American landings such as that under Julian W. Cunningham who commanded Alamo Force landing in the Arawe Islands on 15 December 1943 (Fig. 2.4).[7] The mass of American troops and the amounts of material they brought with them was a profound shock to local people, and it is

Figure 2.4. American troops endeavouring to haul a Jeep out of the water onto the coral shore of the Arawe Peninsula (Australian National War Memorial)

no surprise that the war initiated a marked upturn in cargo-cult activity which lasted until the independence of Papua New Guinea in 1975.

Knowledge was also a crucial part of issues of power and control, and for the European this knowledge was most useful when it took a systematized form. Here anthropology played its part. Chinnery's tasks as government anthropologist between 1924 and 1932 were outlined by McLaren the Government Secretary as: '1) Making a general investigation of the distribution, cultures and conditions of the native inhabitants; 2) becoming acquainted with District Officers, their methods of native administration etc.; and 3) examining the conditions of life and treatment of native labour on various places of employment.'[8] This was not anthropology as a disinterested study, being much closer to seeking understanding for the purposes of governance. This impression was reinforced by the reaction of a purely academic body to Chinnery's appointment. A resolution by the Board of Archaeological and Anthropological Studies in Cambridge University expressed satisfaction at the appointment of Chinnery, a former student, saying that 'Experience has proved that native races are best administered when a sympathetic control is based on a thorough knowledge of native life, custom and religion.'[9] Chinnery was also to give training in Ethnology for new cadets. His talks were to include: 'the history of our native peoples, their distribution and culture; general outline of problems in Territory and instruction in scientific methods of investigating native problems together with advice as to the practical application of ethnographic knowledge'.

'I shall arrange a series of "talks" dealing with the experiences of a "new tribe" from the time of its discovery until it reaches a condition of definite control.'[10] Anthropology had complex relations to administration mainly through the links between power and knowledge. Anthropological knowledge about New Guinea was created in an atmosphere of regulation and governance, so that it is impossible to appreciate what people wrote without taking this into account, even if not all anthropologists were equally enthusiastic about all aspects of colonial governance (Campbell 1998).

Within this mass of colonial relations we shall attempt to situate our anthropologists in future chapters. They came not just to study the natives, but as temporary natives themselves within colonial society, willing in different degrees to abide by its rules and having various levels of knowledge of those rules when they embarked upon the fieldwork we are focusing on here. Lewis, arriving in the German period came upon a newly emerging colonial culture: the government structures had only been developed less than ten years earlier, and plantations were very new to the south coast which was still suffering considerably at the hands of the recruiters. Speiser and Blackwood knew Melanesia, and in Blackwood's case New Guinea, so she moved within a set of social relations in which she knew individuals. Todd was very young, had never been to New Guinea, and was probably unhappy in the field. All of them acted like patrol officers, and this might have been the category of white person into which they fitted in villagers minds. They had New Guinean servants, obvious connections to the structures of government, and went on patrol, taking notes about local peoples and customs which they wrote down. The collection of objects was not unusual, as many whites did this too, including probably some of the patrol officers. Many patrol officers collected information on material culture, such as that which Ian Mack collected for Chinnery 'Lollo and Itne people trade with Arawes with whom they are very friendly. Lollo take Asiu bark for making nets, red paint, armbands and baskets by canoe to Pillilo [sic] and get pigs and coconuts. Arawe–Lollo bargaining done in Pidgin when not expert in each other's dialects.'[11]

Local people would have been far more experienced at dealing with whites than most anthropologists were in dealing with *them,* and this must have smoothed many a transaction. Even so, there would still have been an experimental nature to many encounters, especially for transient visitors like Lewis and Speiser. Both Todd and Blackwood stayed long enough to get to know some people and develop relationships of trust. For local people, relationships with whites were part of the expansion of overall trading links, although connections with whites would have quite different moral and social qualities to those made through the bonds of kinship or trade friends. Whatever the nature of these relationships, trade links within colonial culture were responsible for many thousands of objects ending up in museums around the world. It is to the collections and their collectors that we now turn.

Notes

1. Chinnery Papers, National Library of Australia, NLA 766/5/4 – 8 August 1929.
2. Niall Archive, National Library of Australia, MS 5264.
3. *Melanesian Mission Annual Report* 1935.
4. *Melanesian Mission Annual Report* 1937.
5. Letter from Todd to Elkin 27.12.35, Elkin Papers, Sydney University Archive, MS 4/1/69.
6. Microfilm of patrol reports written by Ian McCallum Mack (PMB 1036) held in Pacific Manuscripts Bureau, Australian National University.
7. Australian War Memorial, Canberra, 54 609/3/3.
8. Letter from McLaren, Secretary to the administration in Rabaul to Chinnery, 11.6.1924 – A5/1. National Archives of Australia, Canberra.
9. Chinnery Papers, National Library of Australia, NLA MS 766/1 – 29.4.24.
10. Chinnery Papers, National Library of Australia, NLA 766/5/2 – 6 April 1925.
11. Patrol Report written by Ian McCallum Mack 5 October – 10 December 1929. Microfilm of patrol reports (PMB 1036) held in Pacific Manuscripts Bureau, Australian National University. Original held in National Library of Australia.

—3—

The Collectors and their Collections

The world's museums are full of objects of all kinds, most collected over the last 150 years. These are said to represent all sorts of possibilities for exploring other times, places and ways of life; but in actual fact there have been few in-depth studies of collections and their attendant documentation. Part of our project was to explore the ways in which collections can be researched, both individually and in combination, and we developed methods to systematically analyse collections to facilitate comparison so that the information could be entered on a database to generate statistics and qualitative comparisons.

Our work is one element in a much broader effort to understand collection practices and material culture as an indicator of historical change throughout the world. Three basic axes influence the nature of collections made in an area: the styles of colonialism that exist in a region; the traditions of museums and of anthropology from which the collectors come; the means of categorizing different parts of the world in terms of the sorts of societies thought to live in a place and the types of material culture they produce. The grudging respect given to African 'art' over the last century has changed Westerners' views of Africa, for instance. The early easy assumption that only 'civilizations' could produce art created dissonance with the notion that Africa was characterized by tribal societies, and such conflicting categories have led to a basic re-evaluation of both social typologies and what constitutes art (Schildkrout and Keim 1998). A concentration on material embodiments of social forces has been creative both in constructing social and material typologies for parts of the world and in breaking them down.

Africa has been a particular focus for the study of museum collections. *The Scramble for Art in Central Africa* is a study of a group of collectors, such as Torday, Frobenius and Schweinfurth who worked in the Belgian Congo at the turn of the nineteenth and twentieth centuries, concentrating on how objects such as carved figures or metal items reflected local social forms. This is a process by which Africa was invented for the West, arriving back in the northern hemisphere stripped of context and presented in private collections and museums so as to create particular impressions of African tribalism and designs. *The Scramble for Art in Central Africa* is a study with considerable similarities to the one we are undertaking here in that a group of different collectors from a single area are considered, albeit by a number of authors in an edited collection (Schildkrout and Keim 1998). However, there are also differences of approach and emphasis. The model of colonialism employed makes a distinction between Africans and incomers, rather than employing a notion of a joint colonial culture such as the one we advocate here. The distinction between Africans and Europeans puts an emphasis on recontextualization as objects move from a black to a white milieu, rather than seeing the flows of objects as the means by which colonial culture was held together. Europeans are seen as external to African cultures, able to invent and imagine them in ways fundamentally influenced only by white philosophies of thought. We explore a different set of tensions and emphasize what happened in New Guinea through sets of local relations which create local forms of thought, as well as the intellectual influences collectors brought with them and in which they became re-immersed on going home. The contexts of the exchange of objects was obviously quite different in central Africa and New Guinea, with the possibility of much more commercialized exchange of objects (and people) prior to the coming of whites in the Congo than anywhere in New Guinea. The invention of Africa (Mudimbe 1988) was a plural phenomenon, so that a variety of Africas was invented on different parts of the continent and at different times. And it goes without saying that the nature of colonial cultures in Africa were also many and various, opening up a vast field of comparative studies of colonialism in Africa and world-wide which can be vitally aided by research into collections.

Such comparative work has started for Papua New Guinea (O'Hanlon and Welsch 2000) where a variety of contributors have explored the mix of motives of collectors in different times and places in Papua New Guinea, from the missionary George Brown to Hubert Murray, the governor of Papua, the arch administrator.

Another area of work similar to, but different from, our own is the means of displaying the results of collections once they arrived in the northern hemisphere. The most thorough and sophisticated piece of work here is that by Coombs (1994) looking at the effects that the display of African objects in Edwardian Britain had on the construction of the national identity of Britain, making the point that it was not just the colonies that were invented through the collection and display of material culture, but the metropolitan centres too. Objects were connected to issues of race and difference, so that the African other became one of the contrasts against which white, middle-class Anglo-Saxon culture was generated. We have concen-trated much less on what happened to objects once they arrived in the USA, Europe or Australia, focusing on relations in the 'field', although we shall pick out issues of display and representation in our future work in this region.

Even this brief summary helps hint at how the analysis of collections can create a broad field of comparative study of colonial relations, inventions and representa-tions. For comparison to be possible, it is necessary to engage in fine-grained, detailed studies of particular times and places. Our present work focuses hard on one region, but keeping broader issues in mind, seeing this as a necessary phase in an on-going pursuit of colonial forms and relationships more generally.

A Century of Collecting

Before we look at the four collectors in New Britain in the period 1908–37 we will examine the preceding period and the years after the Second World War when large scale collecting largely petered out. The collectors illustrated in this book come from a short period of time of almost thirty years, representing roughly a third of the total colonial period in the region. When starting this research project, we had not realized the extent of collecting by German museums and businesses that took place under the German colonial rule, and we have since embarked on a new project to cover the earlier period. We will refer to some of that research here, but it is in the early stages and a forthcoming second monograph will deal with that work more fully.

The four collectors discussed here form a distinct unit compared with those that came before and those collectors that followed. Prior to the annexation of New Britain by Germany, the collecting that took place was mainly done by explorers, traders and recruiters. From 1884 this expanded to include government officials and missionaries, and certainly up until about 1900 most collecting was opportunistic rather than scientific. After 1900 interest in the colony grew and larger collections were sought; our preliminary researches into collections now housed in various museums in Germany show the collectors to be much more varied in background and purposes in collecting than those from later periods. They range from residents in New Guinea to researchers from Germany who were either professionals or self-funding amateurs although West New Britain, unlike the Sepik, was not a focus for major, region-specific, government-funded expeditions.

The variety of collection practices found in German New Guinea reflects the complex set of forces influencing the colony. Germany's late entry into the world of colonialism meant that when the colony of New Guinea was founded, the sovereign power had no long tradition of colonial government, and this is reflected in the rather chaotic arrangements in New Guinea prior to 1900 and the start of Hahl's governorship at the beginning of the last century. The earliest collections came from areas where there were trading stations, and this did not include western New Britain. The main collections we have identified from this period were made between 1900 and 1914. The exception is a collection made by the Parkinsons, plantation owners, recruiters and traders based on the Gazelle Peninsula. Richard Parkinson is well known both for his collections and his writings (Parkinson 1999 [1907]). However, his wife, Phebe, played a largely unacknowledged role in his researches and collections during his life (see Specht 1999) and continued to collect in her own right after his death in 1909. During the period after 1900 the administrative structure used to govern New Guinea was set up, and collectors such as District Officers used their contacts with local people to make well-documented collections, mainly from New Ireland, but with a small component from New Britain. Back in Germany there was much more public interest in the colonies than in Britain, and newspaper articles giving quite detailed ethnographic accounts of Germans encounters with local inhabitants of New Guinea were common. The bond between Germany and the Pacific colonies being set up through the named German individuals reporting home to Germany through articles or objects made Germans at home feel their colonies were an extension of their own country. This was partly the impetus for private explorers and collectors, and at least two men (Mencke and Schoede) appear to have set up their own expeditions to document and collect material on the people, plants, animals and geology of the colony. Schoede, who spent time in western New Britain contemporary with Lewis, will be discussed briefly in Chapter Four. Such private expeditions are much less common from 1914 onwards when the Australians took over the administration of the Territory. The final set of collectors from this period include the members of the Hamburger Südsee-Expedition made up of professional researchers, crew members and long-term residents of New Guinea, and this expedition in itself displays a range of collection practices and interests on the part of its members. The expedition was extremely well equipped and represents part of the professional interest in New Guinea on the part of ethnologists and physical anthropologists at a time when these disciplines were becoming institutionalized in museums and universities in Germany and elsewhere. A last and major influence on all this collecting activity was the growth of German museums. All our collectors had requests from museums for artefacts, if they were not being directly funded by museums. There was competitive rivalry between the various cities of Germany to have the best museum, and objects from the colonies were highly sought after (Penny 1998).

A particular combination of forces came to bear on the German colony of New Guinea which led to a high level of public and academic interest in the region, and this encouraged high levels of collection. The types of collectors briefly summarized above would only have represented part of the collecting activity in western New Britain, with plantation managers and recruiters also collecting. The cumulative effect of this would have made a considerable impact on local people and their systems of production and exchange.

The rich mix of forces led to a diversity of collecting and collectors, which was not be found at later periods in New Guinea. Not only were the large scientific expeditions a feature of the time, but so also were the privately financed trips, such as Mencke's and Schoede's, and there was considerable influence between the two. Longer-term residents of the colony were important collectors in their own right, but also used their local knowledge to aid the professionals, both at the planning stage and in the field. There was thus a dense network of social relations between whites, which shaped and channelled collection.

Following the German collecting heyday, and in the case of Lewis overlapping with some of the German collectors, came the individual museum- and academic-based collectors, four of whom worked in southwest New Britain and are the focus of this study. For each of these collectors, Albert Buell Lewis (visited New Britain in 1909), Felix Speiser (visited 1930), John Alexander Todd (visited 1933–4, 1935–6) and Beatrice Mary Blackwood (visited 1937), we have to understand their personal motivations, how these were influenced by the institution for which they were collecting, and where their type of anthropology fits in with the history of anthropology. These influences are explored in the following chapters.

For each collector we have different sets of documentary evidence. Lewis, Speiser and Blackwood were employed by the museums for which they collected, and in each case southwest New Britain was a short stay in a larger collecting expedition for their museums. Similar museum concerns drew them to the spot, but how these concerns were addressed through their particular sets of expectations will be explored in the following chapters. Todd is distinct from our other three collectors as his collection was made for a university department as part of a PhD project and lacks the depth of documentation available for the other collections. The other three collectors made life-long career commitments to their institutions, and therefore the archives held by their respective institutions include diaries, correspondence and catalogues drawn up and added to throughout the collectors' museum careers. This wealth of information contrasts with the dearth of information available for Todd's collection, and while he published a series of reports (Todd 1934a, 1934b, 1935a, 1935b, 1935c), social issues, and not material culture, were the focus of his writings.

Together these four collectors form a unique picture. They span the first half of the last century when anthropology was undergoing profound change and the status of material culture and collecting was altering. The four collectors came from different 'schools' of anthropology, nationally and sometimes intellectually distinct in their attitudes and approaches to anthropology and yet with cross-cultural academic links. In each of the next four chapters we will look at the intellectual background of each institution from which the collectors came and their institution's collecting policy. The four collections examined in this book are held in four institutions with different histories; tracing each of the histories gives a unique opportunity to provide a comparative, international view of anthropological history.

A.B. Lewis

December 1909 – February 1910 on the south coast of New Britain. Collected for the Field Museum in Chicago and spent a total of four years in the Pacific. On

New Britain he collected a total of 330 objects (37 per cent of the overall objects in the collections we have analysed) and these covered 56 per cent of the total of 117 different categories of artefacts we have defined. Was especially interested in inter-community communication and trade.

F. Speiser

January–May 1930 on the south coast of New Britain. Collected for the Ethnographic Museum in Basel. Collected 110 items overall (12 per cent of the overall objects in the collections we have looked at) and these covered 48 per cent of the total of 117 different categories of artefacts we have defined. Was especially interested in race, migration and material culture as defining culture areas.

J.A Todd

1st April 1933 – 1st April 1934 on the south coast of New Britain. Collected for the Department of Anthropology, Sydney University. Collected 186 items overall (21 per cent of the overall objects in the collections we have looked at) and these covered 33 per cent of the total of 117 different categories of artefacts we have defined. Was not especially interested in material culture – was obliged to collect.

B. Blackwood

March–September 1937 on the south coast of New Britain. Collected for the Pitt Rivers Museum. Collected 275 items overall (30 per cent of the overall objects in the collections we have looked at) and these covered 59 per cent of the total of 117 different categories of artefacts we have defined. Was especially interested in production, technology and skull deformation.

All of the collections studied in this project were subject to criteria that defined the contents of the collections. Some criteria, such as the museums' wants and needs and the collectors' own interests, are easy to assess. However, the communities and regions the collectors visited also structured the collections, and through the material evidence that remains we have attempted to unpick the different threads of agency, both of the locals and of the visitors, in the structuring of the collections and their attendant documentation. The visits of all the collectors in this volume, with the exception of Todd who spent a full calendar year in the region, were subject to the season. Both Lewis and Speiser visited in the dry season and witnessed local ceremonies and customs, whereas Blackwood, who visited in the rainy season, found that the weather hampered local travel and restricted ceremonial practices. Not all collectors covered the same area or villages during their travels, although all were working in the region classed as 'Arawe' (see Chapter Two). As more recent ethnographies show (Goodale 1995; Maschio 1994) there is considerable cultural variation within the 'region' itself, as well as similarity. In addition the social situation in southwest New Britain changed constantly over time as new relationships were forged within colonial culture between the residents of the islands and the colonizers.

To try to make sense of this, each chapter will devote space to the Melanesia of the time during which each collector visited. Commerce, colonialism, the 'opening up' of territories and 'pacification' of groups meant that the region was subject to continuous and rapid change. It is therefore crucial to understand how this affected local people, their residence patterns, their internal trade, their attitude to visitors and other new residents in the area, and the cumulative effect on the region.

After the Second World War this type of research petered out. We will see how Todd, an anthropology student rather than a museum ethnographer, relegated his collecting to an obligatory part of fieldwork, but not essential to his results and personal research endeavours. After the Second World War there was less academic emphasis on material culture, and interest in, and consequently funding for, collections largely dried up. Therefore object collection became an opportunistic by-product of fieldwork rather than its central aim. The momentum behind large-scale acquisitions and the need for collections also lessened as by this stage many museums were well established with substantial collections and there was not the same urgency to fill stores and exhibition cases; instead care of collections and lack of space was becoming an issue. Some museums continued to send out researchers and pursued this tradition for longer, but for the more remote areas such as southwest New Britain the visits by those intent on making major collections had ended. The change in the theoretical foci of anthropology away from material culture was not the only factor influencing the reduction in quantity of objects removed from the area. There was also a new morality and ethics that concerned collectors. The wholesale removal of hundreds of items from one region was no longer justifiable as 'salvage' ethnography. 'Other' cultures had proved to be remarkably resilient and adaptable, and individuals or scientific expeditions found it increasingly difficult to justify the pursuance of large-scale collections either in terms of research potential or ethically.

Anthropologists have continued to collect, and items from the region are still acquired by museums, but they more often come about through items received as personal gifts in exchange relationships by people working in the region or through commissioning individual artefacts or groups from known artists or makers. In the case of Pavlides carrying out fieldwork in the 1980s and 1990s (see Chapter Eight) the decision was made to make household surveys of objects and to thoroughly document them rather than acquiring them to take away. Museum collections made after the Second World War are characterized by being much smaller in number. However, trade and artefact dealers continue to be interested in acquiring artefacts, and this commercial interest though arising from different markets continues to the present day. The rise in interest in Pacific art and tourism means that there is still a market for artefacts and dealers, and tourists still visit the southwest coast to make collections which generally remain in private hands.

Understanding Collections

Some years ago, palaeontologists developed the notion of taphonomy to understand the relationship between an assemblage of fossils and the original plant and animal communities from which they came. Fossils are only ever a proxy measure of the original community, and it is this community and its relationships which is the real focus of palaeontological attention. Organisms with bones or exoskeletons were far more likely to fossilized than those without, but the speed at which sediments were deposited and accumulated was also vital in influencing what became a fossil and when. For many years ethnographic collectors worked with the same implicit notion of what their collections represented, possibly as part of the scientific ethos inspiring collection practice. Ethnographic collections were seen as an imperfect, although valuable, record of native ways of life. These were often seen as ways of life that were fast vanishing, so that the items collected might soon have fossil status.

We think that this taphonomic view of collections is fundamentally flawed. Rather than seeing collections as a proxy, partial and distorted record of something else, such as the workings of 'primitive' communities, we view collections as very good and direct records of the activities that created them; a small, but vitally informative, window onto colonial New Guinea. As we have stressed previously, colonial culture was created through the movement of objects, and what gives that culture some jointness was that all actors pursued their own strategies through the control over objects. Collections were acquired through the trade items and money in common use throughout New Guinea. Collectors utilized social connections within the white sector of the community to guide them, with plantation managers, patrol officers and missionaries providing direction, advice and the contacts through which objects came. For local people relations with whites were often painful and difficult, but their familiarity with collectors and traders provided a fund of knowledge about how to conduct such transactions which they could use to their own advantage when meeting a museum collector.

A man like Aliwa on Pililo (see Chapter Five) was a crucial node in colonial relations. He had widespread contacts with local people throughout western New Britain and as far as New Guinea, which was part of the basis of his wealth and prestige. But he also had wide-ranging and long-term links with whites, not only through his colonial status as a luluai, but also due to the self-confident deployment of his knowledge and local wealth which made him vital to anthropologist and patrol officer alike. The 'famous Mr. Aliwa', as Speiser called him, undoubtedly used his position to attract money and trade goods, which he could then use in a range of transactions with whites and locals to further build his social advantages. Aliwa had connections with whites over which he had some degree of control: he declined to talk to Speiser on first meeting as he had not been told of his coming, and he was the one non-white who did not have to carry anything on patrols. His degree of obvious power in his relations with whites would have increased his local standing even more. Also important was his acquired knowledge about the working of the white aspects of the colonial world, which would have been almost as important as gaining white goods through exchange. Zelenietz's work *After the Despot* (1980) charts the rise of big men along the north coast of New Britain who made autocratic use of their luluai status in the period between the wars. Such processes were probably found more broadly throughout western New Britain and beyond, with Aliwa representing an early and striking example of colonialized forms of authority.

In a different position within the social matrix was Magnin, Blackwood's field assistant. Magnin was not a luluai and, as far as we can tell, did not have an especially high status within the local community. Magnin used his link with Blackwood to sell her a range of objects in exchange for money and trade goods, which would have been in addition to the wages Blackwood paid him. Magnin sold objects to Blackwood, such as pig's-tusk ornaments and gold-lip shells, which she found hard to obtain elsewhere. The sale of socially marked items was a measure of the value Magnin attached to his connection with Blackwood, a conclusion reinforced by the presence of his father's teeth hanging from the pig's-tusk ornament he sold. Magnin benefited materially and socially from his connection to Blackwood, and he may have hoped this would lead to other connections with whites, bringing both more knowledge of the colonial world, together with wealth. Certainly Speiser came across Magnin in 1929, recording his name in a genealogy, although it is not certain how much direct contact they had. For both those at the top of the social structure and the aspiring lower ranks, connections with whites and the goods they brought could be seen as beneficial. Collections are structured by such links and are records of these links, which themselves formed part of a broader mass of relations of colonialism.

There is the wonderful microsociology of a well-documented collection, our best evidence of which comes from Blackwood, because of her detailed documentation of the collection process. Blackwood bought her objects from a wide range of people. She paid out at least £8 7s 6d in money, as is recorded in her diary and note books, although this is probably an under-estimate and most of her objects were acquired using 'trade'. Her most popular form of trade good was a stick of tobacco, followed by knives of different kinds. Some twenty-four people are named as individuals from whom she collected, and the named individuals lived in seventeen different communities that we can distinguish from Blackwood's records. More men are represented than women, but some women, such as Owas, supplied quite a number of items. Not surprisingly she received most items from the people with whom she lived and Magnin sold her fifteen items, more than any other person. Many small or less important items, such as pan pipes or stone axe-heads, seem to have been brought by children who may have been encouraged by Blackwood. We have paid no attention to the human skulls Blackwood collected, but, as a set of items, they do throw light on collection practices. Blackwood collected twelve skulls, and each cost 10s, apart from one of a child, which cost 5s. Eight of the twelve skulls sold were of women, and the skulls were generally sold by men, although the circumstances of the sale could be complex:

> Note. Tunegit left Nos. 8, 9, 10 [sample numbers she gave to the skulls], with me pending the arrival of the permit. He was away when I left, so gave 25/- to Rev. C. Longden, Anglican Missionary on Apui Island, to give him when returned. I subsequently saw Tunegit at Gasmata and told him to ask Longden for the money, he was satisfied with this arrangement.[1]

We wonder about the motives in selling human remains to whites, and whether these were transactions like any other. Given the importance of the skull to people in this part of New Britain, such sales might have been to gain some direct ancestral link with whites, and it is hard to know whether the sale of women's skulls was preferred because a greater connection could be gained through women or to minimize the risk of white sorcery on the male community, as sales of skulls were mainly in the hands of men.

There were differences in the things that men and women wanted from Blackwood as trade. Only women received beads, which were presumably for their own use in making things, although they also wanted money, tobacco and knives. Men received a range of objects including sticks of tobacco, knives, axes and money and the majority of the axes and knives went to men. The commonest payment was a stick of tobacco, and this would buy panpipes, obsidian, an armband or a netting needle. We can note in passing that a carrier for a patrol officer was paid 6d, or two sticks of tobacco, per day. More prized items were only transacted for money, knives or axes. When people in the Kandrian area encountered Beatrice Blackwood in a mood to buy objects, both sides balanced the need for a mutual relationship with the desire for the object. Such favours could extend in both directions: 'Luluai Paiyon brought another blow-tube and a piece of bark-cloth. Shall have to call a halt on both soon.'[2] Skulls, as potentially contentious and dangerous items of collection were mainly from luluais and tultuls and all came at the standard price of 10s each. Local officials were not the only important intermediaries: writing of cassowary-quill belts and dogs' teeth belts, 'If you would like a full belt length of either of these, please let me know by Airmail, as I can easily arrange with Mr. Harold Koch to get me these at as reasonable a rate as possible.'[3] There are two important relationships indicated in this letter: the long-distance directions of Balfour, shaping her collections, and the intimate local knowledge of Koch, obviously drawn upon for the most difficult and expensive of items.

Collection was a process of negotiation:

> Some natives from Alomos village came bringing shields and rolls of bark-cloth which they will sell to these people [of Alu'u village] for gold-lip shell. Tried to buy bark-cloth with tobacco or marks at first, they would not sell them – then one asked for a knife + they liked it. Medium-sized ones I brought from Salamaua, so I got 4 pieces with different patterns.[4]

There are also instances that stimulate the imagination: the woman's black-lip-shell knife sold to Blackwood by a young boy in Möwehafen for a pocket knife on 16 June 1937. These were exclusively women's items, and we can picture the boy's mother searching crossly in her bag for the black-lip shell, while her son hides both the pocket knife and the excitement that the transaction created.

There were changes in people's willingness to sell objects; these are important indicators of historical process. In the 1930s, as the missions were first arriving along the south coast of New Britain, both Speiser and Blackwood were able to buy *mokmok* and *singa*. Blackwood paid between 6d and 2s for the latter and 10s for a *mokmok*. This was a considerable price by the standards of the time (it was the same as she paid for a human skull), but obviously something she could afford even on her slender budget. Lewis has no power stones, noting that the price of one was two pigs, and by the 1980s they were impossible to purchase. It seems to us that the coming of the missions had the temporary effect of devaluing these stones as part of a process whereby people rethought their ritual attachments and spiritual values under the initial influence of christianity. This was a temporary, not permanent, influence, and presumably the reassertion of the old values meant that they had been argued for and discussed, so that this was not simply a reassertion of the old values, but a new means of thinking about the world drawing on older traditions of thought. Collections can hint at subtle and temporary changes which are part of new contexts of life and the revaluation of old values.

Certain things were always difficult or impossible for collectors to acquire. Speiser noted that three items were expensive: large gold-lip shells, curved pigs'-tusk ornaments and black paint used for teeth blackening. The last seems somewhat anomalous and not noted by anyone else, but large gold-lip shells have never been collectible items and most were passed down as heirlooms or used for exchanges of great social moment. One of the notable changes in the post-war period has been the increase in numbers of gold-lip shells along the coast and in the interior (Goodale 1995), but these are all relatively small, playing a quite different role from large shells, the most important of which have names (Chapter Five of this book). Not everything has changed in value in the course of the last century, and we could add dog's-tooth bags to large gold-lip and pig's-tusk ornaments as things which have always been of great worth and difficult, if not impossible, for collectors to purchase. It is this balance of stability and change that we have to weigh in looking at the overall history of people and objects along this coast.

Unsurprisingly, given their different personalities and backgrounds, our four researchers had different modes of collection practice. It was not so much that they collected different objects (as their collections have strong similarities), it is more that they collected quite various forms of information along with the objects, setting the artefacts themselves in quite different contexts. Lewis's mix of motives necessitated balancing items which were informative about connections between regions (his own personal interest) with striking objects which would look good in a museum display (influenced by letters from Dorsey), and collecting a range of objects that would give the fullest possible picture of life in New Guinea (here his systematic and organized personality chimed well with the desire for complete-ness on the part of the Field Museum). The desire to be complete led him to purchase Komine's collection of material from the south coast, not because it was well-documented, but due to the existence of objects within it that had eluded Lewis. Lewis was no theoretician and never derived broader theories of trade and connectedness, preferring to describe the objects, although even this was not undertaken to the same depth as Blackwood.

Speiser writes least about the objects themselves, recording no more than the bare minimum necessary for his catalogue, which included local name, point of collection, sketch and brief comments. However, he does record in most detail the societies from which he collected, and his notes do contain many hints, although not full descriptions, of the ways in which objects were viewed and used. It is necessary to reconstruct from his notes the links between objects and the social process, but there is undoubtedly much information to be gleaned.

Blackwood concentrated on process: the acts of making and using items. Her documentation comes closest to a present-day approach to material culture, trying to set objects in their practical and social contexts. The perfectionist streak in Blackwood's character meant that she felt that she never had enough information. From the perspective of later social anthropology, and by comparison with Speiser's notes from a shorter time in the area, there was a lot of detail on social forces and relations that she did not document. Blackwood also felt that she might be encroaching on Todd's territory, who had completed his fieldwork, but not written up his PhD, at the time she was in Kandrian.

Of Todd's thoughts on material culture we know little. Objects play no great role in his publications, and none of his field notes survive. Todd seems to have taken some care in collecting, as many of the women's skirts and clothing he collected were new and therefore probably made especially for him. The documentation that survives with Todd's collection seems to indicate that he was thorough. Having said that, Todd, in a letter to Beatrice Blackwood, denies any real knowledge of material culture, saying that he has no objections to Blackwood's writing on the material culture of the area. He obviously saw himself as very much a social anthropologist for whom objects were a secondary consideration. Now intellectual fashions have changed again, bringing back objects to a central place in our analyses. It is to the objects that we now turn.

The Material Culture of the Arawe

In each of the following chapters we will highlight specific sets of objects within the collections made by each anthropologist. However, there is not space enough to write about every object that each collector acquired, and we have done this elsewhere in the forthcoming catalogues of the four collections. Therefore, at this juncture will give a brief overview of the material culture from the region. This overview will take the form of a broadly alphabetical list. Where dimension ranges are given they refer to examples in the four collections researched and are not in any way definitive; other variations may occur elsewhere.

Armbands

Turtle-shell armbands are made of flat, thin circles of turtle shell, piled one on top of the other and then bound down two sides of the pile (see Figs 3.1, 4.2, 5.6). The number of thin bands bound together varies but could reach twenty or more. Trochus-shell armbands, with varying degrees of decoration, are also worn. There is a broad variety of woven armbands (Fig. 5.3), ranging from those made of rattan, orchid stem or string, to much more elaborate woven and painted armbands with lappets edged with nassa shell (as Alip is wearing in Fig. 8.2).

Axes and Adzes

Stone axes were hafted using a split piece of cane wrapped over the butt end and bound with rattan. Once the cane dried the haft would become less secure and be replaced. Adzes were hafted on to wooden handles with binding. These items were gradually replaced with metal equivalents.

Figure 3.1. Three turtle-shell objects from Blackwood's collection: a piece of partly worked shell, a completed set of armbands, and two earrings (Pitt Rivers Museum, University of Oxford)

Other Stone Tools

In addition to the above, stones were also used as pestles, in food and pigment preparation (stone barkcloth beaters could also be used in this way).

Barkcloth

Lengths of barkcloth (see Fig. 7.4) are made from the inner bark of a tree. This material is beaten into long lengths (ranging from 900 mm to 6770 mm amongst the examples we researched) and then decorated with red and black pigment. The barkcloth is worn by men around the waist and passed through the legs. Occasionally women wear smaller pieces as belts into which their skirt fibre can be tucked. Old lengths of barkcloth are recycled and used for binding the heads of infants. To make barkcloth, a stone or shell beater is used over a wooden block (Figs 1.2, 4.2, 7.4, 7.5).

Blowgun and Darts

This item (see Fig. 5.1) is typically made up of 3–5 sections of bamboo, spliced together and glued with resin, before being bound. They range from 4m to 6m in length. The darts are generally around 70–90 cm long. The darts are made of wood sharpened to a point at one end, and bound with vine string and decorated with feathers at the other. Today these items are still in use, but the darts are usually made from the sharpened metal spokes of old umbrellas. The blowguns are used to hunt birds.

Bone Spoons

Made from pig or cassowary bones, the bone was ground to give it a thin smooth edge at one end for use as a spoon.

Canoes

Outrigger canoes are imported from the Siassi Islands. However, wooden paddles painted in black designs were, until at least the Second World War, made locally. Woven pandanus-leaf sails, wooden balers and other additions can also be made locally (see Fig. 2.1).

Cassowary Quill and Nassa-Shell Bead Belts

Quills from the cassowary feather are cut into lengths of 2–5 cm and threaded onto string with nassa-shell beads. On occasion trade beads are interspersed throughout the length. These belts are valuable, and the lengths are measured in fathoms (a man's armspan). They are worn by men over their barkcloth belts on important occasions (see Figs 4.2, 7.3).

Coconut-Leaf Bags

Woven from strips of coconut-leaf fibre, the shape defined by thin lengths of wood inserted along the top and sides. A handle may be formed by a gap between the wood and woven sides at the top. Used for carrying food and other produce.

Coiled-Cane Baskets

These circular baskets are generally circular and shallow, with flared sides. They are not made locally but around Cape Gloucester and are made from cane fibre coiled from the centre of the base outwards. Near the rim there may be a section of decorative open work. They are used to hold cooked tubers for ceremonial exchanges and payments.

Cooking Tongs

For the manipulation of food in a hot fire. These tongs are made of a thick piece of bamboo, split to almost its full length, the remaining joined end being bound for reinforcement.

Dogs'-Teeth Bags

String bags are covered on their external surface with dogs' teeth, perforated to become beads. These items are highly valued and are not found in any of our collections (Fig. 8.3).

Dogs'-Teeth Ornaments

Dogs' teeth are strung on woven fibre as belts (see Fig. 4.2) and as forehead ornaments. They are highly valued and are used in ceremonial exchanges and handed on as family heirlooms.

Earrings

The most common earrings are made of a disc of turtle shell, edged with nassa shell beads (see Fig. 4.2) and many examples are worn together. Less commonly they are made from cut and polished discs of pearl shell.

Fire-Plough

Fire was formerly made using a fire-plough, which involves a thin stick being rubbed against a larger piece of wood.

Gold-Lip Shells

These ground and polished shells are valuables and used as payments. Smaller shells can be used in everyday transactions. Larger shells, which may be decorated and have a name, are confined to use in ceremonial transactions. A person may own numerous gold-lip shells of varying value. The decoration usually consists of attachments of string hung with fruit shells, sea shells or trade beads (Figs 4.3, 5.2, 7.3, 8.2, 8.3).

Hair Ornaments

These range from simple strings with a piece of shell or bead at the end, which would be tied to the hair, to large circlets of cassowary feathers which cover all the hair. Some feather ornaments are fixed to combs and pushed into the hair.

Lime Gourd

Gourd, with small opening cut in top for holding lime. Leaf bags are more commonly used in this region.

Masks

There are three types of mask. The first type is coned in shape and painted with a stylized face (see Fig 5.4) and used in the *Kamotmot* ceremonies. The second, the *Kuiunke* masks are made of palm fibre, forming a sack which is pulled over the head. The sack may be irregularly covered in paint (see Fig. 5.5). A further mask, called *Warku* (or *Barku*) is carved from wood in the shape of a face. These masks are rare and are traded into the region.

Musical Instruments

These include the *kundu*, a wooden hour-glass-shaped drum (Fig. 4.1), flutes and panpipes made from bamboo, wooden bullroarers, and whistles made from a folded piece of grass or leaf. The bullroarers, whistles and flutes are often used in conjunction with masking ceremonies and are said to be the 'voices' of the spirits. Rattles of fruit shells are hung around spears and tied around ankles in dances.

Neck Ornaments

Various ornaments can be worn around the neck. Those to be found in the collections included perfumed leaves bound together, filed conus shells forming a pair of circles bound side-by-side and attached to a string, strings of shell beads, and pendants of pig and dogs' teeth (Figs 1.2, 4.1, 4.2, 5.3, 5.6, 7.3, 7.5, 8.2).

Nets

Nets of varying mesh sizes are used for catching pigs, fish and birds. The pig nets are made of strong, thick cord and have a large mesh size. They are kept in the men's house and communally owned. Fish nets, also communally owned, are made from a thinner, lighter fibre, with shell sinkers and coconut husk and wooden floats attached. The wooden floats are decorated by painted designs in red. To make fish nets, wooden needles are used, as are mesh gauges which are frequently decorated or carved, and may be imported from the Siassi Islands. They are hung up on special racks behind the men's house. Nets are occasionally made and used for hunting large birds.

Obsidian Flakes

Obsidian was flaked into small pieces generally used for shaving, scarification and circumcision. These artefacts were largely superseded by manufactured equivalents such as bottle glass and razor blades. Hammer stones were used in the flaking of obsidian. The obsidian came from sources on the north coast of New Britain.

Perforated Stones

These perforated stone discs known as *mokmok*, *mukmok* or *singa* are valuable heirlooms and are owned only by the wealthy. They are occasionally worn by being threaded together and tied over the owner's barkcloth belt (Fig. 4.2).

Pestle and Mortar

Wooden pestles and mortars are found in the region, often imported from the Siassi traders or rough copies of the same. Stone pestles and mortars are also found and can be connected with magic and sorcery.

Pig's-Tusk Ornament

This consists of two pig's tusks bound side-by-side, with a central woven fibre column. They are worn around the neck, on the breast or back, and in dances or fights are held in the mouth as a sign of aggression (see cover illustration and Figs 3.4, 4.2, 5.6, 7.5). These items are highly valued and largely owned by men. A similar ornament of less value is made with two conus-shell disks perforated at the end and bound side to side (Figs 5.3, 7.3).

Pottery Vessels

Spherical vessels, with lip and some incised decoration, used in food preparation. These are made in Sio, Gitua and Madang on the north coast of New Guinea and are traded to the Arawe.

Raincape/Mat

Sewn strips of pandanus leaves, two rectangular sheets are stitched together down one length and across one end. Large mats are used laid flat in a double thickness as a sleeping mat. Smaller versions are pulled over the head to protect people from the rain.

Shell Tools

Various small shells, such as the black-lip shell are used as scrapers or knives, one edge is ground to give sharpness and the whole polished. Depending on the task that it is required for the edge may be serrated. An alternative to the shell scraper is one made from coconut shell, similarly ground or cut to shape and given a serrated edge.

Shell Money

Used both as strings of currency and as necklaces, the variety of shells includes nassa shells and shell beads ground and perforated from a variety of reef and mangrove shells (Figs 1.2, 4.2, 5.6, 8.3).

Shields

Shields are made of three planks of wood, bound together side-by-side with local fibre. The handle is carved out of the centre plank and the front protrudes in a bulge to maintain a standard thickness throughout. Both sides of the shield are decorated, the front carved and painted in red, white and black pigment, the back painted in red and black (see cover illustration). The designs on the front show little variation, consisting either of eight pairs of concentric circles or four pairs of concentric circles interspersed with rows of incised triangles (cover, Figs 2.2, 8.1).

Skirts

Shredded and/or dyed fibre sewn into bundles near one end, they are worn by being pushed into a vine-cord belt around the waist. The bundles can be used in groups of twenty or more, depending on the occasion. The thick fibre is built up mainly at the back so that the skirt forms a soft cushion to sit on (Fig. 3.2). Depending on the occasion a wide variety of fibres may be tucked into the belts, such as perfumed or decorative leaves. These additions would be used once and then thrown away.

Figure 3.2. Mame standing to show off the 'bustle' effect of the skirt she is wearing (Pitt Rivers Museum, University of Oxford)

Sling

Slings of woven and plaited fibre are used with coral pellets as shot. Used for hunting small mammals and birds.

Spear

There are two types of spears commonly found in the Arawe. The first is made of dark hardwood and is carved and polished, examples we saw ranged in length from approximately 2.5m to 4m. Sometimes there is a short decorative panel carved on its length and ornaments of fibre or fruit shells tied to its length. In addition to being used on the pig hunt these spears are also used in dances as a beater against the shield (Fig. 2.2). The second type of spear is the fish spear. This item is made of a length of bamboo, split at one end to accommodate a group of 5–9 wooden (later iron) prongs. They are bound onto the end with rattan.

Vine-String Bags

Looped out of vine string made by women and used by both men and women. These small undecorated bags are used to carry personal belongings (see Fig. 7.6).

Water Bottle

Water was carried in complete coconut shells, stoppered with a leaf.

Wooden Bowls

These bowls, more often known as 'Tami' bowls due to the islands in which they were originally crafted, are imported into the region. They are boat-shaped, of dark hardwood, and are carved around the rim and sometimes along the base. The carved designs are picked out using lime. Some examples have a handle at one end. The bowls are valuable and may be used in bride-price but are also used in the preparation of food, in particular a sago pudding (*sapela*).

The Analysis of Objects

As this is a rather new type of project it is worth spelling out the methodology we have used to analyse the collections and archival material. This will help readers understand and evaluate the results presented here, and may be of help to others embarking on similar projects. Our basic unit of analysis was the individual object, and over the course of the research we examined 901 artefacts. We recorded the information available on each object, usually from the catalogue of the museum concerned, often through photocopying the catalogue cards. We then worked through the collection, object by object, making our own description of each item, with measurements of the main dimensions. This was accompanied by a sketch and a working photograph of every object. Because we are also interested in the process of museum documentation, we recorded everything written on museum labels (often various generations of labels were attached to one object); this often gave us extra important information (Fig. 3.1). We also added any additional information on individual objects contained in accession books or other documents. Photographs were researched, partly as objects in their own right and partly as an element of the network of sources of evidence. Further background information relating to the collector (such as field diaries or notebooks), the collection or the region, could often be gleaned from museum archives and publications, and this information was collated and attached to the database entry.

The database of objects was created using the computer program Filemaker Pro, copying the field structure and terminology devised by, and used at, the Pitt

Rivers Museum. The main database at the Pitt Rivers Museum is divided into searchable fields which facilitate the retrieval of data. We adapted this database slightly and recorded the following details in separate fields (those marked with * are governed by complete thesauruses): Accession Number; Accession Book Number; Region; Keyword*; Local Name*; Class*; Material*; Process*; Dimensions; Weight; Date Made; Maker; Date Collected; Field Collector; Other Owners; Other Numbers; Source; Acquired; Documentation; Notes (see Coote, Knowles, Meister and Petch 1999). The result is that each object is differentiated by accession number, the provenance details are given, plus information on the materials and processes used to form the object, its dimensions and the circumstances of its collection. Original descriptions, plus our own descriptions, can be given in the notes field, together with any other relevant information on the object or its collection. We hope that this database will be of use to other researchers working in New Britain or on similar projects in other areas.

The result is a fully searchable database, where searches can be made on each of the fields, or the notes field. The database combines evidence on the objects themselves, the circumstances of their collection and the processes of curation once they reached the museum. This allows comparisons of the nature and types of object to be made, both within and between collections, and these form the basis of our work on what types of objects were in circulation and use. We can also look at the set of relations linking the process of collection to the point at which we documented the objects, investigating empirically the idea that museum objects are not out of context, but in a new and continuously changing set of relations within the museum.

Once we had compiled an overall table of all the objects (Appendix), to facilitate analysis we divided the objects into categories for study. These categories (hunting and fishing, warfare, valuables, personal ornament/clothing etc.) drew on the typological nomenclature that museums tended to give objects. In particular, we drew upon Blackwood's publication (1970), which was devised for the Pitt Rivers Museum collections and published at the request of a delegation from the Smithsonian Institution, which has since influenced catalogues in other museums around the world. As can be seen in the Appendix, these categories are broad and have been tailored to cover what we class as the main categories of objects related to Arawe culture in the collections. Different categories could obviously be devised for different analytical purposes, but the categories we have chosen to define have been inspired by similar categories imposed on the objects by our collectors. They do not necessarily resemble local Melanesian categories of objects. We then conducted a statistical analysis of the collections, first to examine how many objects fell within each category in each collection, and to use this data to compare the contents of the collections in time and space. In the Appendix we set out the raw data, as we collated it, to make the conclusions and research we have carried out transparent.

In each of the following chapters we will examine the statistics associated with each collection. The aim of this type of analysis of data was to note the presence or absence of certain objects that might provide the key to historical changes in New Britain societies, to highlight intellectual biases on the part of collectors, and to draw out broad themes as conclusions. We have not aimed to use the data to make categorical statements about Arawe society. It is inconceivable that a collector can ever make a 'representative' collection, that includes all permutations of every item present, of the material culture of a region.

In addition to categorizing objects, we also had to count the size of collection. This has proved the most difficult aspect of the statistical analysis. Different museums chose to interpret what was 'one' object in different ways (for example are the two sticks used in a fire-plough one or two objects?). This difficulty meant that the women's skirts, traditionally made up of 20–40 bundles of fibre were categorized either as 'one', where a complete skirt was bought in its entirety, or 'twenty' where several examples of different types of skirt bundles were bought over the duration of the stay. Another common example was jars of obsidian. If they contained 200 artefacts, yet were sold and classified as one object, how did they fit numerically into our schema? After several attempts to construct a system of counting these artefacts, we fell back on our collectors' form of counting. If we removed this and imposed our own universal system, the negotiation and number of transactions was lost to the statistics; this allows us to examine such ideas as number of transactions with male or females, or the collectors' influences more readily.

After these data have been categorized and the units for analysis settled, we also divided up the object types as to whether they were 'mostly male', 'mostly female' or 'ungendered'. Our data for this was drawn from the documentary evidence recorded by the collectors, as it was fairly common for them to note which gender used, made or owned an object. In some cases we relied on the results of Gosden and Pavlides' more recent fieldwork to draw gender distinctions. In other cases there were conflicting data from the various sets of documentation, and those objects were put in the ungendered bracket. None of these categories is fixed or indisputable as none of the collectors examined gender as a particular issue. However, it is hoped that these loose categories provide general insights into the data available.

We also examined the provenance of objects. We will see in the following chapter how important trade was for Lewis when collecting, but it is also an important aspect of southwest New Britain society. While several scholars have recently touched on this issue in their work (Harding 1967; Dark 1979; Pavlides 1988) it has not been investigated thoroughly. We have divided objects into categories of local, local exchange and long-distance exchange. Again, the manner in which the conclusions were drawn is through the documentation made by the collectors supplemented by information from Pavlides and Gosden's fieldwork. This fieldwork was carried out between 1985 and 1992 in the Arawe Islands and mainly involved archaeological excavation, but they also gathered genealogical information, oral histories and carried out surveys of material culture.

Finally, we have tried to estimate relative values of certain objects. All of our collectors note the scarcity or prohibitive cost of items that led to their absence from the collection or the purchase of 'poor' examples as a substitute. The comparison of value across time is difficult but allows an examination of the changing perception of value and changes in the 'hierarchy' of valuables, by both locals and collectors.

At the time of embarking on the project we had identified three major collections from the region, and during the first year a fourth collection, Todd's, was brought to our attention. In fact we belatedly discovered that in several German museums there were large collections from the region that were made during the German colonial period. We have chosen to restrict our current analysis to the four main collections examined here, and have embarked on a second research project, currently in progress, to examine the German collections. In addition to these major collections, small collections of objects were made and deposited in museums all over the world; we decided that these were not large enough to compare statistically alongside the four collections. Instead, in the following chapters we will look briefly at the contemporaneous collectors, such as Lord Moyne who visited in between Todd's and Blackwood's visits, or Schoede, a German collector with whom Lewis was in direct competition, in the context of our collectors. In concentrating on the four collections, which have largely kept their integrity in the years following their collection, we are also able to trace the life and use of the objects post collection, both in the museum and in exchanges, and this will be detailed in each chapter.

Work of this kind is labour intensive and time consuming. During the first year of the project we were based entirely at the Pitt Rivers Museum and worked on gathering together general published and archival material on the region and its material culture and on documenting the Blackwood collection. We worked at the Field Museum in September–October 1997, Gosden for two weeks and Knowles for six weeks. This was on a tiny fraction of Lewis's overall collection, which was curated and stored under excellent conditions making work relatively easy. We were also able to draw on Welsch's work on Lewis (1988, 1998, 1999), which had prepared the ground in many ways. We visited the Basel Museum der Kulturen in January–February 1998, Gosden for two weeks and Knowles for three weeks. As Speiser was a former Director of the Museum there was an extensive amount of documentation relating to the collection, and staff were extremely helpful in allowing us to access this. In August–September 1998 both Gosden and Knowles visited Canberra and Sydney for five weeks. Four weeks were spent in Canberra using the National Library of Australia, the Australian Archives and the extensive library at Australian National University, and one week was spent in Sydney cataloguing the Todd collection and briefly researching the Elkin Papers at the University of Sydney's Archives.

In writing this book it has been difficult to do justice to the mass of information we obtained over the project's length and to integrate this general archival material on colonial background with information on the collections themselves. Small sections of the collectors' material could provide enough data for whole bodies of work in themselves (see, for example, Welsch's work on Lewis's field diaries, 1998) as the majority of the photographs, objects, cinematic film, notes, maps and genealogies were largely unpublished. Thus, in sticking to our primary goal, the understanding of colonialism through the region's material culture, we have woven a large part of this material into the general analysis in the volume. The following chapters, which run in chronological order, are constructed around the interests and work of the individual collectors, which allow us to locate them within their intellectual and institutional histories and the particular historical contexts in New Guinea.

Notes

1. 'List of skulls', Blackwood Papers, Pitt Rivers Museum (PRM) Archives.
2. Blackwood diary, 10 June 1937. PRM Blackwood Papers 8/1/3, PRM Archives.
3. Letter from Blackwood to Balfour, 19 November 1937. Blackwood Papers, PRM Archives.
4. Blackwood diary, Tuesday 8 June 1937. PRM Blackwood Papers 8/1/3, PRM Archives.

−4−

Albert Buell Lewis

We shall use each of these next four chapters to illuminate different aspects of colonial culture in New Britain and the sets of relationships with all parties that our collectors entered into in the course of their fieldwork. Such an analysis of relationships will allow us insights into the collections themselves, but also into the changing nature of colonial culture in the region. Lewis is the earliest of our collectors and the only one who went to New Guinea during the German period. The influence of the colonial government outside the Gazelle Peninsula was relatively recent, as were the plantations and the whole structure of colonial influence. Lewis worked through these structures to a great extent, making the plantation in the Arawe Islands his base whilst on the south coast of New Britain. His overall interest was in how New Guinean cultures interacted over long distances through trade and movement of people. His field notes also demonstrate things that were not of direct interest to him, such as the agency displayed by local people through the process of collection. In considering his collection we must also understand his motivation and attitude towards collecting in the field. We will begin by examining the history of the Field Museum and its position in American anthropology, in order to set the collector and collection in the context of its time. This will illuminate how the collection reflected Lewis and his interests, so that the collection becomes a two-way mirror both on Lewis's place within anthropology and on colonial society in New Guinea.

Albert Buell Lewis was thirty-nine when he joined the staff of the Field Museum of Natural History, Chicago in 1907, as a temporary assistant in the Department of Anthropology. George Dorsey, the Curator of Anthropology, engaged him on the understanding that if and when finances became available he would be made an assistant curator and would be contracted to conduct fieldwork and collect for the museum. This allowed Dorsey to keep Lewis available on a 'retainer', as it were, until a suitable patron could be found to fund the post and an expedition. It seems that Dorsey was impressed with Lewis and keen not to lose him to another employer.

Lewis came to anthropology late, having first had a successful career as a zoologist. Prior to his post at the Field Museum, Lewis had studied for his PhD under Franz Boas at Columbia University, New York. His dissertation 'Tribes of the Columbian Valley and the coast of Washington and Oregon' did not involve fieldwork, but instead was a regional comparison of indigenous groups from the published literature (Welsch 1998[2]: 3–4). Lewis's limited fieldwork experience prior to his arrival at the museum consisted of archaeological excavations in North America, which had provided an income while studying for his anthropology degree, and work with Native Americans in Colorado and California (Welsch, 1999: 453).

American Anthropology and the Field Museum

At the time of Lewis's arrival, the Field Museum was a fledgling institution. Established less then fifteen years earlier as the Field Columbian Museum,[1] it used exhibitions and objects from the World's Columbian Exposition (1893) and funds from Marshall Field, an eminent Chicago retailer, to enable Chicago to retain the many artefacts and specimens that had been brought to the city from around the world and to establish a museum. The World's Columbian Exposition had been organized to celebrate 400 years since the 'discovery' of the Americas by Christopher Columbus.

The Fair's anthropological displays were the responsibility of Frederick Ward Putnam, a leading Harvard anthropologist and Curator of the Peabody Museum. Putnam wanted to use the Anthropology building at the Exposition to define the discipline of anthropology: visitors could have their heads measured by trained physical anthropologists; or compare themselves to the life size figures of a Harvard and a Radcliffe male and female student (Rydell 1983: 57). The displays were complemented by natural-history exhibits and ethnological collections brought from around the world. The fair provided not only a temporary building for the Field Columbian Museum, but more importantly a rich founding collection. Putnam held great sway in the discipline of anthropology, and while responsible for the acquisition and display of ethnographic objects at the World Columbian Exposition he had employed Franz Boas, an up-and-coming German anthropologist, as his chief assistant. It was their exhibits that formed the founding collections of the Field Museum. Putnam was also responsible for instigating the initiative to found the museum, as he did not want to spend time setting up a temporary exhibition with a collection which would be dispersed at the end of the Exposition (Mark 1980: 36). Both Boas and Putnam hoped that Boas would get the curatorship of the new museum. Although he was employed to transfer and install the first exhibitions (Hinsley 1981: 250), the first curatorship instead went to W.H. Holmes of the Bureau of American Ethnology. Another well-known anthropologist, Holmes had been responsible for the innovative life-size groupings of figures of North American Indians in their different environmental settings, which represented the Smithsonian Institution's collections at the Exposition (ibid.: 108). Holmes did not stay long in the post, but by the time of his departure Boas was based at

Columbia University and the curatorship was taken up by George Dorsey, who had also been one of Putnam's assistants during the Exposition.

These early teachers of American anthropology had mainly conducted their own fieldwork in the Americas, and the theories they were constructing were based largely on real experience in a small area of the globe. The differences between the pre-Columbian cultures of North America and the field experience Lewis was to have in the Pacific will be immediately clear in terms of terrain, linguistics and period of contact. At this time there was the general belief that every group, and all cultural traits, could be traced back to single sources: through the mediums of diffusion, migration and evolution, different but fundamentally related cultures appeared over the globe. There was a general assumption that the evidence from North America would provide the overall schema for evidence in the Pacific. Dorsey, in a letter to Skiff, the Director of the Field Museum, wrote, 'We are in a position to do in New Guinea to-day what might have been done, for example, among our western Indians sixty years ago.'[2]

Starting with a 'clean slate', with only small, limited collections allowed staff in the Field Museum to develop a collecting policy: regional collections should be made that would be well provenanced and documented unlike collections made earlier when type, rather than provenance, was the key factor. Equally, objects coming to museums through traders and dealers were often very inadequately provenanced and posed difficulties for curators intent on displaying them by region. Expeditions emphasizing cultural context as proposed by Dorsey were endorsed by the museum administrators who immediately understood that if this fledgling museum was to compete as a centre of excellence and outstanding collections with other established museums it had several decades of collecting to catch up on.[3] Dorsey's programme of collecting aimed to rectify the disparity between the Chicago Museum and those in the East. He persuaded the museum's administrators and outside patrons that by embarking on a series of sponsored collecting expeditions they could build up unrivalled collections economically, not only allowing Chicago to compete with the east-coast museums, but also to form a long-term investment in the future of the museum, for these expedition collections could only accrue in value. Aside from civic pride and the museum's status, for both Dorsey and future curators, this method of collecting had the additional benefit that objects obtained for the museum as a result of specialist expeditions would be well documented, aiding future research and display of the collections.

Dorsey's programme of collecting by expedition was mainly focused on East Asia and Melanesia and he substantially increased the Museum's holdings from these areas. In correspondence with Lewis before a post at the museum was offered to him, Dorsey floated the possibility of several diverse sites for an expedition, including South America, Africa, Polynesia, and the Malay region (Welsch 1998[2]: 9). The focus eventually fell on Melanesia, possibly because it was considered relatively untouched (whereas alternative sites such as Africa had several centuries of colonization, depopulation and slave trading behind them). There was the realistic possibility that in Melanesia there were still 'new discoveries' to be made and the material culture of 'untouched peoples' to be documented. Dorsey was himself a great traveller and in 1908 conducted a round-the-world trip, during which he spent two months in German New Guinea (where he collected 2,000 specimens) and met Richard Parkinson, a plantation owner and amateur ethnologist.[4] Parkinson convinced Dorsey that time was running out if traditional objects were to be collected, as he had already seen items drop out of production and use. This reinforced Dorsey's ideas that Melanesia was where Lewis could muster a singular collection by profiting from the rich, but apparently rapidly disappearing, pickings. At this stage purchase of such traditional artefacts would be within the financial means of the museum, but if they waited any longer scarcity would force up the price of the objects and diminish the Museum's purchasing power.

A patron, Joseph N. Field (the elder brother of Marshall Field and an eminent Chicago businessman), was found, and he was willing to provide $5,000 per annum over three years to finance Lewis's expedition, to be known as the Joseph N. Field South Pacific Expedition. The Expedition was to be the first (and last) wholesale survey of the region of Melanesia ever mounted (Welsch 1998[1]: 558).

Lewis and Dorsey saw this expedition as a last chance attempt to collect items that were soon to disappear. They were working within the salvage paradigm, capturing evidence of 'primitive societies' before 'modernization' changed them, and we shall see from the way Lewis conducted his fieldwork that he was trying to document the 'ethnographic past' (Welsch 1998[1]: 7). For a regional collection, the linguistic and cultural diversity of the peoples living in this region was a crucial part of ethnography. As trade and commerce with the Western world increased it was assumed that the majority of distinctive cultural traits would in time be eroded and replaced by a more unified regional culture. As colonial government took effect, inter-group warfare decreased making movement of peoples less hazardous and at the same time travel was encouraged or enforced by the need for plantation labour.

Lewis's expedition was pioneering for American anthropology, whereas European anthropologists had been making in-roads into the anthropology of Melanesia for decades following the wholesale colonization of the region by various European powers.[5] American input, in comparison, had been limited. Lewis met only one other American researcher in the region during his four years of fieldwork, and that was the zoologist William Patten who collected some Goaribari artefacts from the Papuan Gulf for Dartmouth College, but was not engaged in an anthropological study of the region. There were other American citizens travelling through the area, for religious and commercial enterprises, but Lewis was in a field of his own as regards academia, American anthropology and the region of Melanesia.

Lewis's Melanesia

Lewis is the only collector of the three that we are considering to have visited New Britain during German colonial rule. On his arrival in the region in 1909, Lewis was greeted by Governor Albert Hahl. It was Hahl who had looked after and aided Dorsey in German New Guinea two years previously, and he was happy to welcome Lewis and to further his researches. All sorts of people were being attracted to the region at this time, even if only for relatively brief periods, and Hahl seemed to encourage and welcome scientific researchers in particular. Lewis's first stage of work in Melanesia was a five-month trip along the north coast of German New Guinea.

It is during this period of fieldwork that a picture of German New Guinea begins to develop in Lewis's diaries. The picture painted by Lewis is directly related to his experience of the colony, and a major part of this experience was filtered through his relationship with the expatriate community. There were fewer than 700 permanent white residents in the whole of the colony; these included government officials, missionaries, plantation owners and employees, the majority of whom were male (Welsch 1998[1]: 63). In addition to these residents there were many more people visiting the area, some had scientific motives like Lewis, while others included travellers and traders. A growing Asian community was also establishing itself and was involved in setting up commercial enterprises serving both whites and Melanesians.

The German colony was a maritime one with the colonial community based mainly along the coastal strips. Due to the nature of terrain, even when two villages were linked by land, the likely route taken, except in the case of very short distances, was by sea. This affected the way the colony was run and in turn how Lewis was able to access his 'field', often having to rely on the goodwill of trading or government vessels to take him with them. Ports thus became centres for visitors of any type. Lewis's time in the port of Eitape, on the north coast of New Guinea, as described by Welsch (1998[1]: 66), gives a telling portrayal of the conditions in which Lewis was sometimes collecting.

When the governor and his party reached Eitape on 27 August 1909, the district might have resembled a research park more than it did a forgotten backwater of the German empire. Besides ABL [A.B. Lewis] and Wiedenfeld [a government adviser who was there collecting zoological specimens], the ethnologist Otto Schlaginhaufen from Dresden and the botanist Rudolf Schlechter from Berlin were at Eitape station ... Prof. Dr. Richard Neuhauss, the physician and physical anthropologist from Berlin ... was in Sissano by 1 September ... Yet another researcher, the German anthropologist and philologist Georg Friederici, would arrive in Eitape within two weeks! In addition to these researchers, the warship *Planet*, with a surveying team aboard, also called at Eitape early in September.

However, as well as the transient population highlighted in the above quotation, there were about twenty missionaries in the area, four government officers and three traders as well as the monthly visit from the mail steamer. In addition to these 'residents' and the visiting scientists of varying disciplines, there was undoubtedly an equally large, if not greater, number of trading vessels and crews passing through the port.

As well as the anthropologists and researchers mentioned above, there was a host of others working outside the German colony in the British, Dutch and French territories of the Pacific. In Vanuatu from May 1910 to July 1911 was the Swiss ethnologist, Felix Speiser of Basel's Museum für Völkerkunde, whose later trip to West New Britain will be discussed in the next chapter. Also from Basel was Fritz Sarasin who settled in New Caledonia from 1911 to 1912. From Cambridge University, W.H.R. Rivers returned to the Pacific in 1908 on the Percy Sladen Trust Expedition accompanied by A.M. Hocart from Oxford and G.C. Wheeler from the London School of Economics. Wheeler was to spend ten months in the Western Solomons and Hocart four years on Fiji. In 1910 Gunnar Landtman began two years fieldwork on Kiwai Island, and Diamond Jenness spent ten months in the northern d'Entrecasteaux. While Lewis did not meet all of these people, there is no doubt that he learnt of their endeavours through the colonial and academic grapevines and also on his several visits to Sydney, during one of which in January 1911 he attended the Australian Association for the Advancement of Sciences' annual meeting, where he caught up with Dorsey and was able to meet many of the leading figures in Pacific anthropology (Welsch 1998[1]: 369).

New Britain Notes

Lewis left Humboldt Bay in December 1909 and when he arrived in Herbertshöhe (Kokopo), the Government capital, Governor Hahl was able to offer him passage on a government expedition around New Britain. Hahl suggested he used the government vessel to get to Arawe Plantation at Cape Merkus (on the mainland of New Britain by the Arawe Islands) and from there visit villages on the south coast of New Britain. Lewis took up this offer and spent the next eight weeks collecting along the south coast, the part of his fieldwork on which we have concentrated our research. Once again, Lewis found himself mixing with the residents and other visitors to the coast. His first stop was with Mr McNicol, the manager of Arawe Plantation, a plantation belonging to E.E. Forsayth & Co. Here he also met H. Schoede, a wealthy German, who had chartered a vessel and was spending a year in the colony making large collections, and who, like Lewis, spent Christmas on the plantation (Knowles *et al.* in press). The contrast between Lewis and Schoede's methodology and resources was marked. Lewis was dependent on the goodwill of those who lived and worked in the region to ferry him around the territory, something that would seriously affect his work in the future when relations with the German colonial officers were soured (see Welsch 1998[1]: 226–8), whereas Schoede in his private vessel could drop and weigh anchor whenever and wherever he chose. Compared to the other collectors in this volume Lewis had a generous budget with which to procure and ship specimens back to the museum. However, it is apparent from the style of Schoede's and other museum-based expeditions in the region, that Lewis was a relative 'poor man'. Furthermore, as the competitive stakes rose it seems that collectors not only wanted to secure authentic specimens from 'dying' cultures but they also wanted to procure *all* the authentic specimens to prevent others obtaining similar material (Buschmann 1996: 322). Lewis seems to have felt acutely the relative lack of funds and chartered transport.

What none of the collectors seem to have accounted for in their bids to out-purchase each other was that the artefacts were not becoming obsolete as had initially been assumed would happen. Lewis does not address the issue of authenticity in his diaries, except to note when he rejects items contaminated by the use of European manufactured beads or cloth. However, he frequently states that another collector, Schoede for example in the New Britain villages, had 'bought out' a village at a site where he then proceeds to get a quantity of specimens, which suggests that New Guineans did not stop producing items for which there was so obviously a market, and an enormous one at that.

Before we look more closely at what Lewis collected during the eight weeks he spent on the southwest coast of New Britain, we will first consider some of the different styles of collecting that were current in Melanesia at that time and which may have influenced Lewis's own fieldwork throughout the region.

Lewis was on an *expedition* and was conducting a *survey* of a vast region of the Pacific. He did not have the time, nor was it his remit, to settle down in different places and get to know well his informants and the people with whom he traded for material culture. Aware of this during his expedition, Lewis commissioned collections from over twenty residents in the region (a method frequently used by museums and auction houses which were unable to finance field trips to the region themselves). These 'agents' were required to purchase items for him from areas or groups that either he did not have the time to visit or from which he was unable to collect.

The expedition style of collecting was common in German New Guinea and elsewhere from the late nineteenth century through the early decades of the twentieth century. There was an efflorescence of scientific expeditions coming from Germany to the colony, largely fuelled by inter-city rivalry in Germany itself (Penny 1998: 158). Expeditions such as the Hamburger Südsee Expedition (1908–10) and the Deutsche Marine Expedition (1907–9) overlapped with Lewis in the field and were vast operations with varied aims. Compared to Lewis's own expedition, these were expeditions in the truest sense, combining scientists of different disciplines on board one vessel who were exploring different aspects of the environment and cultures they visited, in which collecting material culture was only a part of their remit. Both Lewis and the German expeditions had the same 'surveying' techniques: they made short stays in many places, pausing only to barter for objects and information before moving on to the next village or harbour.

For the local populations Lewis was just one in a long line of visitors passing through, asking to see objects and then negotiating their purchase. Not every collector encountered by the locals would prioritize items similarly, and Lewis had his own set of priorities, primarily to do with trade and contact between regions, defined by his own interests and those of the Field Museum. Most collectors in this period rarely spent long enough in one area to learn the local language, and instead used pidgin English and interpreters to obtain the information and goods they wanted.

Over the four years in the field, Lewis had three assistants working for him, each drawn from a different area of Melanesia. It is not entirely clear from the diaries as to when the different assistants worked for him. During his time in New Britain he apparently had two people in his employ; of these, one, Kaman of Karsau Island on the north coast of New Guinea, is named in his diary. Lewis employed his assistants to procure food in the remoter areas and carry the trade goods and the objects traded for, while local guides and interpreters were hired in each new region or village, and yet more men, if they were needed, to crew boats or carry more substantial loads. Despite this array of help Lewis rarely is explicit about who is conversing with the producer or seller of an artefact. At each encounter it is possible that Lewis is the questioner, using pidgin or German, or alternatively one of his assistants, or even a local interpreter engaged only for the day. Many of Lewis's diary entries begin with 'We asked . . .' or 'We learnt . . .', and so how Lewis's queries were being mediated by the interpreters is a layer of evidence lost to us.

To throw light on Lewis's relationship with the people he visited on the south coast of New Britain, and the effect this may have had on the collection, we are fortunate to have two accounts of one part of the New Britain collecting trip. Lewis contributed regularly to his diary, a document that he was aware would be typed up and filed with the museum records on his return from the field. However, in this instance, Lewis also filled out what Welsch later published as his 'New Britain notebook' (1988: 1–15), an account of one day during his fieldwork in New Britain sent to the Museum Director, F.J.V. Skiff. This piece of work, unlike the diaries, seems to have been planned as a finished work to be published in the museum's annual report and read by a wider audience, although this never happened. In comparing the two texts we can start to understand the layers of documentation involved with the collection. With this information we can at least speculate more closely on the agency of Lewis, his employees and the locals. Lewis is in his third week on the south coast by this stage and had already collected items that were seen to 'characterize' the Arawe, such as decorated shields and barkcloth. On 6 January 1909 he decided to explore an inland village. On arrival he began to negotiate the purchase of material culture. His diary reads:

> After buying a few things – all I could see around the house (men's house) that they would sell – I asked for the women's house, as I might see something there to buy, but they said it was a 'long way' and my guide said he did not know where it was . . . Just after leaving the house, one of the boys said that the women's house was close by, behind some bushes at the side of the men's house. I now asked the chief-man to go with me, as I did not wish him to think that I would do anything out of the way, and started for the house, my boy going also . . . While looking around and trying to get a look inside (I did not like to go in for fear of too greatly offending them), I neglected the old chief, and when I turned to look for him, I found he had disappeared. My boy said he had gone into the other end of the house . . . taken out some things, and run for the bush, thrusting a present into my boy's hand, as he happened to be near. (Welsch 1998[1]: 175)

In describing the same events the 'notebook' entry reads:

> Most of the other things seen about the house were much the same as I had seen before. This was the men's house, and as I had seen no other, I asked if I could see the family or woman's house. They replied that these were a 'long way' too far for me to go. I had a strong suspicion that this was not the case, but after going out and looking around I could see nothing of them. One of my boys, however, who had also been keeping a look out, told me there was a house just behind some bushes near by. The chief man of the place was close to me, and I asked that he go with me to look at the house, as I did not wish to offend them by going by myself, when they might imagine I was into mischief. So we went toward the house . . . After looking around here a little, I turned to look for my companion, but found that he had suddenly disappeared. I went around to the other side of the house, where there was a door and met one of boys who told me he had just seen him disappearing into the bush, with a number of things which he had taken from the house. The boy also showed me a nice ornament which the man had just given him, apparently as a bribe to let him get away . . . The chief, however, was not again seen, tho he had promised to come to the boat to get payment for an ornament, which I wished to buy, as I did not have with me the articles which he wished in exchange. (Welsch 1988: 21–2)

These two accounts, of the same event, written by the same person, exemplify the problems involved in interpreting the social relations leading to a collection. Despite the quality of the documentation, we still only have the voice of one player, the collector, and the voices of his 'boys' and of the local informants are all mediated through Lewis. This is not surprising but is something that is essential to keep in mind when examining any field worker's notes. In rare cases we may be able to identify a comment from another traveller or resident who has met the collector, but this is unusual. Any attribution of local thoughts, motives or agency is a reconstruction by us, a reading of the evidence available from our intellectual and cultural perspective.

The accounts quoted at length above can give us some insight into the agency of the local big man in his dealing with Lewis. Firstly, Lewis bought all that the big man was willing to sell in the men's house. We must conclude that there were in fact items that the big man was not willing to sell, and that Lewis let them go. In both accounts we read that the locals tried to hide the proximity of the other house from the visitors, and due to the reaction of the big man when confronted with the fact that the visitors were going to visit the house we realise that for reasons unknown to us there were items present that the villagers did not want to sell. The big man, seeing he was no longer able to hide the proximity of the other house and its contents, made a conscious decision to disappear into the bush with the artefacts and to forgo payment for some artefacts which had been exchanged earlier.

There are several ways in which we can analyse the agency of the locals, despite the singular voice of the narrator. To understand the action of the big man we have to understand the nature of gift exchange and trade in Papua New Guinea. In recent years there have been a number of works written on the nature of the gift in the Pacific, in which a recurrent theme is that early contact and collection of artefacts may not have been understood as the straightforward transactions that they were in the eyes of the collector (Thomas 1991: 19). While it is apparent from Lewis's accounts that he was considerate of the big man's feelings about his interest in the women's house and made sure that he accompanied him to it, Lewis may not have understood that the big man's desire to keep him away from the place was his desire to protect objects from being bought. Previous encounters with white populations may have led locals to believe that it was better to avoid confrontation over desire for an object rather than disappoint the visitor with a refusal. Equally the gift, or 'bribe' that was given to Lewis's assistant may have been perceived as such by Lewis, but in the local community it might have been an item of significant importance to make up for the actions of the big man. None of these answers are knowable, but what is clear is that the locals were defining the content of Lewis's collection. We as researchers have to peel through the layers of documentation in an attempt to perceive local agency.

As well as screening objects from a collector, locals might have forced other items on a collector, the items that they were more willing to sell in an attempt to facilitate trade as a whole. These might include objects that had gone out of use due to the influx of new trade items, or other goods that were easy to replace. The type of trade objects that Lewis used was obviously of changing importance in different areas and had a direct effect on the sale of objects. There is not much documentation to tell us about how much trade he had and of what it consisted.

One passage in his diary, while Lewis was in Awar on the north coast of German New Guinea, indicates the range of trade goods he was using, and also gives us a clear idea of just how much Lewis was willing to pay for the *right* object:

> In morning got together trade (14 large axes, 30 tomahawks, 4 claw hatchets, 1 doz. 16 in. knives, 1 doz. 12 in. knives, 1 doz. 6 in. knives and sheaths, 2 doz. planing irons, 1/ 2 doz. razors, and some red cloth) to value of about M. 160, and started in boat for Sisimangum, to see if I could buy one of the masks . . . Took my trade into village and spread it out for the natives to look at, but they declared the masks were not for sale. (Welsch 1998[1]: 287)

This sort of purchase, of a rare, eye-catching, feather mask about 15 feet high, would have been highly approved of by the museum and would have been an expense that his remit would most certainly have justified. Later correspondence between the museum and Lewis, which began to filter through several months after the New Britain work, and when the first boxes had arrived back at the museum, show growing concern on the part of Skiff as to the lack of large and eye-catching items. Lewis's rebuttal of this criticism gives us an insight into his priorities in the field, which sometimes conflicted with those of the museum:

> I do not take it that even a museum should limit itself to <u>show</u> specimens, but should make its exhibit illustrate that sum total of the life and achievements of a people, whether showy or not. I have made a careful study of the whole of New Guinea already explored, in addition to visiting a few places practically unknown. I have talked with most of the men who have been in regions not personally visited, and I can safely say that few men know more about the subject. (letter from Lewis to Skiff, 5 December 1912, quoted in Welsch 1998[1]: 351)

To further understand Lewis's field priorities and how this compares to those other collections that we will examine later, we must now turn our attention to the actual content of the collection made by Lewis on the southwest coast.

Collecting in New Britain

The eight weeks Lewis spent on the southwest coast of New Britain was a fraction of the total time he spent in Melanesia, and the 330 objects he obtained there were only a tiny amount (less than 3 per cent) of the total number of objects he collected on his four-year expedition.

Lewis arrived at Arawe Plantation, Cape Merkus (Arawe Islands) on 20 December 1909. For the first week he remained at the plantation, on occasion suffering from fever. On the 25 December Mr McNicol got together the locals and plantation workers for a Christmas singsing, where Lewis took a series of photographs which subsequently spoiled due to using too warm developing water. On 28 December he felt well enough to start visiting villages, and spent the next few days visiting Pililo and Kumbun islands and travelling up river. On 1 January there was a New Year singsing, along the lines of the Christmas day celebrations, and this time his photographs survive (Fig. 4.1). On 3 January he went eastwards towards Manua (Kandrian), stopping in the Rauto region for two nights. Once in Kandrian (6 January) he explored both the offshore islands and made two trips inland, on one of which 'discovering' the blowpipe in use. He also went to Ross Island before returning to the Arawe Islands on 10 January to await the arrival of the *Irene*, a Forsayth recruiting vessel, to take him to the Huon Gulf. In fact it was not until 11 February that the *Irene* arrived, and during the intervening time Lewis was again indisposed with fever and able only to visit several of the Arawe islands, including Kauukumate (Kauptimete) village on the island furthest to the southwest and Kamangaro village on an island to the north-west[6].

There are two main factors from Lewis's perspective affecting the content of the collection. Lewis's desire to collect and preserve the 'ethnographic past' has already been mentioned. He believed that indigenous technologies and material culture would gradually be eroded under European influence, and that those items that were old or had no obvious signs of outside influence, such as trade beads or paper as component parts, were more representative of the past.

Lewis had a strong interest in inter-community trade and communication and this affected the focus of how he documented objects. An often remarked-upon feature of Melanesian society is that of trading partnerships that may stretch over large areas between linguistically and culturally diverse groups (Welsch, Terrell and Nadolski 1992: 568–600). In pursuance of this Lewis collected and documented the occurrence of objects originating in one village or island and in use elsewhere.

Lewis collected 330 objects in New Britain, and they provide a broad cross-section of the items listed in the previous chapter, the only stark omission being gold-lip shells, which will be discussed below. What makes Lewis's collection substantially bigger than all the others is that he frequently collected numerous examples of certain types of object. This included the more decorative objects, for which Lewis no doubt envisioned display, such as seventeen paddles, six headdresses and five wooden masks. Those items that demonstrated trade, and also considerable workmanship, were collected in number, in particular seventeen 'Tami' bowls, seventeen cane baskets, six pots and eleven drums (which may or may not have been traded into the region). Also collected in number were twelve vine-string bags (although Todd collected eighteen of these) and nine slings. Neither of these latter objects have decorative traits, although the looping of the vine for the bags and the plaiting and weaving of the material in the construction of the

Figure 4.1. Two men celebrating New Year at a *singsing* at Arawe Plantation (The Field Museum, Chicago)

slings show considerable variation in levels of workmanship. Some items that Lewis collected do not appear in any of the other three collections, including two examples of 'medicine' (bundles of plants and leaves), the headdresses and masks mentioned above, a wooden block on which to beat barkcloth, and a wider variety of armbands.

The objects in Lewis's collection from the southwest coast of New Britain allow us to draw some general conclusions about Lewis, his collecting in this area, and the material culture in use by the villagers of this region at this time. The majority (almost 50 per cent) of his New Britain collection was acquired at the Arawe Islands out of the base of Arawe Plantation. Although for part of the time he was confined to the plantation due to fever, and other days at the end of his stay were spent packing specimens, in total he spent six weeks there, as compared to only one week exploring eastwards as far as Kandrian. For this reason he made a significantly smaller collection outside of the Arawe islands. However, it was during his week's trip to Kandrian that he went inland and made his 'discovery' of the blowpipe. Lewis was the most diligent of our collectors in recording provenance of items, perhaps as trade and locations of artefacts were central to his own interests. This allows us to note that at each site named he collected objects, and only twelve items lack provenance.

Of the 330 objects collected by Lewis the key categories are 'personal ornaments and clothing' and 'valuables' at 19.7 per cent and 17.9 per cent of the total collection respectively. Included in the category 'ornaments and clothing' is barkcloth. Used by men as a loin cloth, more infrequently by women as belts and as a head binding for children, it is one of the main local trade items, being produced in the inland communities and traded down to the coast. It is also, with the exception of shields and paddle blades, the only highly decorated object in the community. It is probable that this factor, along with their trade and display potential, led Lewis to collect thirteen full lengths of barkcloth.

The most famous male item in the Arawe region is the three-piece shield. Lewis collected thirteen shields from various sites along the coast. His specimens ranged from 1,295 mm to 1,410 mm[7] in length. Lewis describes then all similarly, and his card catalogue entry for artefact 137385 reads:

> Wooden shield, of three pieces tied together with rattan. Painted on back in red and black designs. Front with incised designs, colored white with raised part painted red and black. Shields of this type are all said to be made in the interior, and are found on both the north and south coasts. The designs vary with the region where made. The carving is said to be done with the beak of the cassowary.[8]

The majority of the other catalogue card entries for shields refer back to this one, the fullest entry for any of the shields, except for shield 137393 which was collected in Solong village near Cape Merkus and which has the additional information that the local name for the shield was *Gil u* or *Gilyu*. While none of the collectors were linguistic specialists they all made attempts to record the local names of items. For shields, both Todd and Blackwood recorded the name *ilo* in the Kandrian area.

Blackwood's catalogue entry for shields is fuller than Lewis's regarding the process of shield construction. She collected two shields and described them as follows:

> Shields are rectangular . . . They are composed of three planks from the tree called *opok*, a species of palm, slightly convex on the outer side, almost flat on the inner side. The middle one is broader than the outer two and the design on it is so arranged as to make it look like two, so that the shield looks as though it were made of four planks . . . The planks are fastened together by four bands of liana, passing right around the shield into a groove cut in the middle plank, under a portion of the wood which is left bridging the groove. The binding is kept in place by bands of liana passing through the wood on either side of this bridge. There may be another pair of bands at the edges. A portion about 12" x 12" on the inner side is hollowed, with the centre bar to form a handle. (Blackwood n.d.: section 'Warfare')[9]

The shields were (and to a lesser extent still are) produced in inland areas and traded to coastal communities, as Lewis noted for the eleven shields he collected. We have few further details of their production than those collected by Lewis and Blackwood, but a variety of different materials and skills were needed to obtain and shape the planks, to bind them and to carve and paint them. Lewis noted that carving was carried out with a cassowary bill, but in later periods this was probably done with metal knives, requiring new forms of relationship to obtain the knives.

Before pacification, shields were a vital part of each man's regalia, at a time when much individual male prestige seems to have been bound up with prowess at warfare. This emphasis was subtly modulated at the beginning of the century, and the situation Goodale describes for the inland Kaulong groups of the 1960s probably obtained in coastal areas much earlier. Goodale (1995: 200–3) describes all night singings in which men with shields and spears took part and which sometimes ended in fighting, but more often acted out fighting in more ritualized form. Shields and spears were used, but in slightly new ways. By the latter part of the last century, shields and spears were not very common in coastal communities, but were still very important in the interior areas, as they remain today. Spears are fairly simple objects in terms of both their form and their mode of production, made from a single piece of wood, presumably by a single individual who made spears mainly for their own use, although occasionally spears may have been traded.

In his diary, Lewis mentions that shields were kept in the men's houses along with other male items, such as spears, fish-, fowl- and pig-nets, and other personal articles belonging to men (Welsch 1998[1]: 181–2). When discussing art he mentions barkcloth and canoe paddles as the only items with designs, and seemingly omits the carvings and paintings that adorned the shields. The current display at the Pacific galleries in the Field Museum, erected in 1990, focuses more heavily on design, and displays shield 137390, with the following label: 'Shield. Painted front and back, this shield is made of split saplings joined with rattan. The designs on the front showed hostility toward an enemy. Those on the back, matching the designs on the warrior's loincloth, inspired him as he fought. Papua New Guinea, West New Britain Province, Cape Merkus. About 1910. 137390.'

The second most numerous category is 'valuables'. Valuables as a category include shell and turtle-shell armbands, dogs'-teeth ornaments, various forms of shell money, cassowary-quill strings, mouth ornaments of both pigs' tusks and conus shells, gold-lip shells (as discussed earlier) (Fig. 4.2), 'Tami' bowls and wooden masks. All of these are used in significant exchange transactions, marriage and other payments. Lewis collected fifty-nine objects in this category. He purchased seventeen decorated oval wooden bowls, which make up over 5 per cent of his total collection from south New Britain. Wooden bowls are not represented at all in either Speiser's or Blackwood's collection although undoubtedly being in use at that time. While all three collectors made visits to the Siassi

Islands, where these bowls were made, while on the south coast, Lewis is different from the other collectors as this did not preclude him from buying the same item once traded, as he was interested both in where objects were made and where they ended up. Blackwood and Speiser, while recognizing ongoing trade, were not interested in pursuing it through the collection of artefacts outside of the area of manufacture, and were perhaps also affected by financial considerations, as trade objects were cheaper when bought at source.

Mouth ornaments were also collected in number, both pigs'-tusk ornaments (Fig. 4.2) and the less valuable conus-shell ornaments (Fig. 5.3). These ornaments, held in the mouth for fighting and at dances and otherwise worn on the breast or back, appear in single figures in the other collections, and Speiser, Todd and Blackwood all comment on how prohibitively expensive they were to acquire. In contrast Lewis seems to have had little trouble in buying five pig's-tusk ornaments and seven conus-shell ornaments. A tusker pig must be specially reared for the purpose, its upper canines removed to allow the lower tusks to curl round and grow into as near to full circles as possible. Someone had to be paid to kill the pig and assemble the ornament. Therefore, for many the pigs'-tusk ornament (*iakron*) was not easy to acquire. Quite why Lewis found it so easy to acquire five of these (plus another six from Komine's collection) is not known to us today, but it is plausible that these artefacts had become devalued due to pacification, with substantially less warfare and therefore less occasion to wear these items. Thus it is conceivable that people were more ready to part with them, although their worth as ceremonial items was reasserted and still continues.

Other 'valuables' that Lewis collected include wooden masks traded from Kilenge (at the westernmost tip of New Britain) to the Arawe. Five examples were collected by Lewis, the only examples of this item to be found in all the collections studied. Again the exclusion of items from elsewhere may be the reason, although unlike the 'Tami' bowls they are not described in the other collectors' notes and only Speiser refers to them. In recent fieldwork Gosden was told that these items were only used for a short period in the history of the region and are not used at all today. It could be that there was increased trade in the late nineteenth century and the early part of the twentieth century due to the pacification of regions under the Germans, and that items new to the area, such as the Kilenge masks, were presented for exchange and for a short period adopted into ceremonial life only to be abandoned at a later date. According to Dark (1979: 147) there were few of these types of mask in existence in 1967 as, according to the Kilenge, the majority were destroyed by the Japanese during the Second World War. He lists a handful of examples that he has located, both in museums and Kilenge, and in this listing identifies the five masks collected by Lewis as being 'Kilenge in style' (ibid.: 149). A further long-distance exchange item that enables us to speculate on change is the coiled basket. In Lewis's time the flat coiled baskets were made 'in the interior

Figure 4.2. Luluai Arulo of Kaleken village wearing his wealth (Pitt Rivers Museum, University of Oxford)

of the island',[10] whereas today no-one in the interior makes such baskets; all are imported from Cape Gloucester on the north coast. An explanation may lie in the colonial government's insistence that bush people move to the coast for ease of administration. Alternatively Lewis could have misunderstood or have been misled. He makes a similar statement for pottery vessels, noting that most were traded from the interior (from mountains in the west), although some were imported from New Guinea.[11] There are no other records of pottery being produced in New Britain in the recent period.

Objects affected by the influx of Western trade goods, were stone axes. Lewis collected five hafted stone axes; of the other collectors Speiser managed to collect two, Todd one, and Blackwood none with hafts, despite asking repeatedly to see examples. By the time of Gosden's visits to the region in the 1980s, only one woman was able to demonstrate knapping obsidian, and stone tools were no longer in use at all. The sharp decline in the use of stone tools is not unexpected. Arawe stone axes did not have ceremonial importance and their replacement with iron was mainly because it was more efficient. Frequent visitors to the region, together with trade stores, kept up the supply of iron.

Some objects drew the attention of all visitors to the area. Lewis pursued the blowpipe despite it taking him into the interior and unknown terrain. Like all the museum collectors in this book, the question of blowpipes, exclusive to the Arawe amongst Melanesians, pricked his curiosity, and while unwieldy to collect and transport, and not eye-catching for display, they were an item of interest for researchers visiting the area. Lewis bought three blowpipes and over ten darts, from the same village in the interior,[12] and perhaps unaware that others (Parkinson 1999[1907]) had previously documented their presence, he publicized the collection of this unusual artefact in his 'New Britain notebook' (Welsch 1988). Lewis felt this set him apart from those like Schoede who passed quickly through a region and made little attempt to explore. Lewis was keen to collect where others had been unable to, and his pursuit of the blowpipe is an example of this.

Part of what Lewis hoped to achieve through collection was to define the cultural area of the Arawe through material culture. When Lewis arrived the only publication on the area was Richard Parkinson's *Dreissig Jahre in der Südsee* (1907), and while several German expeditions had surveyed the area, few resulting reports had then been published.[13] The cultural region of the Arawe was not fixed or determined by others, and there were no 'guidelines' for Lewis to follow. It is likely that he collected similar things from a variety of villages, both coastal, inland and on offshore islands in an attempt to delineate geographically cultural features within regional groups.

Other southwest New Britain items that are catalogued as part of his collection were not actually collected by him. While in the field Lewis purchased 'ready-made' collections if the opportunity presented itself. In total he spent over $7,000 on twenty-two such collections of varying sizes. These collections were incorporated into the 'Lewis collection' on their arrival at the Field Museum. One collection particularly stands out amongst these, not least because of its price tag of $2,269.50, but also due to a subsequent dispute over ownership with Leipzig, Museum für Völkerkunde.[14] This collection, of over 3,000 objects, was made by Isokichi Komine, a Japanese merchant and trader, who had lived in the Pacific since 1890 and had been in the Bismarck Archipelago since 1902. By the end of 1910 Komine was looking for a buyer for his collection, and in 1911 Lewis negotiated its purchase. The collection, primarily consisting of objects from the Admiralties and New Ireland, contained many duplicates of material Lewis had already collected, and so, before listing the full collection, Lewis set aside 402 objects for the Australian Museum (in Sydney) in exchange for 167 specimens from around Australia. The part of the Komine collection sent to Chicago included thirty items from the south coast of New Britain which were accessioned with the items Lewis personally collected whilst in the region.

Komine was probably the most famous Japanese resident in the region at that time, having arrived in German New Guinea in 1902 (Hahl 1980[1937]: 91). Born in 1867, he had first come to the colonies in 1890, working on a pearling ship, based on Thursday Island, in the Torres Strait. It seems he quickly showed an interest in business, leasing his own pearling lugger, acquiring an interest in a boat-building yard, and carrying out expeditions to find suitable plantation land. From 1902 to 1907 he worked for Governor Hahl and Hernsheim and Co. in plantations, trade and shipping. In 1907 he gained a thirty-year lease on land in Rabaul for a shipyard, and this became the part of his commercial activities for which he was most well known, despite also moving into the plantation economy. As a Japanese, Komine recruited compatriots into the colony and was partly responsible for the growth of a Japanese element in the colonial community. Komine's operations survived the First World War and flourished under the subsequent Australian rule. His name figures frequently in *Pacific Islands Monthly* in relation to shipbuilding tenders, and he crops up in many memoirs of the colony (Hahl 1980[1937]: 91–2; Chinnery 1998: 30, 102–3). According to Welsch (1998[2]: 97–8) he was an active member of the social life in Rabaul of the 1920s, and was the most influential expatriate in the Admiralty Islands for the first few decades of the century. On his death in 1934 his obituary in *Pacific Islands Monthly* (1934: 16) described him as 'one of Rabaul's oldest pioneers' and noted that his funeral was attended by the Acting-Administrator (Chief Judge Wanliss).

Of the thirty items from southwest New Britain in the Komine collection, over a third were spears of various types, poorly provenanced and adding little to the eighteen spears Lewis collected himself. Komine also collected several items which fit our criterion of 'valuables'. These 'valuables' are the most interesting aspect of Komine's collection, and it is really only here that Komine's collection can be seen to augment Lewis's. Valuables were obviously expensive for Lewis to buy in the field, and if they were heirlooms, and therefore irreplaceable, were probably not for sale. Unlike all of the other collectors Lewis did not collect gold-lip shells. Gold-lip shells are used as a form of currency particularly associated with exchanges such as bride wealth. Some shells are decorated and fewer still have names, and a history as heirlooms. Both women and men can own shells, and they are one of the most prized valuables in the region. However, Lewis in his notes mentioned that gold-lip shells were worth $5 and £1 at Rabaul (presumably for undecorated specimens imported from Manus). The fact that Komine contributed three decorated gold-lip shells to Lewis's collection filled an important gap in his collection (Fig. 4.3). The absence of this item from Lewis's collection is rather odd, as its importance in the region is noted by Lewis.

Gold-lip shells were rare items that had to be harvested by diving off shore and then ground (to shape them and take off the outer surface) and polished, before being decorated. According to Goodale (1995: 89–90) gold-lip shells were in circulation before German recruiters arrived on the scene, but were few in number, and ownership was the preserve of big men. After colonization, gold-lip shells became more abundant, and shells from the south coast were augmented through imports from Manus Island, the major source within the Bismarck Archipelago as a whole. Today they are used in a variety of transactions including compensation payments for rape and theft (Jim Specht personal communication). In examining why Lewis had no gold-lip shells our attention turned to the collector Schoede.

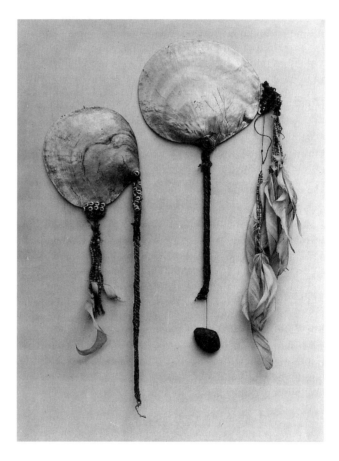

Figure 4.3. Gold-lip shells, bought by Lewis as part of the Komine collection (The Field Museum, Chicago)

Due to Lewis having a fever for several days while in the region, Schoede visited villages in advance of Lewis. Lewis mentions in his diary the quantities of objects Schoede was purchasing, and suggests that some types of object were 'cleaned out' by him (Welsch 1998[1]: 168). We initially thought that perhaps Schoede had bought all available examples of gold-lip shells. However, on further examination we found that Schoede's collection also lacks them. Our recent research in German museums has shown that the members of the Hamburger Südsee Expedition who were in the area for several months in 1908–9 were unable to secure examples either. However, in Linden-Museum Stuttgart there is one example dated 1909, collected by a government officer, Wostrack, and another dated 1920 (although presumably collected much earlier) attributed to Governor Hahl. This leads us to draw the conclusion that these items were rare enough and scarce enough for the locals to price them out of the collector's pocket and that they were only willing to part with them to form relationships with permanent residents or regular visitors to their region. There is the suggestion that Komine was inclined to commission items, at least within the Admiralty Islands (Torrence 2000: 104–41). Komine may have provided the community with new shells and asked people to decorate them, probably in return for further gold-lip shells, of easy access to him with his planta-tions and trading interests on Manus. Goodale (1995: 89–90) notes that the major reason Kaulong people worked on Manus was to acquire gold-lip shells. Links with Komine and his interests in Manus might have facilitated the movement of shells.

Return from the Field to the Field

When Lewis returned from the field in 1913 he was faced with the enormous task of unpacking and documenting the accumulated crates of items he had sent in from the field. In addition to this were the collections Dorsey had made in 1908, including purchases from Richard Parkinson and Captain H. Voogdt, employee of the Neu Guinea Kompagnie, and purchases Lewis had made from German auction houses on his return journey from the field. There were also just over twenty more boxes expected from the 'agents' Lewis had employed on the museum's behalf, the last of which did not arrive until 1919, having been delayed in transit due to the First World War.

When Lewis left Chicago in 1909, the museum's holdings were in the World Columbian Exposition buildings. On his return he expected to enter a brand new purpose-built building financed by a bequest from Marshall Field in 1906. Instead he returned to the same building, suffering from long-term use and lack of space, where the accommodation of over 300 crates of his specimens had forced the closure of one exhibit hall, and with discussions about the new building ongoing.

His task was enormous: some crates had been opened but few had been unpacked, and none were numbered or catalogued. Lewis had preparators and assistants to aid him, but the prospect must still have been a daunting one. A year after his return from the field, Lewis was able to answer demands to see the collection when he put on an exhibit of thirty-seven cases of material from Fiji, the New Hebrides and the Admiralty Islands. In January 1919, after five years, Lewis finally completed the cataloguing of all his material, and in 1920 the museum moved into its new home at Grant Park. On this site Lewis could finally implement the displays he had envisioned while collecting in the field. In May 1921, the Joseph N. Field Hall of Melanesian Ethnology (Hall A) opened, a full eight years after Lewis's return from the Pacific (Welsch 1998[1]: 547–9). This exhibit was to remain untouched until the 1950s when the cases were illuminated and half of the objects on display had to be removed to accommodate the lights. Despite this no wholesale changes were made in the interpretation or layout of Lewis's collections until 1986 when the whole Pacific exhibit in the museum was dismantled and replaced.

Lewis's publishing record on his return from the field was poor. Apart from several short articles (Lewis 1922, 1923, 1924, 1925, 1931), he did not publish his major work, *The Ethnology of Melanesia* (Lewis 1932), a guide to the Museum's Melanesian Hall, until twenty years after he returned from the field. This was more than a guide, expanding on the information available in the galleries to give an overview of the region and its material culture, the only one of its kind to be published. Written for a popular, rather than professional audience, it was well received by the general public and a good seller. It did not receive critical acclaim from academia, which was largely critical of its lack of sociological analysis (Hogbin 1932: 114–15). However, the book was reprinted twice posthumously as demand was great, particularly by the families of those servicemen sent to the Pacific during the Second World War, who knew little about the region and for whom the book became a popular source (Welsch 1998[2]: 570–1). Lewis was obviously keen to publish when in the field, and despite this book it is frustrating that such extensive fieldwork was never written up into something more theoretical that examined such issues as trade, and the 'ethnographic past' more closely. By the time that Lewis was ready to write, Malinowski had already published his landmark volume *Argonauts of the Western Pacific* (1922) which had an enormous impact on the discipline and is credited with changing the future of anthropological fieldwork. This did not stop other anthropologists such as Speiser (1923) publishing the results of their fieldwork in the more traditional descriptive style. It seems that time and museum work overtook Lewis more than the changes in academic anthropology, and so while several other journal publications did emerge, even the 'New Britain notebook' (Welsch 1988) never saw publication in his lifetime.

The Melanesian collection held at the Field Museum became famous in the museum world from its conception. The early display on the old site and subsequent opening of the new gallery in 1921 provided access to scholars of Melanesian ethnology. The collection, and those made by Dorsey and others, produced some duplicates. We have already noted that Komine's collection was not preserved in its entirety even before leaving Oceania. In 1918 the Peabody Museum at Harvard, purchased fifty-eight New Britain items from the Field Museum, comprising artefacts from Parkinson's, Lewis's, Dorsey's, Komine's and other recently accessioned collections. Lewis supplied the attendant documentation and presumably selected the material. Between 1918 and 1939, all within Lewis's time at the museum and therefore presumably under his direction, twelve other Lewis items were exchanged with other institutions as part of an exchange network between individuals and institutions.

Other aspects of the collection have more recently been researched in a manner that both Lewis and Dorsey envisioned when they first proposed a field expedition to Melanesia. Since the 1980s, the Field Museum's own New Guinea Research Project has used the data-rich material collected by Lewis to address questions of cultural and linguistic diversity, through both a re-examination of Lewis's material and a comparison with data collected in the same field area on two fieldwork expeditions to the north coast of Papua New Guinea in 1990 and 1993–4. This work attempts to understand the means by which peoples speaking a variety of different languages interact and exchange objects over a distance of several hundred kilometres. The Lewis collection allows the comparison of historical material and contemporary data to try to understand trade and indigenous settlement of the area from prehistory to the present day (Terrell and Welsch 1991; Welsch 1996; Welsch 1998[1]: 575–7). One of their main conclusions is that the network of trade partners in existence in 1910 was still a major element of life in the 1990s.

The sheer scale of the total collection means that it has never been analysed in its entirety. However, in 1998 Welsch published a transcript of Lewis's field diaries and much of the attendant documentation alongside a valuable 'Who was who' in Melanesia, which situates Lewis within colonial New Guinea. This enormous work provides the first published overview of the collection and its documentation since Lewis's own *Ethnology of Melanesia*, and made available hitherto inaccessible information. Such a publication has facilitated studies, such as this one, which focus on only one small area of Lewis's regional survey.

Lewis is important for our purposes as he illuminates the type and nature of social links in German New Guinea. Lewis was part of a broad research community in the field in German New Guinea which was composed of large numbers of German researchers from many disciplines and which was never recreated again in quite the same way. The American Lewis was unusual in the German-speaking scholarly community and had variable relations with that community, mainly due to Dorsey's interventions from afar. Lewis provides us with a glimpse into the newly established plantation and administrative worlds. Equally importantly he gathered evidence of the old order of things among local people, with the *warku* masks he collected being some of the last evidence of male-only cults, which were also linked to the male warrior society. By the time Speiser arrived in the late 1920s this world had gone and was only remembered by his informants as a world they had lost. Between 1910 and 1929 Arawe communities were restructured and reformed through changes in settlement pattern, the impact of recruiting and the expansion of local trade. Other aspects of the broader colonial world had also altered, with the Australian administration setting up a larger number of patrol posts, instituting regular foot patrols and linking in to a much larger and influential plantation economy. It is to this new world of the 1920s that we now turn.

Notes

1. The Field Museum was originally called the Field Columbian Museum after its founder and financier, Marshall Field, and the name of the Exposition from which it was born, the World Columbian Exposition. The title of the museum changed to the Field Museum of Natural History in 1905.
2. Letter from George Dorsey to Director F.J.V. Skiff, 22 December 1908. Correspondence Folder, A.B. Lewis Archives, Field Museum of Natural History.
3. At this time the Smithsonian Institution, Washington (founded 1846), Harvard University's Peabody Museum of Archaeology and Anthropology in Cambridge (founded 1866) and the American Museum of Natural History, New York (founded 1869) were leading the field in anthropology.
4. Parkinson was the brother-in-law of 'Queen Emma', the Samoan-American owner of E.E. Forsayth and Co., one of the most profitable trading companies in the region.
5. For example, the Hamburger Südsee Expedition which visited the region almost exactly one year before Lewis arrived (December 1908 to April 1909).
6. We were unable to locate exactly which island Lewis was referring to in this instance.
7. These values are converted from those recorded by Lewis in feet and inches (4'3" – 4'7.5").
8. Taken from the card catalogue for object number 137385, courtesy of the Field Museum of Natural History, Chicago.
9. This quote is taken from an unpublished manuscript for a proposed Occasional Paper with the working title *Notes on Arawe Material Culture*. The manuscript, of approximately thirty pages in length, is divided into sections on aspects of material culture, but remains unpaginated. The original is to be found in the Pitt Rivers Museum Archives, reference RDF 1938.36.1050–1334.

10. From exhibition label for 'Coiled baskets' as written by Lewis and used in the display in Melanesian Hall A. Courtesy of the Field Museum of Natural History, Chicago.

11. From card catalogue entry for 137882, and exhibition label for 'Cooking pots' as written by Lewis and used in the display in Melanesian Hall A. In addition, in the Accessions List (in collector's file 1113) Lewis remarks that 'the natives in several places affirmed that pots were made in the interior'. Courtesy of the Field Museum of Natural History, Chicago.

12. Lewis does not name this village. The only hint of its location is that it was less than one day's walk from Kandrian. In the Accessions List (in collector's file 1113) Lewis describes the blowpipes as coming from 'Bush villages near Manua (Moewehafen)'. Courtesy of the Field Museum of Natural History, Chicago.

13. The Hamburger Südsee Expedition had made the most comprehensive and scholarly examination of this region several months prior to Lewis from December 1908 to April 1909. However, the New Britain fieldwork was not published until 1954, and even then formed a mere summary in comparison to other of the twenty-five volumes published as a result of this expedition (Thilenius 1927; Reche 1954).

14. Several letters referring to this dispute survive in the Field Museum Archives. It seems that Hernsheim & Co., acting on behalf of Leipzig Museum, sent word to Komine to purchase the collection. However, this notification was received by Komine after Lewis had bought the collection. As the German museum had sent word sometime before this occurred, Leipzig felt that they had a moral title to the collection. Leipzig threatened the Field Museum with legal action, but after the submission of a report on the purchase by Lewis, the Museum refuted their claim to title and legal action was not pursued. See letter from Lewis, 91[sic] June 1912; from Skiff to Lewis, 18 April 1912; from Director Weule to Field Museum, 26 March 1912; correspondence folder, A.B. Lewis Archives. Courtesy of the Field Museum of Natural History, Chicago.

–5–

Felix Speiser

Lewis was an American in German New Guinea, whilst Speiser was a German-speaker in Australian New Guinea. Both had the ambiguous status of being outsiders to aspects of white colonial culture, and Speiser linked into the still existing German community in Rabaul that had survived the expropriation of German plantations and other difficulties. In terms of his fieldwork practice, Speiser produced the most detailed account of Arawe life through discussions with local big men such as Aliwa on Pililo. This ethnography has never been published, and although it strongly reflects Speiser's own interests in culture history it is a most valuable account of the region and its changes. We have not been able to do the ethnographic accounts full justice here, but we use them to illuminate the sets of relations surrounding Speiser's collection practice. An important element of these relations was links to the white dimensions of colonial culture, and Speiser's meetings with Harry Bond, a local plantation owner and long-term New Guinea resident, provide us with more detail of the workings of colonial culture. We shall use the nexus between Speiser, Aliwa and Bond to provide a detailed view of some of the relations which sustained New Guinea in the late 1920s. An important new element as far as the south coast of New Britain was concerned was the arrival of the missions, which had complex effects, one of which may have been to temporarily devalue sacred objects which Speiser was then able to collect, but which were not sold in later periods. This brief period of sale of ritually important objects shows that values in the region were being continually discussed and debated, with no fixed conclusions deriving from such debates. For New Guineans the colonial period represented a series of social and material experiments, the outcomes of which fed back into people's future practices. Speiser's collection and fieldnotes help throw light on some of these debates.

Felix Speiser was forty-nine years old when he arrived in the Pacific to carry out his second regional study of Melanesia. Born on 20 October 1880, he came to the discipline of anthropology at the age of twenty-six having already trained in chemistry and pharmacology and having resigned from his post at J.R. Geigy & Co. in New York. While living in the United States he spent four weeks on a Hopi reservation, and this kindled an interest in ethnology which led him back to Switzerland, to his maternal uncles, the evolutionary natural scientists, Fritz and Paul Sarasin. They encouraged his change of direction, and in 1907 he enrolled at the University of Berlin to study physical anthropology and ethnology under Felix von Luschan, Director of the Berlin Museum für Völkerkunde. With Luschan's encouragement Speiser went to Vanuatu on fieldwork from 1910 to 1912; this resulted in his major work, *Ethnology of Vanuatu* (1996) an exemplary study of material culture (originally published as Speiser 1923).

From the moment of completing his degree Speiser's career became formally linked to Basel University and the museum. In 1914 he was appointed university lecturer in ethnology and in 1917 this became a professorship. He was also Curator at the Basel Museum für Völkerkunde.[1] Between his first and second trip to Melanesia Speiser carried out fieldwork in South America, but intellectual questions regarding the history of Melanesians, drew him back to the Pacific, and in 1929 he set off on a regional survey, a trip which took him to the Northern Solomons, south New Britain, northeast New Ireland and the Sepik region. His efforts swelled the collections of the Basel museum and resulted in several publications (Speiser 1936, 1938, 1941, 1945, 1945/6, 1946) and an exhibition, but no major monograph. Speiser died in 1949 while in post as director of the museum.

Speiser's life and work has parallels to Lewis's. Both came from scientific backgrounds, Lewis in zoology, Speiser in chemistry, and once in the field Speiser also conducted a survey, and like Lewis was interested in inter-community contact. As they both came from museums they were collecting with their institution's specific interests in mind. However, Speiser was also trying to solve a theoretical issue – the construction of the history of Melanesia through a comparative analysis of its varied cultures, in particular as expressed through material culture, art and religious ceremony (Kaufmann 1996: 413). Unlike Lewis, Speiser went to fewer places in his survey and so was able to spend more time travelling along the south coast of New Britain and to visit the whole 'cultural area' which he defined as extending from Lindenhafen in the east to the Arawe Islands in the west (Speiser 1945: 22), conducting a broad survey of material culture and cultural traits. Despite their similarities, Speiser's intellectual background differed markedly from Lewis's as his theoretical approach had developed within the German school of anthropology.

The Museum at Basel and the Discipline of Anthropology

The history of 'German anthropology'[2] is central to understanding the intellectual background of Speiser and other figures instrumental in the creation of the ethnographic collections of Basel Museum. Basel Museum, through its personnel, was intimately linked to developments in Germany and particularly in Berlin.

Basel ethnological collections and the ethnographic museum developed from the work of two sons of the city, Fritz and Paul Sarasin. From the mid-nineteenth century ethnography began to interest academic circles and, under the influence of evolutionary theories, drew in the Sarasins as zoologists. In 1888 the brothers presented a collection, which they had assembled whilst in Ceylon (Sri Lanka), to the museum which attempted to show the relationship between tools, technology and culture. This gift stimulated a broader interest in ethnology amongst the intellectuals of Basel. The General Museum of Arts and Sciences had opened in the city in 1849 and from the beginning had key ethnographic collections, but it was not until 1892, after the arrival of the Ceylon collection, that a special committee for ethnographic collections was set up. In 1896 the Sarasin brothers were assigned the direction of the Museum Committee and went on to play a key role in the growth of the museum and its ethnographic collections. Paul Sarasin was director of the museum until 1926 when Fritz took over and held the post until his death in 1942; he was in turn followed by Speiser (Jeanneret 1969: 58–63). The museum's focus on Melanesia began in 1902 with the receipt of a substantial collection from a F. Wanderes, who had worked for a long time in New Guinea as a plantation manager for the Neu Guinea Kompagnie and later as chief of police for the German government (Ohnemus 1998: 22). However, it was the expeditions by Speiser to Vanuatu and by Fritz Sarasin to New Caledonia that reinforced this focus on Melanesia which has persisted up until the present day.

The Sarasin brothers supported Speiser's change in career and directed him to Berlin (where the brothers had worked previously), and here his main foci were physical anthropology and collecting. The agenda of Berlin ethnology and museology had largely been set by Rudolf Virchow and Adolf Bastian who led the formation of the *Berliner Gesellschaft für Anthropologie, Ethnologie und Urgeschichte*. This group, founded in 1870, eclipsed its national German equivalent and had a broad membership that stretched as far as the Sarasins in Basel. A key to the society's influence was their journal *Zeitschrift für Ethnologie* which was read widely and quickly gained an international reputation (Smith 1991: 163–73).

The *Gesellschaft* gradually acquired an artefact collection which soon outgrew the available space, and as private museums with ethnographic collections developed in other German principalities, the need for a designated, state-funded 'national' museum in Berlin was brought to the attention of the authorities. In 1886 the Royal Museum of Ethnography (Königlichen Museen zu Berlin, Museum für Völkerkunde) opened in purpose-built premises. Bastian was appointed director and concurrently promoted to honorary professor of ethnology at Berlin University (Buschmann 1999: 31).

Once Bastian was in post he was able to create museum assistantships, and in the 1880s recruited the first generation of professionally trained ethnologists, which included Franz Boas and Felix von Luschan. It was Luschan, a physical anthropologist, who stepped into Bastian's shoes on his death. Luschan was no theorist, but a great gatherer of empirical data, encouraging large-scale collections and expanding the Berlin museum's collections considerably.

In 1907 when Speiser looked for a school which combined museum studies and anthropology, Berlin was the logical choice. However, from an examination of Speiser's academic work, we conclude that Luschan, as his teacher, had little influence even on his early work as regards theory. Luschan's heart was in physical anthropology, he worked also in archaeology, and his regional speciality was Africa. Yet, it was Luschan who suggested Vanuatu as an area for fieldwork, and in this he influenced Speiser's early work, to a similar extent to the Sarasins, as initial research plans aimed to analyse 'cultural evolution from the standpoint of *biological variation*' (Kaufmann 2000: 289, our emphasis). However, Speiser was an independent thinker, who grappled with theoretical issues directly rather than accepting the received thinking of the day or his mentors' opinion, which made him a far more interpretative fieldworker than perhaps Lewis or Blackwood ever were. Once Speiser was in the field he began to formulate his own threads of enquiry, his attention focusing on material culture, and art styles and ceremony in particular. His attempts to order this information into a series of comparative data sets culminated with his final work in 1946. Here he set out six basic principles of art and used them to plot regional influences in Melanesia, concluding, for example, that two of his six styles were indigenous to Melanesia and had evolved there, and another came from Indonesia and mainland Asia and had been imported into northern New Guinea. Supplementing this was the diffusion of ceremony, in particular initiation, and material culture forms. Together these studies attempted to order the history of Melanesia in relation to Indonesia and Polynesia, and were the main thrust of Speiser's life's work.

Speiser's Melanesia

This was not Speiser's first trip to Melanesia, so he had experience of fieldwork in the region and had already developed a fieldwork methodology. To understand the Melanesia of 1929 as seen through Speiser's eyes, his theoretical approach and expectations, we will first have to take a brief overview of his experience and work in Vanuatu in 1910, a shared British and French colony. Although Vanuatu was not a German territory, German influence was at its height in the Pacific around that time, making the 1929 experience a sharp contrast to this earlier work.

Speiser published his major monograph on his Vanuatu fieldwork, *Ethnographische Materialien aus den Neuen Hebrides und den Banks-Inseln*[3] (1923), six years before his work in New Britain. The monograph focuses specifically on material culture, and in it we have a resource that surpasses all of the other collections, as in the introduction he discusses the process of collecting and makes insightful comments on the tasks and aims of a collector. For the other collectors discussed in this volume we can assume that they had wrestled intellectually with the practicalities and morality of collecting, but we cannot know how these issues affected their collecting methodology as they undoubtedly did for Speiser.

Speiser's two years in Vanuatu were spent constantly moving between islands in an attempt to get an overview. At no point did he attempt an intensive study of one village or even one island. In his opinion, to gain the broadest and best collection for the museum it was expedient to move around. This also fitted in with his theoretical approach that developed during his time in the region. According to Kaufmann (2000) he set out with the aim of carrying out a biological survey of the region, and the survey would provide him with the statistical data to test the theory that particular biological groups would have specific material-culture traits. This aim fed into the twin themes of diffusionism and evolution, which in the German school of anthropology were not necessarily mutually exclusive theories (Buschmann 1999: 10). During fieldwork the emphasis changed, and instead Speiser examined these themes through material culture, and gradually came to regard objects and certain cultural traits as ways of devising regional cultural complexes and understanding the migratory (or local) history of the whole region of Melanesia.

His Vanuatu collection was obtained almost entirely from the indigenous population. Speiser's recorded principle was to acquire everything that could still be obtained of the objects constituting the native culture. Yet when he arrived in Vanuatu he described the culture as being in a state of decay and noted he was only just in time to 'salvage' some remnants of a formerly rich culture, and had to substitute poor modern examples of items that had already been lost (Speiser 1996: 2).

In the acquisition of items he is candid about his own shortcomings: '. . . the traveller cannot rely on the initiative of the natives but will, as a rule, manage to see only what he wants to see, and will therefore be able to acquire only what he has actually set his eyes on, either through chance or through systematic research' (Speiser 1996: 2).

As Speiser moved around he was unable to learn any of the local languages and instead relied upon *Bislama*, the lingua franca, to communicate. Acknowledging that it did not give him the vocabulary to discuss issues pertinent to an anthropologist's investigations, he relied on interpreters. This hampered Speiser's ability to form a rapport with his informants, something he found difficult even without language barriers, and he frequently felt in the dark as to the nuances of situations he found himself in. He notes:

> After the first few days I even refrained from asking the natives to give me the names of the articles collected, for I had begun to realize that they were supplying me with every kind of nonsense and obscenity. As I had no means of keeping a check on their statements (my servants naturally helped the natives or did not know their language), I preferred to give up collecting native names for things rather than introduce into scholarship designations that made no sense (ibid.: 3)

Few scholars are this honest about the problems with fieldwork. It is clear that Speiser was very aware of the influence of the locals as regards his treatment, and in the results of his research he adds: 'Here already we find evidence of the passive resistance which the natives show towards any white person they do not know well' (ibid.: 3).

It is clear that locals lied or confused the researcher. If Speiser was not on hand to see an artefact in use, information on everyday artefacts was imparted that was 'palpably false' (ibid.: 4). What is impressive about Speiser is his ability to admit that the locals had the skills and ability to deceive the white man, and that he wrote this into his introduction. It is difficult to think of a more candid discussion of collecting until the recent account by O'Hanlon (1993: 55–77) regarding the problems of collecting in Papua New Guinea today. For a European to admit in the colonial era that the indigenous population were involved in 'passive resistance' is unusual.

The results of Speiser's work in Vanuatu and the subsequent publication caused him to mull over several intellectual concerns about culture, history and material culture. Subsequent fieldwork in South America proved unsatisfactory in resolving any of these issues and it was not long before the Pacific beckoned again. The Pacific was the focus of much intellectual interest in 1929, but Speiser felt the emerging functionalist school was neglecting certain issues that he felt remained pertinent, and he sought the opportunity to resolve them.

By the time of Speiser's second trip to Melanesia, a completely different colonial landscape to that which he had experienced around 1910 was in place. Some aspects of the German rule of the colony still echoed across the colonial landscape, such as the use of luluai and tultul, but Australia had now held the colony in various guises for almost fifteen years. During this time a comprehensive system of District, Patrol and Medical Officers was established across the Territory and patrol stations set up at strategic points to bring areas under 'control'; thereby enabling the administration to conduct regular patrols and collect head tax (Campbell 1998). In 1929, when Speiser arrived on the south coast, the patrol station at Gasmata had been up and running for twelve years. The system differed greatly from the German arrangement. Then it had been Governor Hahl's interest in anthropology that promoted studies and supported visitors, but under Australian rule, as the patrol system was set up around the territory, anthropology was seen as one thread through which an effective understanding of the region, and therefore effective control, could be achieved.

In 1920 the post of government anthropologist was established in Papua; in 1924 the Territory of New Guinea followed suit, and E.W.P. Chinnery was appointed first government anthropologist. In his capacity as Government anthropologist Chinnery carried out several surveys of the Territory (Chinnery 1925, 1926) and two of these took him along the southwest coast of New Britain in 1925, where he was able to take a photograph of the blowpipe hunters of the region (Fig 5.1). Chinnery published this picture and a one-page commentary on the object and the people in *Man* in 1927 (p. 208) and as this preceded Lewis's guidebook it may be the first information about this object published in English.

For Speiser to function in the Territory he had to gain research permits from the administration, and, like Lewis, he relied on government vessels and the goodwill of residents to help get him around. Like Lewis, his nationality and mother tongue set him apart; Lewis an American and an English speaker in a German colony, and Speiser a Swiss national and a German speaker in an English-speaking colony. While both Lewis and Speiser spoke both languages, the nationality barrier did separate them from their respective colonial hosts. In Rabaul Speiser was grouped with the German expatriates; he was expected to socialize at 'The German Club' and stay in the hotel that was owned and run by a German. Therefore, while his administrative business relating to his trip was carried on with the native English speakers, his social circle was largely made up of German speakers. Rabaul was a nationally divided town, with the British and Australians, Germans, Japanese, Chinese and locals all forming distinct social groups. How much his nationality affected his reception and the amount of help he was given in the region is difficult to assess, but from surviving correspondence it seems that Speiser operated through a very formal relationship with the administration and armed himself with letters of introduction from academics in Britain and Australia to ease his passage. Before leaving for the colony he had written to Alfred Cort Haddon in Cambridge (with whom he had an ongoing correspondence), to ask him to write letters of introduction to Murray, among others, for him.[4] He also gained Radcliffe-Brown's support and letters of introduction while staying at Sydney University before going 'up' to New Guinea.[5] Despite his having had prior experience in the region, the administration was different and new networks had to be set up. Speiser knew that the key to any research work was having the right introduction and contacts. In New Guinea this meant Chinnery, who, in his capacity as government anthropologist, acted as a 'gatekeeper' to the region for all anthropologists.[6] All researchers had to apply for permits to carry out their work, and Speiser's applications are still extant in the colonial records in the National Archives of Australia. In them he sets out his planned expedition 'for the purpose of making an anthropological and ethnological study of the natives of New Britain'.[7] and indicates that he will be accompanied by a zoology student, Heinrich Hediger. The many other anthropologists in the Territory of New Guinea would have had to go through this process. In 1929 and 1930 there were anthropologists from all over the world in the field including Reo Fortune and Margaret Mead on Manus, Beatrice Blackwood in Buka and Bougainville,[8] and Hortense Powdermaker in Lesu, New Ireland. Each one of them had liaised with Chinnery and other officials on their arrival in the Territory.

Figure 5.1. Geglip 'boy' demonstrating how a blowpipe is used (National Library of Australia)

The south coast of New Britain was not the remote territory that it had been for Lewis. Apparent from Speiser's diaries is that, throughout his field trip, he was staying with, conversing with and drawing on the expertise of missionaries, patrol officers, plantation owners and managers and traders, in addition to liaising with locals in their capacities as servants, interpreters and informants.

Speiser's stay lasted from January to May 1930 and was centred at three base points: Gasmata government station, where he spent the month of January; Kandrian, where he spent six weeks; and the Arawe Islands, where a further six weeks was spent, during which time he spent several weeks visiting Umboi Island and the Siassis. At each point of residence Speiser made short trips inland and along the coast. There were villages he visited several times and others he visited only once while on expeditions. At each site Speiser interviewed those living there, which included both the whites and local people who were willing to speak to him and had stories to tell. During his researches several male local informants stand out as being the source of the largest quantity of data, and in the majority of instances these men had the officially sanctioned posts of either luluai or tultul, while also having a big-man status in their village. These interviews were typed up and together form about 350 pages of ethnographic data. Amongst these informants are two in particular who stand out in his personal record, and a description of them will allow us to understand the dynamics of the region at this time.

New Britain Portraits

Once in the rural areas, there were no national boundaries amongst the white population. Here any European was a welcome source of entertainment or interest, and Speiser's visit led to close contact with residents. In addition to the help and friendship of these whites, Speiser had considerable contact with the locals, who were to be his key informants.

As in Rabaul the first point of call when Speiser reached a new area was to check in with the *Kiap* (patrol officer). In this area he was based at the sub-district office of Gasmata where there was an office, hospital and jail. At the time of Speiser's visit District Officer B. Calcutt was in post, and Speiser stayed with him; he proved to be interested in Speiser's work and willing to help. According to Speiser, Calcutt was trying with some success to pacify the people and was collecting taxes (a sign that an area was under government 'control'). Calcutt offered Speiser the daily use of the government schooner *Hermes*, with police soldiers to accompany him, and a patrol officer agreed to lead them inland both at Gasmata and Möwehafen.[9] Calcutt was able to supply Speiser with the 'boys' he needed to move around the region. Their main task to carry his equipment and act as servants for cooking and washing. Interpreters and guides were hired as and when they were required.

Although the government station at Gasmata was the first port of call for Speiser, he soon moved westwards to Möwehafen to make the acquaintance of Harry Bond, owner of Aliwa Plantation and a long-term resident, having arrived in the region in 1912. Bond's links to, and knowledge of, the local community and landscape surpassed that of any patrol officer. Bond was a port of call for anyone in the area, Chinnery had liaised with him on his visits and recommended him as a contact to Speiser when he had advised him in Rabaul.

Bond was the sort of character described as 'colourful'. Our research about him began with the mention of his name in Speiser's own notes, but then his name cropped up in a wide variety of sources including the news publications from the region at the time. Bond's reputation preceded him. Despite the recommendation, Chinnery also warned Speiser that if he chose to spend time with Bond, to be sure to keep any alcohol he carried well hidden.[10] The following brief account of his life is a blend of these various sources. His biography is probably not that dissimilar to the stories of other single white men who came to the region seeking a new life (and probably escaping from an old one). As a plantation manager, and perhaps a misfit, he found the colonial life and its attendant ambiguities in the remoter areas fitted his lifestyle.

Bond came to the Territory before the First World War and gained employment with the German firm Hamburgische Südsee A.G. (HSAG/Hamburg Southseas Inc.). This company headed by Rudolf Wahlen had bought out Queen Emma's company in about 1910. Bond was manager of their Arawe Plantation, and after the war he continued to manage it for the Expropriation Board before leaving to start up his own coconut plantation, east of the Arawes at Möwehafen, which he named Aliwa.[11]

Like many other single male residents he took a local wife, and he had at least one child. Bond's contacts with colonial society would have been with visitors passing through the region and with other plantation residents (at Arawe plantation to the west, past Gasmata at Lindenhafen plantation to the east, and Bill Money's plantation on Rooke Island off the western end of the island), and would have been infrequent as would have been his trips to Rabaul. Bond did, however, have a trade store in Mandok in the Siassi Islands. In addition there were recruiters scouring the south coast looking for plantation labour, and Bond helped them or at least socialized with the visitors. The most constant white contact would have come from the members of the patrol post at Gasmata, as patrols aimed to go along the coast every 3–6 months, and they used his boat to patrol in the 1920s. By far his greatest contact would have been with the local community, who provided the majority of his workforce, and through his relationship with his wife's kinship ties. It is impossible to gauge exactly how the locals viewed Bond, who by the time Speiser arrived seemed to lead a fairly dissipated life and was gradually falling into debt.

By May 1930, only days after Speiser's departure, a notice appeared in *New Guinea Gazette* stating that as the result of a writ issued by Carpenter & Co. against Harry Bond, presumably in an attempt to cover debts, the 200-acre Aliwa Plantation would be up for sale by auction in June of that year. The next official record of Bond is the following letter to the Prime Minister's department in Canberra:

Subject:- Estate of Harry Bond, deceased.

I am informed that upon an Inquiry held by the Harbour Master in accordance with the Wreck and Salvage Ordinance 1902, on the 11th Oct last, concerning the loss of the auxiliary cutter 'Aliwa,' the Harbour Master found that Harry Bond, late of the Aliwa Plantation, was drowned. The only evidence available was that of the survivors of the native crew, from which it appears that the vessel was in charge of the deceased, who was the Master and owner and the only European on board, and that the vessel foundered in heavy south-east weather encountered near the Siassi Group while proceeding from Kauptometi Island Yungpum. So far as can be ascertained, the 'Aliwa' foundered late at night on a date towards the end of the first week in September last, and the deceased went down with her.[12]

This is followed up by a further letter regarding his will nine months later in which it is noted: 'The deceased is described as having been of roving disposition and not at all likely to have made any testamentary arrangements.'[13] In the event some relatives in Sydney were found and a will had been lodged with them. The remaining legacy (after expenses) was handed over to them, and Harry Bond left the public record.

The circumstances of Bond's death are mysterious. No one else died in the accident; all the native crew survived and made it to shore. This begs the question of why Bond was the only casualty. Was he drunk and unable to save himself? had his debts caused him to commit suicide? or did the local crew decide to kill him? The overall tone of the government letters suggest that all these options were considered as possibilities and the real truth could not be ascertained.

Through Bond, Speiser was directed westwards up the coast to visit Aliwa,[14] an old man who was a big man and luluai[15] on Pililo island, and whose influence spread right along the coast. He is one man whose legacy remains today. In 1985, more than fifty years later, his achievements were recounted to Gosden.

Speiser wanted to know the history of the area. It was crucial to the way he understood the landscape and its people and to the picture of migration and development of material culture that he was working on. Up until this time Speiser had been moving between a variety of willing informants, some were big men, some luluai and others tultul, but was continuously frustrated by their lack of knowledge and by the commonly spoken phrase 'The old men knew, we do not know any more.'[16] Aliwa was to become Speiser's most important informant as he was able to tell stories of the past which few around him remembered; on several occasions other local men and boys listened in on the sessions as many of them had never heard the stories before.[17]

While Speiser was in Möwehafen he was already banking on the reputation of Aliwa, noting in his diary a full two weeks before he met him, 'I now pin all my hopes on old Aliwa in Arawe, but I will probably experience disappointment with him. He is said to be very communicative and knows a lot.'[18] When Speiser finally met him he was frustrated as Aliwa had had no prior warning of his arrival.

> In the afternoon I went then to Umtingalu village where I met the famous Mr. Aliwa – an old, very worthy and self-confident man, whom I made my compliments to. He still knew nothing about me – officially – Harry Bond had naturally forgotten to speak to him about me . . . however he was stalling . . . he said all kinds of things to me, that I still hadn't seen – and he wants to come again tomorrow.

In his field notes Speiser described Aliwa as a large man of about seventy years of age, with a large family, and with the status of 'upper'-luluai. He suggested that he was coming to the end of his career and was very ill, probably with lung disease. Speiser attributes Aliwa's lessening influence on the coming of the whites. The tone of Speiser's notes suggest that he felt sorry for Aliwa. With the passing of tradition and the passing of his power, he interprets Aliwa's willingness to pass on information as an acknowledgement of its lessening relevance to the Arawe today.[19]

To understand the significance of Aliwa one has to go back in time. The first published record of him that we have found is in the first volume of the publications of the Hamburger Südsee Expedition (HSE), which was in the region in 1908 (Thilenius 1927). The expedition members were not the first, nor the last, visitors and white residents to forge links with Aliwa for their mutual benefit. According to Müller, a member of the HSE, they met Aliwa when he was enjoying the height of his power. Müller draws particular attention to Aliwa's influence derived from his wide trade connections: he was one of the few men in the region to have actually travelled to New Guinea, and had strong connections with the Siassi Islanders, the main trading partner, and one of his sons resided there. The HSE researchers likewise made close links with Aliwa, staying in his village and later hiring him to accompany them up the Pulie River to pave the way with the locals there. Their main need for Aliwa was as guide and interpreter. Müller noted that he had favourable relations with the people they were to visit and a knowledge of all the languages and dialects spoken in the surrounding area for quite a distance, of which he was justly proud. As an acknowledgement of his status, Aliwa did not have to carry any cargo during the expedition, and his brother only had to carry a small pack. This was one of the earliest, if not the first, exploratory crossings of New Britain to Talasea, and Aliwa made sure he was a key part of it.[20]

Aliwa's influence was long lived. In a patrol report by Ian McCallum Mack for a patrol to the Pulie district from 12 February to 12 March 1928, he noted meeting Aliwa whom he described as the paramount luluai, who had accompanied Mr Merrilees and Chapman (two patrol officers) on their crossing of the island in 1926. Mack also reported Aliwa's help with his own work in mustering labourers and speaking to people inland 'at great length and making a favourable impression' on behalf of the officers. When they met those he had mustered, Aliwa had already left to visit other regions, which suggests he had his own business in the area and was not always beholden or morally contracted to the officers.[21]

Aliwa's social standing was also defined by his material wealth, and this was recorded by Speiser. Of great significance were the thirteen named gold-lip shells that Aliwa owned. These gold-lip shells, of the type Lewis found so hard to procure, were larger than those used as cash. They were partly inherited from his father (although some of his father's shells went to his brother) and some had been fished for off-shore and polished (an increasingly rare occurrence as they were more often traded in from Manus at this stage). The name of each shell was widely known in the district, as was their association with Aliwa. Aliwa was happy to allow Speiser to photograph them, and they were laid out in a long line in front of a house in order of size and each named in descending order of size (Fig. 5.2). No other collector was able to make such a thorough list of a man's wealth. Speiser was impressed by this collection, describing the shells elsewhere as all having a lateral ornamentation and beautiful cords, the value placed on them by Speiser was 5–10 shillings each, but in real terms it was probably far greater as he was unable to buy any of them.

According to Aliwa, only the big men were truly independent personalities and had the following rights: they were the sole owners of *mokmok* and tusker pigs; they did not need to fight; they alone could kill as they pleased; they governed the whole social life of the village and controlled almost all the possessions of the village, including having a percentage of the commoners' wealth through killing pigs; they alone had many wives and could rape women as they pleased; they had their own group of followers and stood above political distinctions.[22] When Aliwa listed these attributes for Speiser he was secure in the knowledge that he had them all. Whether these attributes were indeed attributes of big men we do not know, but what seems certain is that a man like Aliwa could consolidate his position by stating those criteria he fulfilled to the anthropologist or government officer, and omitting those, if any, he did not.

One had to be a skilful player at many social games to become a successful big man. In an interview with Speiser on 17 March 1930, Aliwa explained the position of big men, their hereditary title and their rights. Significant to Aliwa was that only big men had the right to breed tusker pigs for ornaments. These men had special reputations in their villages but their influence could spread out along the

Figure 5.2. Gold-lip shells belonging to Aliwa and laid out in front of the house (Museum der Kulturen, Basel)

coast if their personality was strong. Aliwa noted that inheritance passed from father to son and that the land belonged to the big men. Speiser suggested that this meant that the big men represented the village rather than they owned it and that in telling this to him Aliwa was trying to skew the information to his advantage.[23] This may have been perfectly true. Aliwa had had a long contact with the whites in the area, and his influence, and the respect afforded him by the white community is obvious. If Aliwa formed the main line of communication and interaction between the two communities there is no doubt that he, as a skilled diplomat, would have influenced white men's perception of the community and his authority, and would have used this to his advantage.

According to histories told to Gosden during fieldwork in the 1980s, Aliwa founded three men's houses for the different purposes of war, sorcery and trade, at a time when other men only founded one, which emphasized his influence in three key areas of Arawe political and economic life.

From the various roles Aliwa played in the colonial community and his traditional community over his lifetime, it is clear that he was no white-man's pawn. While he had been made paramount luluai by the colonizing government, he was also a big man in his own right with all the attributes needed to hold and maintain the position in the village. There is no doubt that Aliwa was highly intelligent, and when warfare was outlawed – and therefore part of the big-man system destabilized – he improved his abilities in trade and sorcery, two other important areas of expertise (Zelenietz 1980). Aliwa's trading connections were impressive, made more impressive by the skilful deployment of a large family (Fig. 5.3) and his knowledge of pidgin, as well as the dialects and languages of the surrounding regions. As luluai, he was not beholden to his tultul to interpret for him, and he was a valuable resource for any expedition – making him first on the scene when any new areas were opened and instantly affiliated with the white man's power and protection. It is obvious that Aliwa manipulated the expectations of both communities, becoming the ultimate colonial player and enhancing his own position in every arena. Zelenietz (1980) pointed out that there were unusually powerful big men on the north coast of New Britain in the 1920s and 1930s who were able to manipulate their local links and government positions to give them an unusual degree of power. Aliwa made similar use of local and government connections to gain power and influence through all areas of colonial culture.

The lives of Bond and Aliwa were heavily entangled. Bond, as perhaps the longest-term white resident in the area, had a relationship with Aliwa, the most powerful man in the district. Bond began work on Arawe plantation, before creating his own plantation, 'Aliwa', eastwards down the coast. Speiser was frustrated that Aliwa after their first meeting travelled down to Möwehafen to visit Bond. While at Arawe Plantation Bond would have been in close and frequent contact with Aliwa. Bond as an employer, recruiter and tradesman was vital to the community, particular in their desire for currency and certain Western goods. For Bond the co-operation of Aliwa was essential for the success of the plantation; Aliwa could advise, help or hinder work depending on his commitment. Bond and Aliwa represent pivotal colonial figures – Bond with his local wife and son had many local contacts and real ties to the community – Aliwa with his status in the village and amongst the Europeans. Their actions held colonial culture together, whilst each pursuing their own interests. Both were acutely aware of the situation and played it to their own strengths and benefits. They had learned how to operate this colonial culture into which they had entered in adulthood, as well as in the cultures into which they had been born.

Speiser on the South Coast

Speiser's specific interests in the region were the occurrence of the blowpipe, head binding and circumcision, and at Gasmata, Kandrian and the Arawe Islands he documented these in detail. Despite these main focuses his notes are not solely about these aspects of life and instead seem to form a catalogue of everything that Speiser managed to glean information about. A comprehensive list of the subjects he covered is too long to cite here, but we will try to give the broad themes of the information he collected before concentrating on data unique to Speiser's investigations. Speiser focused on the material culture and gave short descriptions of objects and their use; the sociological aspects of life, including kinship, law, politics, totems and the everyday activities of agriculture, cooking, transport and housing; the ceremonial, from the life stages of birth, marriage and death, to skull cults and masking ceremonies; and physical anthropology, from descriptions and measurements to body deformation. These interviews and observations on these topics are supplemented with maps, word lists, vocabulary and kinship lists. While none of it is analysed or arranged in anything other than by region, it provides a detailed account of a myriad of aspects of life. Most of his informants were older males, but young men, and in a few cases women, were also interviewed.

Speiser focused on the history of peoples and cultures and took the view that art styles were historical, in an evolutionary sense, and therefore bore witness to the history of the society of which they were part. Despite this idea, barkcloths, shields and paddles, the main decorated items of the region, did not hold his attention; it was the objects and ritual practices which had first drawn him to the regions, and blowpipes, pig's-tusk ornaments, circumcision and head deformation that became his main focus. Speiser's collection of 110 objects contains material relating to all these themes. His collection is the smallest of the four as he generally collected only one or two examples of each type, so his collection shows little evidence of variation of type. Exceptionally, he collected five vine-string bags. Despite the small number of objects, there are several items not present in the other collections. In particular, two examples of snail-shell hair ornaments. These consist of a piece of fine local string, hung at one end with a perforated snail shell. Most important in our research were three *Kuiunke* masks, only found in Speiser's collection, which will be discussed in detail below.

Speiser took an holistic view and could not view material culture as separate from the sociological; for his research he had to have knowledge of the whole to understand and utilize each part. He also realized that as his intellectual interests might shift he needed the broadest base of data for interpretation. Speiser was acutely aware of the limitations of his material, which was partly because of his lack of knowledge of the local language and due to the limited amount of time he had in each area. He was to write later that although government control was not complete in the region, the effects of the whites on material culture was already 'strong enough to show', yet he did not deny that there was still a lot of material to be examined. In addition, Speiser outlines his reservations about the reliability of informants, noting that old members of the community were often suspicious of the visitor, and that once willing to be interviewed they did not speak pidgin well, whereas the young did not know enough about the traditional life, so they would happily make up stories to fill in their lack of knowledge.[24]

On 27 May 1930 Speiser sat down in Jacquinot Bay and wrote a letter to Alfred Cort Haddon in Cambridge giving him a summary of the work he had just completed on the south coast of New Britain:

Figure 5.3. Aliwa's daughter at Umtingalu, Arawe Islands (Museum der Kulturen, Basel)

Concerning the natives of the south-coast here, I reckon that they represent about the most primitive form of the Melanesian culture. This is to some extent the consequence of a general degeneration here, owing to a severe epidemic of measles, which some 40 years ago has swept away all the old people and with them the tradition, so that it has to be newly built up by the living ones. The Ceremonies are partly still practised, but they have no meaning any more to the people, and ever and ever I must hear: The old men knew, we do not know anymore. And this cannot be accounted for by the influence of the whites, as this has been very small up to the last years.[25]

It is clear from his notes and the resulting publications that the majority of Speiser's informants were men. Not only that but Speiser's interest in the movement of cultural traits meant that he concentrated on ceremonial and material similarities between the Arawe and Indonesia and other Melanesian groups. Contrary to Lewis or Blackwood, this led to a concentration on the ceremonial in the collection he made, despite his fears that they had significantly degenerated.

We now propose to draw on Speiser's own publication, which was produced as a guide to the exhibitions on New Britain (Speiser 1945). This allows us a glimpse of Speiser's developed view of Arawe material culture.

Of significance to Speiser were the two masking ceremonies – the *Kamotmot* and the *Kuiunke*. Of particular interest is that while the *Kamotmot* ceremony had been documented by Chinnery (1926), the *Kuiunke* ceremonies are not documented by any other visitor to the region known to us. Speiser saw the *Kamotmot* masks at Arung in Möwehafen and described them as not very beautiful, but more to the point noted that they were not for sale, as according to informants, no one knew how to make them anymore, which caused him to remark on the cultural degeneration of the area since white contact.[26] None of our collectors managed to collect these very distinctive masks (Fig. 5.4), and while they do appear in some collections of earlier date, they were generally hard to come by. The ceremony still takes place today, but even now the conclusion of the ceremony should be the weighting of the masks with stones and their disposal in the sea, making sale to a collector an unlikely outcome (Christin Kocher-Schmid personal communication). Todd took photographs of the *Kamotmot* ceremonies as well, but did not make any collection (Chapter Six).

The *Kuiunke* masks are far more intriguing. Made of palm fibre, the masks are supplemented with a costume of leaves which veil the body (Fig. 5.5). When in costume the *Kuiunke* spirits bark like dogs and use the secret leaf whistle (*kopkop*) to unsettle people. However, Speiser suggested that at that time the masks' power was often abused and used by young men to frighten woman at night and extort meals from them, whereas in the past they would have been used as village sanctions and in the enforcement of village law (Speiser 1945: 18). Perhaps in support of their lessening value as a sanctioning device, Speiser was able to purchase three examples (Vb 8727, Vb 8728 and Vb 8729).

Figure 5.4. A group of three masked *Kamotmot* dancers at Aviglo (Museum der Kulturen, Basel)

In addition to these two types of mask, the *Barku* (called *warku* by others) was also mentioned by Speiser (ibid.: 30) in relation to the initiation of young men. Speiser stated that this special mask was only imported some generations earlier from New Guinea, and this supports the information available relating to the wooden masks collected by Lewis (see Chapter Eight).

Speiser collected many examples of musical instruments, which formed 9 per cent of the total number of objects. This can be explained by his personal interest in music, but in addition because they were used in conjunction with the masking ceremonies.

Despite the local variation in masking ceremonies and use, Speiser defined the area as a cultural whole from Lindenhafen westwards to the Arawe Islands using principal traits. He collected objects that supported this delineation of the area and fixed it as a cultural region to compare to others. Foremost amongst these cultural traits Speiser listed head binding, which although he concluded was done to conform to the local ideal of beauty, suggested that this aesthetic could not have developed independently and must link the region with Vanuatu.

A second culture trait was the pig's-tusk ornament, which we described briefly in the previous chapter. Speiser managed to collect two examples of this item (Vb 8413 and Vb 8564) and two of the cowry-shell versions (Vb 8147 and Vb 8563).

Figure 5.5. *Kuiunke* dancer (Museum der Kulturen, Basel)

Like the head binding, significance was given to a similar object in the New Hebrides. These artefacts still hold great cultural significance – their production requires a considerable investment of time and their ownership signifies status and wealth. Speiser attempted to thoroughly investigate their place in Arawe society. The following is a summary of the main points in the published pamphlet. The main structure of the item is the circle of pig's tusks, and these were grown by removing the upper canines ensuring that they did not wear down the tusks. They continued to grow and eventually the tip met and perforated the pig's cheek, and in the most extreme cases was encouraged to form a double circle. The tusks meant that the pigs could no longer eat, and to root would damage the tusks. Therefore women took over feeding them. Particular animals that have well-developed tusks were renowned throughout the region, and people made special visits to see them as Speiser noted: '. . . as we would travel to museums to admire works of art' (1945: 26).

Once the desired shape of tusk was achieved the pig was sacrificed. The meat was eaten and the tusks cut out and touched by the big man's children who sat by the sacrificed pig, giving the children the right in the future to breed their own tusker pigs and sacrifice them. Through these ceremonies a man's status and reputation increased. Once the celebrations were over the tusks were taken and bound into the ornament, which the big man gave to his son, who had to kill someone while holding the ornament in his teeth. The blood of the victim was then smeared on the teeth and the ornament brought back to the father who hung the teeth around his neck (Fig. 5.6). From then on they would serve as an amulet in a fight. Speiser stated that further ornaments could be made and distributed to his followers to ensure support. Any surplus tusks were sold at a high price to the Siassi people, and they traded them into New Guinea where they might move as far as the Papuan Gulf.

Speiser judged that this ceremony, while different from that found on Malekula, could not have developed spontaneously, and he linked it culturally with Nias (an island to the west of Sumatra), to Arawe and then to Malekula (ibid.: 26–7).

A further custom which referred to Indonesia was tooth blackening, which a young man must undergo if he wanted to marry, as white teeth were unattractive. The colour was achieved by painting the teeth with a black powder (manganese oxide) and took two days and nights. During that time the boy had to sit with his mouth open and could not eat or drink (ibid.: 28). Speiser's collected a jar of the powder and tucked the following note in it: 'Vb 9187: Möwehafen. Yumyelo. Earth to colour the teeth black if soaked in a plant-juice. It would be traded along the coast from the west (Siassi) and is very expensive.'[27] All of the other collectors bought an example of this, but none noted its exchange from Siassi or its cost, nor does Speiser expand on why this ceremony was also evidence of a link with Indonesia.

In addition to the ceremonial, Speiser concentrated on the valuables related to men. Of these, *mokmok* stones were noted as being particularly precious and were listed by Aliwa as being one of the conditions of a big man's status. The *mokmok* was described by Speiser as being of grey stone, up to the size of a chicken egg, and artificially perforated through their centre. They were not made locally, but were said to come from river beds; in Speiser's case he was told they came from the Pulie River, and had belonged to the ancestors (1945: 28). Their value was

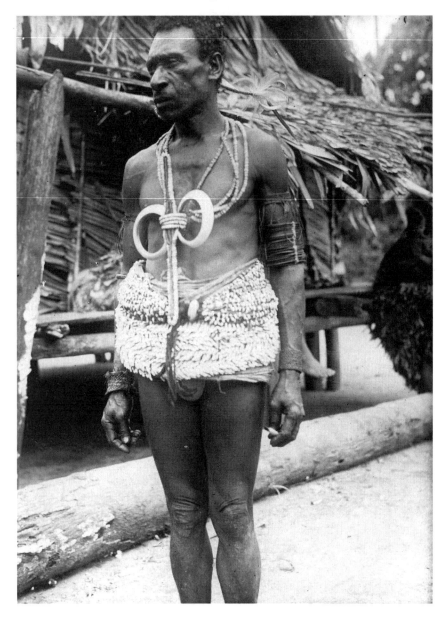

Figure 5.6. Arulo, Luluai of Kaleken village (Museum der Kulturen, Basel)

reflected in the fact that Speiser only collected one example. They were displayed by being worn over the barkcloth belts of men, along with dogs'-teeth belts (Speiser was unable to purchase an example of these).

Return to Basel

What sets Speiser apart from all other collectors discussed in this volume is the importance of his southwest New Britain work in relation to his later work. Unlike all the others, New Britain was a central example in all his later writings on Melanesia. In addition, as noted above, he curated an exhibition devoted entirely to the areas he had visited in New Britain.

However, before the exhibitions could be opened and catalogues published, the basic task of accessioning, numbering and creating card catalogues for every item in the collection had to be completed. It is clear from the distinctive handwriting on the cards and the rough sketches of some items that Speiser himself recorded each object for the museum's records. Speiser, unlike the other collectors, had financed his field trip and collection with his own funds. On his return to Basel he sold his collection of artefacts to the Museum to offset the cost of the expedition. In addition, *Dubletten* or duplicate objects were set aside for exchange, or more importantly for sale to other institutions. The duplicate specimens were chosen by Speiser in conjunction with another museum employee, and were never accessioned to the museum's collections, but were already siphoned off before the cataloguing began so that there could be no complications with the sale. The museum, which purchased the central collection from Speiser for 25,000 Swiss francs (an approximate cost of 20 francs per item), came to the arrangement with Speiser that they would help him sell the duplicates for a percentage of the revenue he generated. The remaining collection was estimated at a value of 30,000 francs, and the share in the profits of each sale was set at 80 per cent to Speiser and 20 per cent to the museum. If an exchange, rather than a sale, took place then Speiser had to be given 80 per cent of the item's estimated value by the museum.[28]

The museum was happy with the negotiations. In a first draft of the contract and correspondence between museum staff, the author noted that 'even if Professor Speiser is a somewhat tough salesman, then I must confess nevertheless that our museum is close to his heart, and he naturally wishes for the collection to come to this museum and makes no attempts nor wishes to sell the collection to any other museum'.[29] Despite their wishes to have the collection, the museum had to raise the funds for its purchase, and in the event that this money was not paid after four years the outstanding balance would be paid to Speiser with interest of 4 per cent a year.

In a letter to the museum from Arawe at the end of his sojourn on the coast Speiser commented that he had collected approximately 350 artefacts.[30] What remains in the collection today is 110 objects. While we did not count or examine the number of items collected at Rooke Island and Siassi (and a significant proportion of the collection comes from there), even if a similar number were collected (in a significantly shorter period) it suggests that possibly as much as one half were classed as *Dubletten*, as Speiser valued the *Dubletten* collection as equal to the collection the museum acquired.[31]

The exchange of items was not uncommon. We have already examined those items that Lewis exchanged and sold from his collection at the Field Museum. However, what is interesting in Speiser's collection is that he specifically collected items for exchange and sale. He was weighing up Western values while in the field and picking out the best for his museum and duplicates for others. While in Buka he met with Blackwood, and they discussed the possibility of an exchange between their museums.[32] Both were willing to part with rare objects because they could see their way to procuring more than one during their work in their respective regions. The Blackwood exchange was discussed in the field but did not take place until 1934.

The division of the collection into a core collection and duplicates before it was catalogued poses problems for our analysis. Effectively Speiser was collecting both as an anthropologist and as a commercial dealer, and from the moment of embarking on the fieldwork the commercial aspect was written in. However, as the repercussions of the Wall Street financial crash reverberated round the world markets, finances became a worry for Speiser, and more thought had to be given to the commercial aspects of what he was doing and its impact on his personal finances.

What sets Speiser's and the Basel museum's attitude to the sale of items apart from the purely commercial is that they were not for profit but for the museum's gain. In practice what happened with the *Dubletten* collection was that items were exchanged and rarely sold for cash. As noted above, when this occurred the museum paid a percentage of the item's perceived value to Speiser, but the option to exchange meant the museum's bartering power was significantly increased. How widespread this practice was with other collections in the museum we have not discovered, but it provides a concrete means of charting academic networks.

Speiser was a prolific publisher, and almost immediately he began to write up his south-coast work. He had gone to the region to gather empirical evidence that would help him prove his theory of migration and development of material culture. Thus on his return he set about using this evidence to defend his hypothesis. Speiser not only collected and provided future generations with research data, he also used the information and items he had gathered to form his own interpretation of the data relevant to contemporary concerns in the academic field.

In 1934 he spoke to the Royal Anthropological Institute in London on 'Observations on the cultural history of New Caledonia and the New Hebrides' which drew on the links that he had outlined with the south-coast work: head deformation, the creation of rounded boar's tusks and ceremonial pig killing (Speiser 1934: 74) In 1938 he presented a paper at the Second International Congress of Anthropological and Ethnological Sciences held in Copenhagen, during which he discussed

'Cultural connections between Indonesia and Melanesia'. This was followed by a paper given by Blackwood on head deformation. However, it was not until 1945 that he tackled the material culture fully and published a guide to the New Britain collections exhibited in the Basel Museum. This volume covered the whole area that Speiser was able to visit, and outlined his theoretical approach in lay terms, but despite being for the general public it was still the most comprehensive survey in print of material culture along that coast.

Despite his publication record, Speiser was never able to publish a volume like that which accompanied his Vanuatu work. However, in his archives, as mentioned above, was a manuscript that was intended for publication. The introduction to the manuscript gives us some idea of why no substantial publication was forthcoming immediately after his return from the field. He notes that the nature of collecting meant that he was unable to spend time really getting to know a region and the people. While he recorded material culture he did not feel he truly got to grips with the minds of the people, and therefore his work was not worthy of a major publication. By the time of writing the manuscript the Second World War was over, the effects of which he feared had probably changed the situation in the visited regions irrevocably, so that his work, even with deficiencies, should be published as an historical record.[33] The effects of the war were also felt on Speiser's attitude and approach to anthropology. He abhorred the stance of colleagues in Germany,[34] and he also came to the conclusion that the designation of Melanesia as a region or a race of Melanesians was false and that his work and researches had succeeded in 'exterminating' them.[35] However, he never fully published or explored this new ground.

Overall, Speiser's collection represents the usual mix of economic constraints, intellectual interests and the influences of the people who sold him material. Speiser's interests appear today to be a mixture of themes, some of which appear out-moded and others still have contemporary relevance. His attempt to define culture areas within New Guinea on the basis of differences of race and material, and as influenced by migration, seem very much in tune with his times. However, the relationships between art, ritual and material culture have much more resonance today. The element of Speiser's collection still in Basel is not large, representing 13 per cent of all the objects we looked at in the project as a whole. Almost a quarter of his collection was made up of ornaments and clothing, objects which are relatively cheap and easy to acquire, and were items which might be swapped with other institutions or sold at some profit. Over half of his objects were connected with men and the majority of his informants were men, particularly older men. Speiser collected the smallest numbers of objects that featured in long-distance exchange, and those he did collect were important in ritual. His notes, which are far more extensive than those of any other collector, and which we have not been able to do justice to here, dwell on ritual and ceremony. Speiser collected objects, such as the *Kuiunke* masks, not even mentioned by our other collectors. This may have been due to his deeper interest in ritual, or possibly because there was a fluidity in ritual forms at the time, which made for constant change.

Speiser's collection has the fewest objects but the greatest amount of anthropological detail attached to it. He records information on ceremonies, such as those involving *kamotmot*, *kuiunke* and *warku*, helping to document the change from male-dominated rituals, such as *warku*, to those involving the group as a whole. Speiser's focus of interest was with the local group, rather than longer-distance trading connections, so that his interests contrast with those of Lewis, but coincide with Todd's, the next collector we consider.

Notes

1. The museum has gone through various name changes, but recently changed from the Museum für Völkerkunde und Schweizerisches Museum für Volkskunde, Basel to the Museum der Kulturen Basel.
2. By 'German anthropology' we refer to the German-speaking part of Europe including all those states which were unified into a German nation, as well as the Austro-Hungarian Empire and Switzerland.
3. The direct English translation would be *Ethnographic Material of the New Hebrides and the Banks Islands*.
4. Letter from Speiser to Haddon, 27 May 1930, in which he thanks Haddon for writing and organizing letters of reference. Haddon Archives, folder 2044, Cambridge University Library.
5. Letter from Speiser to Radcliffe-Brown thanking him for his support, 28 July 1930. Elkin Archives, Series 13, Item 132, Sydney University Archives.
6. There was a general feeling among anthropologists that a field site had to be 'negotiated' with Chinnery. In her memoirs *Blackberry Winter*, Margeret Mead wrote of Chinnery: 'On his [Gregory Bateson's] first field trip in 1927, E.P.W. [sic] Chinnery, the government anthropologist, had refused to let him work on the Sepik and had insisted that he go to the Baining' (Mead 1972: 203).
7. From a request, by Speiser, for a research permit to carry out work in the Territory. Series A528/1, No. K806/1/3, National Archives of Australia, Canberra.
8. When Speiser visited Buka, after leaving New Britain, he met Beatrice Blackwood on fieldwork on the island (1929–30).

9. Letter to Fritz Sarasin, 23.1.30 [Gasmata] third day of expedition. The patrol officer stationed with Calcutt is not named in the letter. Archives, Museum der Kulturen, Basel.

10. Field notes, 16 December 1929. Speiser Papers, Archives, Museum der Kulturen, Basel.

11. *Rabaul Times*, 23 September 1932.

12. Letter from Acting Administrator in Rabaul to the Prime Minister's Department in Canberra, 13 December 1932. National Archives of Australia: Series A518/1 No. Z808/1

13. Letter between two State Departments, 8 August 1933. National Archives of Australia: Series A518/1 No. Z808/1

14. In this chapter we will follow the more usual spelling 'Aliwa' for the luluai. Speiser's spelling Aliiwa, for the big man and luluai may have been for his own benefit making it easier to differentiate between the man and Aliwa for Bond's plantation. In all other sources the spelling remains consistent as Aliwa so we have chosen to use it here. Quite why a man, a plantation and also a village near Kandrian were all called Aliwa, and whether Bond named his plantation after the man or village, is unclear.

15. Speiser uses the terms 'big man' and 'luluai' interchangeably. While it is true that luluais were frequently big men, not all big men would have been luluais. This distinction is not made clear in Speiser's notes.

16. Letter to A.C. Haddon from Speiser, 27 May 1930. Haddon Archives, folder 2044, Cambridge University Library.

17. Field notes, February to April 1930. Speiser Papers, Archives, Museum der Kulturen, Basel

18. Speiser's notes for 26 February 1930. Speiser Papers, Archives, Museum der Kulturen, Basel.

19. Speiser's observations on Aliwa are to be found in his notes made while interviewing him and others in the field. Speiser Papers, Archives, Museum der Kulturen, Basel.

20. Drawn from the typed manuscript of Müller's diary for February 1909. Archives, Hamburg Museum für Völkerkunde.

21. Patrol Report of Ian McCallum Mack. Microfilm of patrol reports (PMB 1036) held in Pacific Manuscripts Bureau, Australian National University. Original held in National Library of Australia.

22. Field notes, Arue 5.IV.30. Speiser Papers, Archives, Museum der Kulturen, Basel.

23. Field notes, Arue Aliwa 17.III.30. Speiser Papers, Archives, Museum der Kulturen, Basel.

24. Taken from the introduction to a manuscript produced by Speiser on his 1929–30 fieldwork c. 1940. Speiser Papers, Archives, Museum der Kulturen, Basel.

25. Letter to A.C. Haddon from Speiser, 27 May 1930. Haddon Archives, folder 2044, Cambridge University Library.
26. Letter to F. Sarasin, 24.2.30 Arung, Möwehafen. Archives, Museum der Kulturen, Basel.
27. This information is taken from a noted tucked inside the jar which holds the powder. Item Vb 9187, Museum der Kulturen, Basel.
28. Letters between Speiser and a number of museum officials, 1930–2. Archives, Museum Kulturen, Basel.
29. Museum memorandum, 25 September 1931. Archives, Museum der Kulturen, Basel.
30. Letter to Fritz Sarasin 30 April 1930. Archives, Museum der Kulturen, Basel.
31. Letter to Fritz Sarasin, 30 April 1930. Archives, Museum der Kulturen, Basel.
32. Letter from Blackwood to Balfour, 7 July 1930. Blackwood Papers, Pitt Rivers Museum (PRM) Archives.
33. Taken from the introduction to a manuscript produced by Speiser on his 1929–30 fieldwork c. 1940. Speiser Papers, Archives, Museum der Kulturen, Basel.
34. Letter from Speiser to Blackwood, 11 October 1942. Blackwood Papers, PRM Archives.
35. Letter from Speiser to Blackwood, 11 October 1942. Blackwood Papers, PRM Archives.

−6−

John Alexander Todd

Todd is essentially a shadowy figure. He spent long periods of fieldwork in New Guinea, but unfortunately his notes, diaries and most of his photographs are lost. We feel, however, that he had a particular relationship to colonial culture which we can gain glimpses of through what he collected in New Guinea, but also what he took there. His collection shows that he had excellent local relations, linking into the activities of women who formed the basis of communities at a time when many men were leaving the villages to find work. His second visit to New Britain may have been an attempt to enter white colonial culture so as to gain employment there in a time of depression in Australia, and he seems to have set up house in the manner of a plantation owner, throwing light on this aspect of colonial culture (see Gosden 2000 for a fuller account of Todd's relationship to colonial culture). The fact that Todd's collection exhibits so much women's material confounds any straightforward notions of the influence of gender on collection practice, as Blackwood, our only female collector, had relatively little female material culture. Todd was on the south coast at the time of the coming of the missions, and his extant letters contain indications on the impact of missionaries on local life. It is ironic that his collection, which was a relatively minor element of his fieldwork, should be its major surviving result, and Todd's career was very much shaped by the early history of Australian anthropology and its funding difficulties.

John Alexander Todd was born on 19 February 1911. His birthplace is unknown but was either in New South Wales or New Zealand, as his family seem to have been New Zealanders, but were probably resident in Sydney at this time. Between 1923 and 1927 Todd attended North Sydney Boy's School, and in 1927 (at the age of sixteen) he went on to the University of Sydney where he earned a BSc degree in science specializing in the chemical and biological sciences, his scientific interests falling somewhere in between those of Lewis and Speiser. Following his BSc Todd took Anthropology I and II as a post-graduate diploma, presumably in 1930 and 1931 under Ian Hogbin and Raymond Firth, with some success as he was awarded the Frank Albert Prize in Anthropology for Anthropology II.[1] For the year 1932 Todd worked for eleven months as a research assistant on Australian National Research Council (ANRC) funding, under the supervision of Firth, who was acting-chairman of the department of anthropology. During the year's work Todd wrote two reports: 'Criteria for the classification of cultures' and 'Affinal relationships in Melanesia'. He might not have completed either as he resigned before completing the twelve-month post to go into the field, at the age of twenty-two, to the south coast of New Britain (1933–4). On this trip Todd made a collection and took over 1,000 photographs, all of which were given to the university department on his return.[2] This fieldwork was written up in five preliminary publications (1934a, 1934b, 1935a, 1935b, 1935c), and although Todd returned again to the south coast for a further year in 1935–6, no record of this time remains except the receipts lodged with the ANRC accounts (Gosden 2000).

Todd is unique amongst our collectors for having been a student, and his institutional affiliation was with Sydney University and not a museum. Having come to university straight from school, and to anthropology at the age of nineteen, he was the youngest by far of all our collectors (Lewis, Speiser and Blackwood were all in their forties at the time of their research in the region) and the least experienced. Todd was required to collect for his home institution, and was given a budget of £30, but it was not the part of his fieldwork on which he would be most closely judged, and material culture was certainly not what took him to the field. On his return to Sydney, Todd left anthropology and chose to study law, which he felt would provide him with a more stable future. He left behind his collection, and the subsequent history of the objects unfolded independently of him.

Todd at Sydney University

Todd began his anthropological career, carried out fieldwork and left the discipline to study law all within a decade (1927–37). Todd studied in the new department of anthropology which was founded at Sydney University in 1927 with Radcliffe-Brown as Chair. The establishment of the department was in part a response to strong recommendations made by the Pacific Science Congress in 1923 (Elkin 1943: 4–7), but was also due to considerable lobbying on the part of colonial administrators and academics. The motivation for setting up the department of anthropology, as argued for vociferously in the Anthropology and Ethnology section of the Congress, was:

> The preservation, progress, and welfare of the native population of Oceania, which is a charge under the terms of the mandates granted to the Commonwealth of Australia, can best be carried out by a policy based on the investigation of native conditions, customs, laws, religion, and the like which is a study not merely of academic interest and importance, but points the way to a sympathetic method of dealing with and governing such peoples . . . this knowledge can best be gained only by intensive investigations by trained students. (quoted in Elkin 1943: 5)

The recommendations were supported by the ANRC, and by 1926 the money was in place to support a Chair and department of anthropology at Sydney University. At the same time the Rockefeller Foundation agreed to support fieldwork and provided grant aid (and it was this money which would benefit Todd). The amount of the grant and the lack of definition of how the money was to be used made the Sydney Chair an attractive proposition, and Radcliffe-Brown, having already set up a department in Cape Town, was appointed. Others influencing the creation of a Chair included Sir Hubert Murray, Lieutenant-Governor of Papua, who had seen anthropology and the administration of colonial territories as important interlinked disciplines. For him applied anthropology meant the training of missionaries and colonial officers. Unfortunately, although the Rockefeller funding lasted through a large part of the Depression, it diminished considerably after 1935, affecting Todd's ability to continue in anthropology.

From 1926 on Radcliffe-Brown attracted students of anthropology to his department from all over the globe, either for study or for a stopover and advice before going to the field. These included Camilla Wedgwood and Raymond Firth (who became members of the department), Speiser (who thought Radcliffe-Brown arrogant), Margaret Mead, Hortense Powdermaker, Gregory Bateson and Reo Fortune. Todd, while a diploma student and later an employed researcher in the department, would have also drawn on the wealth of experience and contacts available to him through the department. Along with the academic goals, a key aim of the department was to educate colonial officers in the field in anthropology so they could better understand the locals in the environments in which they worked. These visits meant that a young student like Todd would have met up-and-coming anthropologists such as those listed above, who could impart advice from their own fieldwork, but also colonial officers like Chinnery who could advise on choice of field site and the opportunities in the Territory. It is likely that the idea of New Britain as a field area came from the published works of Chinnery (1925, 1926) on that region, but it is equally possible that he could have had further correspondence and advice through Chinnery himself when he visited the department (Gosden 2000).

By the time Todd completed his second year of fieldwork (1935–6) and returned to Sydney in 1936, the department had changed fundamentally. Radcliffe-Brown had moved on, and in his wake A.P. Elkin was appointed Professor, and Wedgwood, Hogbin and Firth, had moved into arenas more fitting to their theoretical perspectives. In addition Rockefeller funding had been withdrawn and grants became much harder to come by, resulting in Todd leaving the discipline by 1937, and abandoning any real hope of writing up his work.

Todd's New Britain

Unlike any of the other collectors discussed in this book, Todd took an active interest in the colonial rule of the Territory, probably because he had had most contact with colonial officers and those representing the colonial government during his time at Sydney. One of the four published articles about his fieldwork deals solely with the subject of 'Native offences and European law in south-west New Britain' (Todd 1935b). This paper gives us a unique insight into one of our collector's perspectives on a local aspect of colonial rule, and in this section, rather than looking at the wider issues of colonial New Guinea and the region of Melanesia, we will use Todd's work to look closely at his interpretation of the local effect of colonial rule.

Todd's paper considers both the interests of the locals and the government. The paper tends to concentrate on categories of crime and how they are viewed and resolved by the local and administrative community, comparing differing approaches and suggesting ways in which a more mutual understanding could be reached. However, more importantly from our perspective, in the footnotes Todd gives snapshots of the administrative personnel in the region.

At the time of Todd's stay the administrative district was the sub-district of Gasmata, and the Government Station was based at the village of that name at the eastern end of the district. According to Todd (ibid.: 437) the local population was estimated at approximately 15,000, although only the narrow strip of coastline within the district was completely under government control, with locals inland only partly under government influence, and those yet further inland being largely uncontacted. The white population was based at the government post and among seven plantations and three or four mission stations, and spread along the 250–300 miles of coastline that constituted the district. The actual organization and effect of the government officials is explained by Todd:

> The Assistant District Officer at Gasmatta normally had under him a Patrol Officer and a Cadet Patrol Officer . . . For portion of 1933 there was an Acting Assistant District Officer only in the sub-district . . . During the twelve months April 1933 to March 1934 government officials paid five visits to Möwehafen [where Todd was based] but only two of these were regular patrols involving the yearly collection of head tax, adjustment of the village census and medical treatment as well as judicial work. A third patrol was stationed for some time at the police post in Möwehafen whilst en route to the bush peoples inland. On the other two occasions the official merely passed through on a schooner. The nature of the wet season makes patrol work impossible in the months May to September. It will be seen then that the amount of contact of the natives with the officials is not very great . . . The influence of the Government is, however, augmented by the continual coming and going of natives travelling up and down the coast, some returning from periods of indenture as labourers for the European, others engaged in

trading and visiting . . . most of the younger men have served a period as indentured labourers for the European both British and Germans. (Todd 1935b: 438)

Todd paints a picture of a region where there is a lot of travel along the coastline, regular contact, but little stability in the type of contact. For a time, when Todd was in the region, the headquarters were under-staffed, and successive copies of the *New Guinea Gazette* which lists the officers working in each area, show that this was not uncommon.[3]

In addition to giving an overview of the white control in the region, Todd also outlines the locals' involvement in it in their capacities as police boys, luluais and tultuls. The police boys work under European officers and are given firearms. Where there are permanent base camps police officers often manned them alone for the majority of the time and were visited only occasionally by their white superiors. According to Todd, in the past the police worked in their own villages, which gave young men an enormous amount of power at odds with traditional social structure, so that due to this, by the mid-1930s they were generally posted outside of their area to cut down on any abuses of power. Luluais and tultuls, however, were drawn from their communities and based within them, but 'natural' leaders, such as big men were generally chosen for this role. However, this could lead to similar abuses of power. Todd describes two different examples, one a seeming success for the government and the other not: 'the headman of the village of Aviklo at Möwehafen was a man of exceptional personality and energy and he acted as a kind of liaison officer for the district officials over a wide area. Outside his own village however he always emphasised that he derived his authority from the government' (Todd 1935b: 441), the implication being that this man held his role with the government in a separate capacity to his headman status, and did not abuse the power it gave him.

In contrast, when discussing the introduction of 'paramount luluais' (who ranked above several ordinary luluais) in some parts of the Territory, he notes: '. . . there was a paramount luluai at Arawe in the west. He was not a great success' (ibid: 441). This may be a reference to Aliwa, whose obvious ability to manipulate his position between the government and the local situation might have resulted in an uneasy feeling about his loyalties.

Todd's Collection

Todd was based at Kandrian (the new name given to Möwehafen) during his first year of fieldwork (20 March 1933 – 1 April 1934). Arriving at the start of the rainy season his first six months were characterized by inhospitable weather and consecutive days when it was impossible for anyone to leave their houses (Todd 1934a: 83). He spent the first week on Aliwa plantation, and he was able to move to settle in the village of Aviklo on Geglep Island (now called Aviklo Island), where he lived in a house built especially for the purpose. Apart from a week at the end of 1933 spent in Gasmata, he remained for a full twelve months. Todd returned to the region in 1935 and stayed for a further year (19 July 1935 – 24 June 1936) at Melenglo and Kandrian. Although he planned to go to the Arawe Islands he never did, probably hampered by illness (he was hospitalized in Rabaul, 4–8 February 1936). Todd's collection and publications relate to his first field trip, which we will concentrate on here.

We do not know how much Todd spent on individual items, but in his project budget drawn up for the ANRC he includes '£30 for specimens', which at a time when the most valuable object would have cost about 10 shillings would not have restricted his choice too much. The major structuring influences on his collection would have been his own intellectual interests, any instructions on what to collect from his Sydney department, and his relations with local people. Collecting appears to have been a relatively minor aspect of his work as a whole, and he obviously saw himself as a social anthropologist for whom objects were a minor consideration. His later publications (Todd 1934a, 1934b, 1935a, 1935b, 1935c) concentrated on kinship, social structure, land tenure, ritual and law.

Todd's collection follows some of the patterns of our other collections in that it includes the distinctive 'Arawe' items such as shields, blowpipes and barkcloth, but in addition it has several examples of coiled cane baskets, 'Tami' bowls, drums, nets (including items used in their production), cassowary-quill belts, vine-string bags, panpipes and skirts. In addition he has one clay cooking pot (only Lewis among the other collectors also managed to collect these) and is unique in managing to acquire examples of dogs'-teeth ornaments (four belts and one forehead ornament).

Despite his confessed lack of interest in, or knowledge of, material culture[4] Todd produced a sixteen-page document as a catalogue of his collection.[5] This catalogue seems to indicate that he was thorough, listing 'Name', 'Description', 'General information' on context or use and 'Local Name'. Not all the information was available for every object, and our general feeling is that the catalogue might have been composed from memory on his return to Sydney when he handed over the collection, as some information is given with the caveat 'were probably used . . .' or 'apparently'. For someone in the region for so long, this reinforces the idea that he was not focused on these issues in the same way that he might have been on social issues. This may also be something to do with age and experience; perhaps Todd relied on his memory more often than he should, something that seasoned fieldworkers like Speiser and Blackwood had learned not to do from bitter experience.

Todd had a good sense of how valuables were used and how they ranked above each other, giving an idea of the relative value of items. Todd would have witnessed many transactions of valuables and been able to assess for himself the spheres in which valuables were deployed in relation to the occasion and each other. Lewis, who collected several examples of the 'Tami' bowls, did not attempt to give them a value, whereas Todd notes for example E.85002: 'These bowls are extremely valuable and become family heirlooms to some extent, this one is said to have cost Five pounds in cash in Siassi.'[6] For the dogs'-teeth strings he notes: 'These come via Siassi from the mainland of New Guinea . . . They play an important part in ceremonial exchanges and are often handed on as family heirlooms. Only wealthy men of the community own more than small amounts.'[7] Of cassowary-quill belts he writes: 'These strings are regarded as "valuables" and are inherited, they may be occasionally restrung, added to or portions sold. They are much commoner and less prized than the dogs teeth.'[8] Finally, on the *mokmok* stones he writes:

> Even small ones . . . are very valuable and seldom seen. Only the wealthiest and most important men are said to own mukmok though lesser individuals may own a small one. They are heirlooms par excellence and in addition unlike other valuable articles such as gold lip shell, black 'tambu' strings, boars tusks, large food bowls etc they are not used for trade or exchanges. Only very important and pressing circumstances will cause a man to sell a mukmok which has probably been in the possession of his family for generations[9].

Todd's collection is structured partly by its absences: he showed no interest in stone tools (one item collected). Many at the time were working within a salvage paradigm, which stressed that local cultures were being erased by colonial influences, and the change from stone to steel was seen as one of the best instances of this process. Nor did he take any notice of the production of materials (what we have down as craft production). On the other hand he did show a marked interest in the everyday: utensils for food preparation and eating, and containers are very well represented. His major interests seem to have been in the areas of ornaments, clothing and valuables.

For us, looking at the region from an historical point of view, one of the strengths of the small published corpus of Todd's work is its description of ceremonial activity, which can be linked to artefacts which were just about to go out of use with the coming of the missions. Todd was obviously interested in ceremony and the structures of belief that lay behind it, and his second piece of fieldwork seems to have been partly aimed at looking at the ritual complex to the east in Melenglo, which he considered to be the border of this complex.

It may also reflect the structure of Todd's local relations, which might have been very local. Although on both field trips he aimed to travel, illness and the difficulty of moving around appear to have prevented him from doing so. For his first visit we have no evidence that he left Aviklo and the immediate area, except for his Christmas holiday to Gasmata. The structure of the local community and Todd's own sedentary habit could have been the major structuring principles behind his collecting. Given the number of men away at work on plantations, these communities were probably held together by women. The gender bias in the collection may indicate that he had good relations with local women and either took a real interest in their lives or took the path of least resistance and collected the items which were easiest for him. Todd seems to have taken some care in collecting, as many of the women's skirts and clothing he collected were new and therefore probably made especially for him. This again contrasts with all our other collections where most of the personal items collected had been worn and used.

Tracking Todd: His Legacy

Todd's immediate legacy was his four publications; while the first two were only intended to be preliminary field reports, the overview they give of Todd's work is tantalizing as regards what might have been if Todd had managed to write his work up fully. Todd's work is only partly published, and on leaving anthropology he took his notes and diaries with him, and these are currently lost from the anthropological record.

When Todd returned from the field he gave 245 objects with a typed list to Sydney University's anthropology department. Todd lost control and sight of his collection, and as the foci of anthropology changed so did the relevance of these collections to those teaching and learning anthropology. In 1957 all of the Sydney University collections were transferred to the Institute of Anatomy, Canberra for the National Ethnographic Collection, where they remained until the transfer of all the non-Australian material to the Australian Museum, Sydney in 1985.[10] Over this period sixty objects went missing, and today only 186 objects, approximately three-quarters of the original collection, remain.

In February 1937 Todd started studying law, and in 1939 he was admitted to the New South Wales Bar. The final academic word we have of him is in a letter to Elkin (22 November 1939) in which he says he will start writing up his notes over the long vacation and that he is fairly physically fit, but washed out after study. We know from records of the legal profession that he was a barrister between 1940 and 1951. A record of a conversation with a former colleague[11] suggests that some of his photographs were used during the war by the war office in planning manoeuvres along this coastline. Todd gave up practising law soon after 1956, when he was about forty-five years old, possibly for reasons of ill health. Todd died 22 December 1971 at Lower Fort Street, Sydney, aged sixty.

Todd attempted to link into the white colonial society in New Britain, and his publications are anthropology from an administrative point of view, pursuing questions of law and order and the problems that the administration might have in controlling the local population. His lost ethnography must have contained much detail on other matters, and this influenced Blackwood who worked in the region shortly after Todd. Blackwood felt that there was little point in pursuing certain avenues in her fieldwork in New Britain because Todd had already covered them. Blackwood had quite a different view of colonial New Britain to Todd, and where he sought links with the white world Blackwood was exasperated by the number of white visitors who disrupted her work and altered her relations with local people. The contrast with the period when Lewis was in Arawe is considerable. In 1910 the white presence in Arawe was fledgling and fleeting. By the late 1930s there were regular visits by patrol officers, missionaries, traders and plantation owners, together with travellers pursuing science or pleasure, thus creating a very different form of colonial culture.

Notes

1. For the majority of the biographical information in this chapter we owe thanks to Tom Harding. Research by him to find Todd's lost papers and details of his biography in the 1980s resulted in a folder of biographical information which is lodged in the Anthropology Division of the Australian Museum, Sydney.
2. Although handing over the collection and the negatives of photographs taken in the field was a condition of the grant that Todd was given, we have only managed to track down the objects related to Todd's fieldwork. The whereabouts of his notes and photographs is currently not known.
3. *New Guinea Gazette*, 1923–40, nos. 62–592.
4. Letter from Todd to Blackwood, 16 December 1937: 'I shall not I think deal specifically with material culture for one thing I don't know enough about it.'
5. This 'Catalogue of specimens from south west New Britain. J.A. Todd' is lodged with the collection in the Anthropology Division of the Australian Museum, Sydney.
6. Entry 19 of 'Catalogue of specimens from south west New Britain. J.A. Todd', Anthropology Division, Australian Museum, Sydney.
7. Entry 60 of 'Catalogue of specimens from south west New Britain. J.A. Todd', Anthropology Division, Australian Museum, Sydney.
8. Entry 65 of 'Catalogue of specimens from south west New Britain. J.A. Todd', Anthropology Division, Australian Museum, Sydney.
9. Entry 88 of 'Catalogue of specimens from south west New Britain. J.A. Todd', Anthropology Division, Australian Museum, Sydney.

10. For a more detailed account of the history of the Sydney University collections, see the unpublished report by Leonie Oakes (1988), held in the Anthropology Division, Australian Museum, Sydney.
11. See notes compiled by Tom Harding, Anthropology Division, Australian Museum, Sydney.

−7−

Beatrice Blackwood

Blackwood's is the best-documented collection of those that we looked at. She was interested in the processes, physical and social, through which objects were made, and her notes and diaries provide a mass of detailed information on her local relationships with men like Magnin and women like Owas, two key local informants. Blackwood's material, as we have seen in earlier chapters, provides rounded views of material culture in production and use and the local sets of exchange relations through which objects moved. Because she named many of the local people from whom she obtained objects, and indicates the items of trade she used, we can gain a detailed view of local people's relationship with one particular white woman, which helps us understand colonial relations more broadly. As the latest of our collectors, Blackwood also helps us understand how much had changed in all elements of colonial culture since Lewis's visit early in the century. Blackwood's collection is both a detailed snap-shot of one time, and can be compared with the earlier workers to get a sense of change to the nature of communities in the Arawe region, but also of the stability in the forms of material culture.

Blackwood was born on 3 May 1889 in London. In 1908 she won a scholarship to Somerville College, Oxford where she was awarded a degree in English in 1912. However, it was not until 1916 that she again attended Oxford University, to undertake study for the Diploma in Anthropology. It took her two years to complete as at that time she was already employed by Arthur Thomson[1] at the University Museum as his research assistant. In 1924, as a Laura Spelman Rockefeller scholar she embarked on a three-year anthropological investigation into the relation between intelligence and physical type in North America. On her return to Oxford she became University Demonstrator in Ethnology, a post that was transferred to the Pitt Rivers Museum in 1935.

She began fieldwork in the Pacific in 1929 when she visited Buka and Bougainville, funded by the American National Research Council. The resulting publication, *Both Sides of Buka Passage* (1935), integrated social anthropology, material culture and technology, reflecting her ability to combine methodological approaches. In 1936, under the aegis of the Pitt Rivers Museum, she was sent to investigate the production and use of stone tools amongst the Anga of the Upper Watut, from where after nine months she travelled to the southwest coast of New Britain to analyse the process of head deformation on new-born babies.

Blackwood, Oxford and the Pitt Rivers Museum

The formalization of British anthropology into an academic discipline was entwined with the foundation of the Pitt Rivers Museum in 1884. The gift by Lieutenant-General Pitt Rivers of his collection of artefacts to the University of Oxford to found the Pitt Rivers Museum and the stipulation that came with it – the funding of a lectureship – gave the discipline an institutional foothold and paved the way for teaching of diplomas in anthropology (Oxford 1906, Cambridge 1908).

The creation of the teaching post at Oxford, taken up by Edward Burnett Tylor, was a direct result of Pitt Rivers' search for a home for his ethnographic and archaeological collection. This collection had previously been on display in London's Bethnal Green branch of the South Kensington Museum (the forerunner of the Victoria and Albert Museum), and was displayed typologically in evolutionary series which demonstrated the development of mankind and the material arts. As Pitt Rivers added to the collections and they outgrew the space allocated to them, relationships with South Kensington Museum broke down and Pitt Rivers searched for a permanent home where his collection could be used to educate the masses and as a research tool for scholars (Petch 1998: 82–3). After prolonged negotiations the collection was gifted to Oxford University in 1884. The deed of the gift laid down that a new museum be built to house the collections as an annexe to the University Museum (of Natural History) and which emphasized his evolutionary theory, then seen as a logical extension of Darwinism. In addition to housing and displaying the collection in accordance with Pitt Rivers' typological series, he required that someone should be available to lecture on the subject, and a post was instituted, although H.N. Moseley, Professor of Comparative Anatomy, was put in charge of the collections. Two of Moseley's students, W. Baldwin Spencer and Henry Balfour were involved in the removal of the collection to the new museum. In 1887 Baldwin Spencer left Oxford to become Professor of Zoology in Melbourne, where he was to become famous for his work with Frank Gillen among the Australian Aborigines. This left Balfour to work on the construction of the displays, and in 1891 he was appointed as the Museum's first Curator (Blackwood 1970).

When Tylor took up his post as Reader in Social Anthropology at Oxford (later Professor, 1896), his period of anthropological achievement, characterized by the publication of *Primitive Culture* (1871), lay behind him, and issues in anthropology were moving on. Although he was at the height of his reputation and influence, he was no longer setting the theoretical agenda in anthropology (Stocking 1995: 3). By 1906 when the first diploma students were instructed in anthropology at Oxford, they took lessons from Balfour, now lecturing in ethnography, material arts and technology; Robert Ranulph Marett, Fellow of Exeter College and Reader in Social Anthropology; and Professor Arthur Thomson, for physical anthropology. Material culture and museums was the centre to the Oxford discipline, and Balfour made museums the focus of his Presidential Addresses to the Anthropological Institute (1904) (van Keuren cited in Herle 1998: 99).

Beatrice Blackwood was a product of the early Oxford school of anthropology. Blackwood was an Oxford anthropologist, all of her academic training and qualifications were from the university, and subsequently she was employed continuously by the University Museum and the Pitt Rivers Museum respectively from 1927 to 1958. Like Lewis and Speiser, Blackwood had a broad academic background, beginning with reading English, with a paper on the etymology of Scandinavian and German languages as an undergraduate, then the Diploma in Anthropology and a BSc in Human Anatomy. While coming relatively late in her life to the discipline, by the time she made her second research trip to Melanesia she was a seasoned fieldworker. Those that influenced her training and initial interest, Thomson, Marrett and Balfour, were linked to the early years of the Oxford department, but by the time Blackwood reached the field in 1929 these three were 'elder statesmen'. With her early background in linguistics she was well equipped to be a traditional all-round anthropologist, with every aspect of society intellectually available for her study. Despite carrying out fieldwork in a period of great ferment in the discipline after the publication of *Argonauts of the Western Pacific* (Malinowski, 1922), and when many new students were directed to London to get the most up-to-date teaching,[2] her fieldwork and publications remain firmly anchored in the Oxford school. While she did change her approach away from surveys to intensive study (the contrast between her American and Buka fieldwork) she was unable ever to truly grasp the nettle of theory and challenge the new publications which marginalized material culture, and which made her uncomfortable (Knowles 2000). By the time she returned to the field in 1936, Thomson and Marrett had died and only Henry Balfour remained, and the appointment of Radcliffe-Brown as Professor of Social Anthropology in Oxford, which spelled the end of the Pitt Rivers Museum's role as sole centre of Oxford anthropology, was only months away.

Blackwood's Melanesia: An Established Colonial Society

Blackwood arrived in New Britain during the hey-day of colonial society. There was a whole host of long-term white residents in Rabaul, including a number of women.[3] As Blackwood is the only female anthropologist looked at in this study, we will explore how her gender may have affected her experience of colonial New Guinea and working relationships with the local indigenous populations in the field.

All the anthropologists in this volume and others who visited the colony, had to engage with the colonial society. This was not only a question of etiquette but necessity; transport and supplies to the various remote parts of the territories, favoured by anthropologists, relied totally on the infrastructure created and maintained by the white residents in their various guises as traders, government officials or plantation owners. However, unlike the American Lewis or the Swiss Speiser, Blackwood (an English woman) came from a country that was intimately linked to the shaping of the colonial structure in the Territory.

This was Blackwood's second trip to the Pacific, so she had already met most of the main figures in Rabaul society, at least those who held sway in the anthropological field in 1929. Her arrival in Rabaul in July 1936 allowed her to catch up with old acquaintances and draw on their support for her future endeavours. For the residents, she was a known quantity and someone who brought first-hand news and gossip, from Oxford and England, and from Sydney. Her arrival was recorded in the *Rabaul Times*,[4] as Sarah Chinnery, wife of the government anthropologist, threw a small tea party to welcome her back. The local paper described Blackwood as the 'guest of honour', and the party was attended by several leading figures of Rabaul society, including the Governor General McNicoll and his wife, Archdeacon and Mrs de Voil, and Mr and Mrs Wauchope (who were later to help her with fieldwork near their plantation on the Ramu river).

For Sarah Chinnery, entertaining visitors, particularly visiting anthropologists, was crucial to her role in Rabaul society. Of paramount importance was maintaining E.W.P. Chinnery's place as the leading academic influence in the region. It also kept him up-to-date with developments in the discipline, keeping his own academic connections alive with an eye on the possible future development of his career. Sarah's recently published diaries (1998) record her frequent social interaction with anthropologists and plantation owners, both being crucial to Chinnery. When Blackwood arrived in Rabaul in 1936 she was not the first female anthropologist to visit the Territory; she herself had visited seven years earlier and Hortense Powdermaker (1929), Margaret Mead (1928–9, 1932–3) and Camilla Wedgwood (1933) had all passed through Sarah's home and relied on her and Chinnery for advice and entertainment. The majority of the women that were in the Territory at this time had arrived as wives of men who had employment in the region and were dependents of them. The resident women had to carve out in the society a role that would support their husbands and adhere to the social codes of the colonial society. This dependent relationship was not experienced by the independent anthropologists, and so altered their experience of life in the colony.

For the transient women visitors, be they anthropologist, artist, traveller or natural historian, the expectation of their role was far less fixed, and ultimately they had less responsibility to fit into this society. Bulbeck (1992) notes how transient visitors posed a perennial problem, as they did not always share the white residents' opinion of the indigenous populations, and did not have a vested interest in maintaining the racist ideologies which perpetuated the status quo. Those women who had preceded Blackwood as anthropologists in the field had caused comment, and their attitude to the indigenous population was paramount in their assessment by the residents. 'Going native' was seen as the most dire consequence of an anthropologist's work. Sarah recounted in her diary a conversation with Margaret Mead about Hortense Powdermaker's field attitude and, in particular, her dress. She wrote: 'I don't know why she should wear shorts and stockings rolled below her knees, and wear a boy-scout knife on a belt around her waist' (Chinnery 1998: 51–2).

Blackwood, came to the field as a mature woman (she was forty-eight during her time in the Arawe), with long-standing connections with the fathers of anthropology. However, her dress in the field was not above comment either:

> Unconventional in dress – didn't seem to care about it, was completely bound up in her anthropology, though she always denied her great knowledge – she wore what suited her work, rough useful clothes. She was laughed at, at first, by the native police but later on she was very highly respected by them – and by the natives in the villages – for her capabilities, knowledge and courage. (Ken Bridge quoted in Simpson 1954: 67)

The issue of dress was a central theme to all facets of New Guinea society, as we discussed in Chapter One, and Ken Bridge's comment on the initial attitude of the police to Blackwood's dress exemplified the fears felt by residents of the possible results of the eroding of the rigorous hierarchies between classes of white residents and indigenous populations. By wearing something that amused the locals a person immediately crossed the barrier of status and respect which was essential in keeping the structure of colonialism intact, at least in the minds of those whites resident there (see Gosden 2000).

For the residents there were strict codes of dress and behaviour, and for women practices such as wearing gloves and hats for tea, the use of calling cards for introduction, and formal dress, did not fully die out until the mid-1950s when such practices would have been absurd elsewhere. For men dress was also prescribed and, regardless of financial means, a man was expected to conform to the colonial dress code of 'whites'. Isabel Platten, the wife of a poor Methodist missionary described how her husband 'had to be decked out in what was the uniform for all males – long white trousers, long-sleeved white shirts, white socks and polished black shoes – and for any formal occasion a white coat' (Bulbeck 1992: 12). For the long-term residents in the colony there was no possibility of giving up these material signifiers of the colonizers' 'civilization'. Todd entered into this, perhaps because he saw his future in the Territory and not in the academic discipline at Sydney (Gosden 2000); Speiser and Lewis had also worn broad approximations of 'whites'. However, not all anthropologists adhered to the dress codes, particularly when out of Rabaul; it depended very much on how the anthropologist wished to position him- or herself in relation to the local community and the white community, in his or her field area.

The innate British roots of Australian colonial society and its newly 'civilized' aspect made it a popular choice for the more intrepid, rich tourist. From time to time exciting public figures passed through the district on pleasure cruises or research. One of these visitors, Lord Moyne, came two years prior to Blackwood's time in the field, on his yacht the *Rosaldo*. The first Baron of Moyne had made his fortune as the head of the Guinness family; he was part of the aristocratic set that was young and 'fast' and epitomized the swinging 1920s and 1930s. He had an interest in anthropology and exploration, and made collections during his travels which were divided between the Museum of Mankind, Cambridge Museum of Anthropology and Archaeology, and the Pitt Rivers Museum. His guests included Lady Broughton, who acted as photographer and collector of live animals for London Zoo, and Clementine Churchill, wife of Winston Churchill. The voyage resulted in the publication of an account of his travels (Guinness 1936) which used the design from an Arawe barkcloth on its front cover.

This cruise, although it visited the southwest coast of New Britain, said far more about the perception of New Guinea 'back home' than about the anthropology of the region. It makes apparent that New Guinea had become a place that it was possible to visit, to take a 'cruise' to, and that it had been 'tamed'. These travellers were not going to risk their lives in the territory. The town of Rabaul was an established colonial capital offering all the amenities, and the most visible aspects of the local population spoke pidgin, were willing workers, and were part of the integral structure of this society. The days of punitive raids that echoed the German colonial era were largely over, and New Guinea was open to the tourist.

Colonial Melanesia was centred around Rabaul and some of the major trading posts or mission stations. Where Blackwood was to work, although there were plantations, was outside of the social protocols of Rabaul. Blackwood's time in Arawe took place after she had spent a year in the territory. Her main reason for travelling to New Guinea had been to make collections in the newly opened up Highlands. In fact she was only able to get as far as the Upper Watut, near the patrol station of Otibanda, as the Highlands had already been declared 'uncontrolled' by the government. The Anga region of the Upper Watut was a frontier site, and it had taken a considerable amount of persuasion for Blackwood to be allowed to settle there. When, after nine months, she left the region to take a break, a Chinese storekeeper was killed and the area was declared uncontrolled, preventing her return.

This style of frontier fieldwork was exactly what Blackwood enjoyed. She thrived on the isolation from whites and on building relationships with the locals. In her earlier fieldwork in Buka and Bougainville she had moved her fieldsite to somewhere more remote and less accessible after three months in the field because the missions were a permanent fixture in her site and she was viewed as part of the white community to the detriment of her work. The Arawe region was to frustrate her with its permanent white residents, patrol post and regular shipping.

The visit to the southwest coast of New Britain was forced upon Blackwood by circumstance and by Henry Balfour, the curator of the Pitt Rivers Museum, who wanted head-bound skulls, decorated barkcloths and blowpipes from the region to 'complete' typological series in the museum. As she was only collecting, and did not have time for a full anthropological study, she knew she would only be in the field for a short period (she planned a maximum of three months), and therefore had to stay in the *haus kiap* built at Kandrian on the mainland. This permanent structure was built for the use of patrol officers and their staff when on patrol through the region. By situating herself here she was instantly identified with the colonial regime, a fact she was aware of, was uncomfortable with, but could see no way of avoiding.

In addition to Blackwood's presence in the region, there was a series of other new arrivals. The trickle of change had begun at the end of Todd's first year in the region, but by the time Blackwood was there the change was in full swing. Prior to Todd's fieldwork period, the white influence on the southwest coast was felt mainly through the actions of the plantation owners or managers, and the white presence there was fairly constant. In addition, there had been regular government surveys of the coast and labour recruitment and trading vessels passing along the coast. While the government representatives now came on foot, their presence was relatively infrequent and perhaps only amounted to twice-yearly patrols. At this point, however, the missions were moving in, and with them came a permanent set of white residents dispersed through the region; they made quite different demands from anyone else already encountered.

Missionaries had been monitoring the southwest coast for some time, and there had been a mission station at the Arawe Islands for some years, but it was only in the mid-1930s, after accusations of neglect,[5] that the missions leapt into action around Kandrian. In the month prior to Todd's departure, Roman Catholic teachers arrived and the missionization of the region began. By the time Blackwood had settled in, the fight for souls in this region had taken on something of the elements of farce, with the erection of wooden crosses in the 'Roman' villages and threats made to anyone supplying the 'English' with food, and villages changing allegiance between the various denominations as threats and persuasions poured forth.[6]

An Anglican minister, Reverend Longden, who arrived at Kandrian one week after Blackwood, took four weeks to find an unclaimed village at which to make his base. During this period he regularly dropped in for respite and a chat with Blackwood, keeping her up-to-date with the fight for souls, and on one occasion appealing to the patrol officer for government support against the tactics of the Catholics. Despite the obvious antagonism of the various religious groups

(Anglicans, Methodists and Roman Catholics) they were but a small white minority in a 'wild' place, and for social occasions they did get together. On these occasions the Europeans would gather on Koch's plantation, where mail arrived, and hear 'all the news of the world' whenever Koch returned from the metropolis of Rabaul.[7]

Harold Koch was the main personality in the region, as the new owner of Aliwa plantation (having taken over from Harry Bond) and the most permanent resident, although he had a manager and spent long periods away from the district, he provided an anchor and a base for all those passing through. Koch was able to supply food, trade items and advice, making a stay in the region easier. At the time Blackwood was in the region Kandrian had become a busy point on the south-coast trail. Where Todd, perhaps keener on white company, had been able to preserve some privacy in his house on Geglep Island, Blackwood became allied with, and in the middle of, the administration, both by taking up residence in a government house and by having to entertain and give hospitality to anyone passing through the region who had similar rights to use the house.

Todd and Blackwood would have presented completely different types of collector to the local population. It was only a year after he had finally departed (still cherishing the hope that he could return again) that Blackwood arrived in the area. Her planned stay was short, six weeks to three months. However, the eruption of one of the volcanoes at Rabaul caused sufficient disruption to shipping that she ended up stranded in the region, and her stay was eventually four months. Working in the shadow of Todd, who had published several articles relating to the social anthropology of the region, she concentrated on material culture and head binding (physical anthropology), following Balfour's wishes and her own desire not to 'poach' on a colleague's territory.[8] Along with this, passing 'collectors' went through the region, the most notable being Lord Moyne and his entourage, who spent one day collecting and negotiating purchases before weighing anchor and moving on.

Collecting in New Britain: Trade and Exchange

Blackwood spent nearly four months on the south coast (18 May to 3 September 1937). Unlike Lewis and Speiser she never went as far west as Arawe. Instead she left Salamaua, visited Tami and Umboi Islands before travelling straight to Kandrian, arriving on 1 June. She settled in Kandrian for sixty-four days, then moved east to Gasmata for a fortnight (between 4 and 17 August) and on to Lindenhafen for seventeen days while awaiting transport (17 August to 3 September). At both Kandrian and Gasmata she made daily trips to the villages in the area and the offshore islands. At Lindenhafen she stayed put because a ship might turn up at any time and she needed to be ready to leave at a moment's notice. In Kandrian she made two trips of several nights each inland. The first visit was to Mibolok and Alomos villages, where Blackwood hoped to source and photograph the production process of barkcloth and shields. The second visit was to Lapalam and Aliwa villages. In Gasmata she was mainly in the company of the district officers and A Rulo, a local luluai (whom Speiser had met), and spent time with him visiting villages nearby.

As she had done on all previous occasions, and as was the norm for anyone setting up home (however temporarily) in the Territory, she employed two servants from the local region, recommended by the patrol officer, to run her household. When these did not work out she accepted the offer from Magnin, a local man and relative of one of the other servants, to work for her. Magnin was to become her main informant in the field, her means to accessing the objects she wished to collect, and someone to liaise with other locals on her behalf. At the time that Blackwood arrived in the region she was a fluent pidgin speaker and experienced fieldworker. However, the locals were also experienced in handling fieldworkers and the relationships with them. Certainly after the prolonged visit by Todd, there was little doubt in the minds of the locals as to what to expect from an anthropologist, and they immediately accommodated her and her role.

Blackwood collected a similar set of items to the other collectors, but due to being in the region during the rainy season clearly found it hard to collect material evidence of things that were not in use at that time of year. For example, she did not collect any fishing nets, and shows less variety in her collection of ornaments, probably due to the lack of ceremony. She was unable to buy or even record much detail about masks. However, she did collect a group of nine objects she classed as 'Toys' which were totally absent from all the other collections. Blackwood's collection of objects was skewed in a number of ways. She clearly collected far more stone tools than anyone else (over 30 per cent of the total). Blackwood had been sent by the museum to study stone-tool usage amongst the Anga, and the incidence of so many stone tools in the Arawe collection is probably a hangover of those concerns. Faced with an abundance of abandoned stone tools in the area, and with the possibility of acquiring them quite easily, she chose not to pass up the opportunity.

There are certain omissions in Blackwood's collection as well. There are no conus-shell ornaments of the type that echo the pig's-tusk ornaments. Looking at the museum documentation we discovered that Blackwood stopped for several hours at Aliwa plantation in 1930 on her return from Buka and here she acquired one item, an ornament of this type. Therefore, when Blackwood returned to this site seven years later, she was safe in the knowledge that the museum did not need a conus-shell ornament. In fact, as Blackwood found the procurement of valuables particularly difficult, it is likely she was relieved that she could immediately, metaphorically, tick one item off her list.

Blackwood was centrally concerned with process. We will discuss this further below, but it is worth giving an overview here. Unlike all the other collectors, she went to great lengths to acquire examples of partly made or completed items and examples of the raw materials and tools needed to make items. This is particularly true for the items Balfour expressly desired her to acquire, for example, barkcloth, blowpipes and deformed skulls (see Table 7.1). However, Blackwood did not confine this thoroughness to items of Balfour's choice; she similarly collected evidence of process for the production of obsidian flakes and turtle-shell arm rings. For other categories of artefact, where the procurement of numerous comparative specimens would have been difficult, and they would have been difficult to transport, she recorded what details she could. While she only brought home two paddles she copied the designs of approximately ninety paddles, from throughout the region, into a sketchbook (Fig. 7.1).

In this section we would like to focus on transactions between local people and the anthropologists. Blackwood, while having no budget for the purchase of specimens, so having less need to justify her allocation of funds, set up a table in the back of her diary recording the date, number of items purchased, description of the item, the seller and the cost (Fig. 7.2); while on closer inspection this record

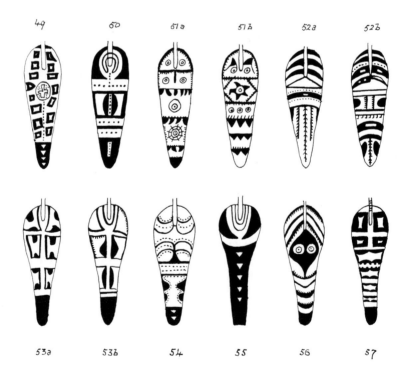

Figure 7.1. A page from Beatrice Blackwood's field sketch book reproducing a dozen canoe-paddle designs (Pitt Rivers Museum, University of Oxford)

Table 7.1. Numbers of Items Collected as They Relate to the Production of Various Objects

Type of Object	Raw Material	Tools	Stages of Production	Finished Product
Barkcloth	15	8	4	13
Paint for barkcloth	4	3		
Blowpipes	4			4
Head deformation		2		12
Obsidian flakes	4	4		15
Turtle-shell arm ornament			1	1

is of only about a third of all 275 objects purchased, it does give a very clear view of the type of trade goods desired, and the range of values attached to local objects.

Blackwood took a variety of items as trade goods to the region, which included money (both German marks and Australian shillings), sticks of tobacco and manufactured goods (razor blades, laplaps, glass, knives, whistles, harmonicas and beads). Tobacco was used in the payment of police boys by patrol officers, and along with currency it also seems to have been Blackwood's main item of

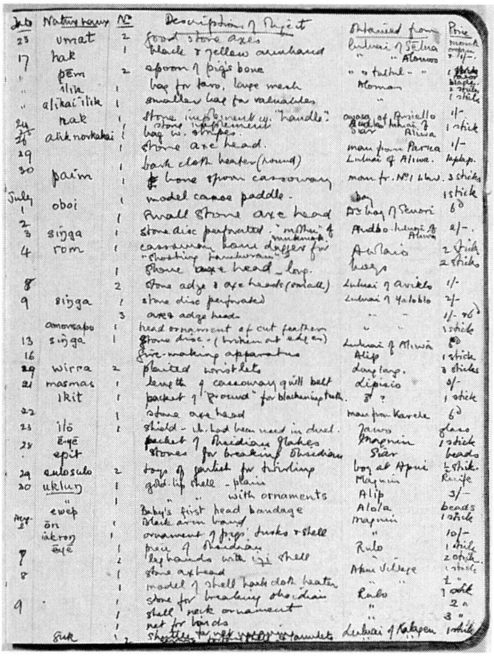

Figure 7.2. A page from the back of Blackwood's field diary where she recorded the items she collected (Pitt Rivers Museum, University of Oxford)

payment. She had brought a greater amount of marks than shillings and was worried about funds running out when only shillings were desired by the locals. This may have been because the coastal area was considered completely in the control of the government and therefore a head tax of 10s was levied on every man and there was a need for shillings (particularly if it allowed one to choose whether or not to labour for coin). In each transaction Blackwood, like all collectors, was trying to negotiate the most competitive price while also dispensing of her trade goods and money in the most profitable way possible. This process involved trial and error, when men came from inland villages with barkcloth to sell to the coastal Arawe, Blackwood initially tried to make the purchase with tobacco and marks, though shields and barkcloth were usually paid for in gold-lip shells (Fig. 7.3). When this offer was was refused, Blackwood had to reveal her other trade items, the only one of which accepted as an alternative to gold-lip shells being knives. Twenty-five years later when Jane Goodale settled with the Kaulong she took tobacco and shillings for purchases but found that some people were only willing to exchange food or services for gold-lip shells, so that she had to obtain gold-lip first in order to enter into a transaction (Goodale 1995: 25).

The Arawe are sophisticated traders maintaining extensive networks of exchange stretching to the north coast of New Guinea. All our collectors entered into these networks of exchange in their desire to collect and also for their daily needs such as food. For Blackwood, we have a specific record of her interaction with individuals. Paramount among these was Magnin. Blackwood's commercial, and to some extent social, relations in this region were set up by Magnin. Magnin seems to have acted as intermediary between other sellers and Blackwood, in general acquiring items Blackwood sought from his own relatives and thus in turn consolidating his position within his kin group and probably their place in Kandrian society. In Kandrian there was also a female informant, Owas, the wife of Alip, luluai of Alu'u, who helped Blackwood gather some information and collections, but by demonstration or sale rather than brokerage. In Gasmata her main informant, apart from the patrol officers, was A Rulo, a luluai, who had been Speiser's main informant seven years earlier, had constant contact with the patrol officers based in his area, and was obviously comfortable with the role. Magnin had also appeared in Speiser's notes seven years earlier,[9] in genealogies and village records, although none of Speiser's interviews seem to have been with him.

This continuity is not surprising. Those who spoke pidgin well and were comfortable with visiting whites were likely to be the main points of contact for all visitors. In addition, those who were well respected in a community or had power were likely to be sought out by the anthropologist. In the case of Magnin, he was not a big man, but might have had ideas of elevating his status in the group through association with visitors. While he was unable to do this with Speiser, experience, and the passage of others through the region, such as Todd and Moyne,

Figure 7.3. Woman of Kanglo Island, seated on ground and surrounded by her wealth (Pitt Rivers Museum, University of Oxford)

meant that he was familiar with what would be required of him and could assess the possible benefits for himself, his family and kin group before becoming enmeshed in any social and financial relationship.

As noted earlier, Blackwood recorded in detail approximately a third of all her transactions in the region. In this list Magnin featured frequently as a seller. However, what we cannot see, but which comes across from the diary entries, is that he was also engineering or seeking out other items for sale and was brokering deals. Magnin's influence was most significant in the case of valuable items. As discussed in previous chapters, there are a number of items that are significant social signifiers, and Blackwood found it particularly hard to get hold of examples. From Magnin she bought, several perforated stone discs, one *mokmok*, which cost 10 shillings, and two *singa* which cost 2s 6d each (which are very small sums, especially when compared with other valuables). One possible explanation for people's willingness to sell *mokmok* and *singa* in 1937 was the initial impact of the mission. Early missionary activity might have meant a change in attitude towards objects sometimes used in sorcery, although it is clear that if this change of attitude took place, it did not last. These stones were the ultimate heirloom in that they appear to be prehistoric and might well have been dug up from prehistoric sites, or eroded out of the same and into river beds from where they were recovered. It is clear that the mysterious origins of these objects was an important part of their power. Goodale (1995: 51) notes in regard to her fieldwork in the 1960s and 1970s that 'Stone valuables . . . are considered an ultimate measure of one's social power, but they are rarely displayed or used in any transaction today,' whereas in the past they were used specifically in 'the exchange of pork and the granting of permanent sexual rights in women' (ibid.: 89).

Next in value, from a community perspective, were the curved pig's-tusk ornaments, and Blackwood's only example was purchased from Magnin. The pig's tusks were bound to a stick of wood, edged with nassa shells and held in the mouth using a mouth-piece attached to the back of the piece of wood. As discussed in Chapter Five, the most socially charged element of production of these is the growing of a pig with curved tusks suitable to make *iakron*. Blackwood described the object itself, its production and significance:

> Men are frequently seen wearing an ornament consisting of two boar's tusks, curved into a circle, joined by a band of plaited fibre edged with *iyi* [nassa] shell, which extends above and below the tusks in two long points. This ornament is *iakron* and is worn at the back, suspended from several strings of *iyi* shells. For dances it is turned round and held between the teeth. (Blackwood n.d.: 'Currency and valuables')

Blackwood's *iakron* also gives us a key insight into her relationship with Magnin. She obviously had considerable difficulty acquiring an *iakron*, which she desired as a key valuable item. Her diary for Monday 2 August records 'Magnin brought a pig tusk ornament which he let me buy for 10/- – a small one and not a full circle – but am lucky to get one. It has two of his father's teeth attached to it.'[10] Six weeks later she wrote to Balfour

> The pig's tusk ornament (iakron) is a small one, but quite typical. The best, perfect circles or more than circles, are valued at £1 per tusk and 10/- for the centre work, which I thought excessive. Even at this price the natives are generally unwilling to part with them, it was a special favour from a particularly friendly native that enabled me to get even this small and not very valuable specimen.[11]

Blackwood was obviously slightly disappointed that she could not obtain a more magnificent specimen, or at least this is how she expressed her thoughts to Balfour. If this was her feeling, she might have under-played the personal nature of the act of giving by Magnin. Not only was he willing to part with something most others in the region would not, but Magnin also sold an object with some personal link to himself, in that it had his father's teeth hanging from it. Blackwood had earlier been unable to purchase a cassowary-quill bead belt (*masmasi*) because it was decorated with several of the owner's father's teeth.[12] This reinforces the point about the special nature of Magnin's transaction of an *iakron* decorated with his father's teeth. In selling this particular object to Blackwood, Magnin might have hoped to cement the personal tie that had grown up between them in the field and to make it more likely that they stayed in contact once Blackwood had gone home. In exchanges with whites, a mixture of motives may have pertained: some objects were rarely sold, due to their personal and ritual significance, and the inducement to sell them might not have been primarily monetary, but rather the nature of the relationship that existed or was desired. Even the most sensitive European (and there seems little doubt that Blackwood was very sensitive, by the standards of the time) might have misread or been totally unaware of the motives underlying acts of giving or receiving. Colonial relations linked Melanesians and Europeans, but not always in the manner each party desired.

Blackwood also managed to collect two gold-lip shells, one from Magnin in exchange for a knife. Again, these items were not easy to come by, or at least one had to take what examples were offered. The second gold-lip shell came from Alip, luluai of Alu'u. Blackwood wrote in her diary for Friday 3 July: 'Went to mainland to collect gold-lip shell promised by Alip – he had not fixed up the one I chose but sold me another for 3/-.'[13]

In 1937 there was a whole range of objects Blackwood found it difficult to collect; most of these were objects of heirloom status.[14] The small number of socially marked items she did buy are of special significance to our understanding of her social relations and to the standing of white people in general. Blackwood had a close relationship with Magnin, who was more inclined to include Blackwood in the full range of his transactions than were other people. There was probably a series of whites along the south coast of New Britain who had special relationships with some local people, including long-term residents such as plantation managers and missionaries, and frequent visitors such as traders, recruiters and government officials.

Notes on Arawe Material Culture

After returning from New Britain Blackwood wrote a manuscript on her work in New Britain, which she planned to publish as an Occasional Paper initially with the working title of 'Notes on Arawe material culture'. This was proposed to be changed to 'Patterns and techniques of the Melanesians of south west New Britain' for the published version. The paper was mentioned in the Annual Report of the Pitt Rivers Museum in 1956 but was never actually produced. The manuscript was to be based on a compilation of material from Blackwood's fieldwork. For our purposes, the unpublished manuscript provides an excellent snapshot of the material culture and social relations in the Möwehafen and inland areas in 1937, which can be compared with the situation both earlier and later, a comparison which we will make in the next chapter. We have taken the manuscript as the basis for our discussion, but we have also used diary entries and information from the catalogue to provide a rounded picture both of the artefacts in use at the time, and also of Blackwood's own collection practices.[15]

A key aspect of Blackwood's account is her stress on the processes of production, which fit in very well with the idea of *chaîne opératoire* which we discussed in Chapter One, although there is no evidence that she was intellectually influenced by Mauss or the French interests in production more generally. In what follows we will concentrate on the key items of male and then female dress, looking at the chains of processes lying behind their production, where these can be discerned from Blackwood's account. Concentrating on dress will give us a good insight into the mass of social relations surrounding key sets of objects, their production, trade and use.

Blackwood paid particular attention to the production of barkcloth, partly because of its dual importance as an element of male dress and for head binding, but maybe also due to accidents of fieldwork which provided her with a mass of information on this object. We will base our account on quotes from Blackwood from material that she hoped to publish on her fieldwork, but never did. The overall sequence of events necessary for the production of barkcloth is shown in Table 7.2.

Barkcloth is made by the natives of villages a short distance inland from Moewehafen, and also, I was told, by those still further inland. The coastal people do not make it, but buy it from bush natives. That made at the villages of Mibolok and Alamos is regarded as particularly good, and it was in those two villages I saw it manufactured. (Blackwood n.d.: 'Bark cloth')

A number of different tree species could be used and a strip of bark is cut from a branch. The bark is cut round with a knife and prised off using a pointed stick, which is less likely to damage the bark. The inner layer of bark is pulled off using both hands, with another person holding the strip. Blackwood collected eight small specimens of bark from a variety of trees used for making barkcloth.

The inner bark is beaten out using a stone beater known as *hringe* on the coast and *ninnin* in the inland – Blackwood collected six of these (with Lewis and Speiser collecting one each) and three shell beaters from the Lindenhafen area. The stone beaters were, Blackwood notes, oval or round, incised with criss-crossed lines and obtained from the beds of rivers (Blackwood n.d.: 'Bark cloth'). She noted in her diary: '14th June: *hringe*: 1; Bark cloth beater: Magnin: small knife,'[16] and in her field notes she adds, 'These stones are sometimes bought by the coast natives for cracking nuts, as they have no hard stone available' (ibid.). 'The cloth is beaten on a wooden block (*lapilamulu*) about a foot in diameter at the top, but cut down to a pointed stick at the lower end, and of such a length as to bring the top on a level with the operator's lap as he sits on a bench in the men's clubhouse, where the cloth is usually made' (ibid.). When the strip has been beaten out (Fig. 1.2), it is folded and beaten again, wrung out to rid it of sap and hung up to dry. When dry it is painted with red and black designs, starting with black outlines and then the red infilling. Amongst her set of samples showing the processes of production Blackwood collected one partially beaten barkcloth and one that was fully beaten but unpainted.

> The black paint (*kawene*) is prepared as follows: – the resinous exudation of the canarium almond [a common food nut] is burnt on a slow fire over which has been placed a large flat stone (*hangar*). The smoke produces soot which collects on the under side of the stone. It is scraped off with a piece of the inner bark of the *la* tree, which is folded over and chewed in the operator's mouth. The resulting black saliva is spat on to a leaf which is laid in half a coconut shell. A piece of the outer bark of the *la* tree is cut to an oblique point and dipped into this mixture and used as a pen. (ibid.)

Blackwood again collected a specimen of canarium resin and the inner bark of the *la* tree as reference samples. This paint was also used on canoe paddles and other objects. Painting was done at some speed, to traditional designs, which were rendered from memory and never copied. Many people painted, 'but some men's lines were less fine and neat than others. Sometimes a man will hand over to someone else to continue, or several people will work at different places on the same strip' (ibid.). There is no concept of individual production or artistry at work here.

> Red paint is prepared as follows:– A small piece of bark of the *epe* tree is laid on the leaves of a fern *tingi*. Lime is sprinkled over both and they are chewed with betel pepper leaves, spat into a piece of bark cloth and the 'juice' squeezed into a receptacle made of leaves. It must be used at once as it dries quickly. The brush is a peeled stem of the *mimos* plant. The red is used only to fill in certain spaces between the black lines. It is often done rather carelessly, over-running the edges. (Blackwood n.d. 'Barkcloth')

Once again, Blackwood collected specimens of all the components of the red paint, plus the brush used to apply the paint.

To complete her set of samples Blackwood collected fifteen finished barkcloths (compared with thirteen each by Lewis and Todd and three by Speiser). These had a variety of designs, some of which had some story attached to them. Specimen 1938.36.1214 had a design called *megiok*, 'said to illustrate a story of a brother and sister who went to a dance. The women tore the man's loin cloth in half along the line down in the middle [sic]. The right hand part (holding the cloth at the

Figure 7.4. Sections from three pieces of barkcloth (plain, black, decorated) showing the stages of decoration, from blank canvas to completed design (Pitt Rivers Museum, University of Oxford)

broad end) was taken by the man and the left hand part by his sister.[17] Other designs refer to pigs' teeth, the interstices of a fishing net, creepers or snakes and so on, but it must also be stressed that the exact meanings of the designs were less important than the manner in which they reflected a man's persona, as there were links between the designs on a man's barkcloth and the back of his shield (see below). The sizes of barkcloth varied considerably, and Blackwood noted a variation of between eight and two yards in length. However, their uses were few:

Table 7.2. Stages in the Production of Barkcloth

Process	Tools	Number of people
Remove bark from tree and remove inner bark	Knife and pointed stick	2
Beat bark, fold and beat again. Repeat 2 or 3 times	Wooden block and beater (stone or shell)	1
Dry	Rack	
Prepare black paint – *canarium* resin and soot chewed and spat out	Fire, stone, *la* tree bark	1
Apply black paint	*La* tree bark	1 or more
Prepare red paint – *epe* bark and *tingi* fern chewed with lime and betel pepper and spat out.	None	1
Apply red paint	Stem of *mimos* plant	1 or more

Both bush and coastal natives use the cloth for two purposes only: in small strips to bind the heads of their babies, in order to produce the characteristic elongated deformation, and as loin cloths for the men. Two or more pieces are worn. The under one passes between the legs and tightly over the genitals, enclosing them as in a bag. It is then wound round the waist several times. One end is often left hanging down between the legs behind, like a tail . . . The covering extends up to and sometimes beyond the umbilicus. The folds are used to carry small personal possessions such as areca nuts (Blackwood n.d. 'Barkcloth')

Elsewhere in her manuscript she noted 'The folds of this sometimes very voluminous loin cloth are used to carry small personal possessions, such as areca nut and packages (or, now-a-days, cigarette tins) containing lime. (Quite large and heavy stone implements were produced from these folds in which they had been carried in from the bush)' (ibid.: 'Dress and ornaments').

There was a regular trade in barkcloth between the inland where the barkcloth was made and the coast, where it was not made. Even inland villages that made their own cloth sometimes obtained barkcloth in trade, often from villages even further into the interior (presumably those of inland Kaulong and Sengseng where Goodale and Chowning worked twenty-five years after Blackwood was at Möwehafen).

The price of a medium-sized piece of bark-cloth is usually one small or medium-sized gold-lip shell . . . Now-a-days a trade loin-cloth will sometimes be given in exchange.

These are valued by the natives at about 2/- and the shells at two to five shillings according to the size. The very large gold-lip shells would not be used to purchase bark-cloth. (ibid.: 'Bark cloth')

The exchange of loin cloths for barkcloths presumably represents the greater availability of store-bought materials on the coast and the unrequited desire for these on the part of the inland peoples. We should also note in passing the unusual contact history of these inland communities, from which people were obviously travelling to the coast for trade several decades before the first patrol went into their areas. These uncontacted tribes had taken it into their own hands to contact the outside world well in advance of the outside world coming to them.

Blackwood herself participated in the exchanges to buy her museum objects, and had to negotiate not just type, but amounts of objects.

Some natives from Alomos village came bringing shields and rolls of barkcloth which they will sell to these people for gold-lip shell. Tried to buy bark-cloth with tobacco and marks, at first they would not sell – then one asked for a knife and they liked the medium-sized ones I bought from Salamaua, so got 4 pieces with different patterns.[18]

This quote shows clearly the range of different exchange media in use at the end of the 1930s and the negotiations necessary by all parties in order for objects to change hands. We also now have a sense of the amount of effort and the range of social interactions needed to make and exchange four pieces of barkcloth, so that lying below Blackwood's four specimens was a mass of action and interaction.

Blackwood provided exemplary documentation on many aspects of barkcloth, recording the processes of production on both still and cine film, so that it is possible to link objects, her verbal accounts and the visual record to create a full picture of the situation in 1937 and of the various items as they exist today.

We have dwelt at some length on the production and exchange of barkcloth, partly because it shows the detail of documentation and objects collected by Blackwood, but more particularly because her accounts demonstrate the mass of actions and relationships involved in making and exchanging barkcloth. Not only do the various raw materials for the cloth need to be gathered, but also objects like barkcloth beaters have to be exchanged and made. Each step of production and exchange requires sets of physical and social skills, and the decorations on the cloth reflect vague but important forms of symbolism, with stories attached. Barkcloth was a vital part of male regalia in the 1930s and before, even though it was by then being superseded by store-bought *lavalava*. Today barkcloth is worn, but only for ceremonial occasions. Not only have barkcloths become less common, but the set of relations through which they were produced has atrophied. In partic-ular, this will have disadvantaged inland areas, where much barkcloth was produced,

Figure 7.5. Five men holding up barkcloth for sale, Kandrian (Pitt Rivers Museum, University of Oxford)

changing their sets of connections with coastal areas. As more items from the coast, such as gold-lip shells, have made their way into the inland in the course of this century, the interior communities would have suffered from a balance-of-relationship problem, being less able to set up and maintain relationships on their own terms as the items through which relationships were created went out of use.

Moving to women's clothing and finery, we should immediately note that many of the objects used by men were also used by women. Belts, shields, spears were solely male items, and it was only on rare occasions that pig's-tusk ornaments were worn by women. But the perforated stones, *mukmok* and *singa* (see Chapter Five), were owned by men and women, and prestige was a more important determinant of use and ownership than gender, so that big men and big women owned and deployed larger amounts of these stones than did those of lesser rank. A number of items were heirlooms, again passed down through either the male or the female line, and these included the cassowary-quill money and large gold-lip shells (Fig. 7.3).

Only women wore skirts, and these were commonly collected items. The wearing of skirts was obviously general in Blackwood's time, but has declined steadily since then, so that now only women in inland areas ever wear a grass skirt on a daily basis. Blackwood's description of skirts is an evocative one and ran as follows:

> Women wear around the waist a tight girdle (*edel*) consisting of several rounds of the stem of the bush vine *alikuiyi*, or sometimes a twist of barkcloth. Into this girdle are tucked wisps of grass and leaves, in front and behind, leaving the flanks bare. At the back there is a great bunchy mass of leaves, grass and flowers, sometimes reaching almost to the ground. It serves as a cushion when the wearer sits, as women usually do, on the ground with the legs straight out in front. For special occasions both back and front are made still more bunchy by the addition of specially dried and prepared grasses and shredded leaves, covering the flanks also. Parts of these may be dyed red with the skin of the root of a tree called *ipsi*, which is mixed with lime, bruised between the hands, rubbed over the grass, and then dried in the sun. A variety of grasses and leaves are used in women's skirts, including the young leaves of the lawyer cane, and a species of pandanus. Large leaves are shredded by being rolled on the thigh. Little boys go naked up to the age of five or six, then they wear a piece of bark cloth . . . Girls, except the infants, usually wear a smaller edition of their mother's 'skirts'. There does not seem to be any ceremony connected with the first putting on of these garments. (Blackwood n.d.: 'Dress and ornaments')

She collected six skirts (compared with twenty-seven that Todd collected). Two of these were known as *baluluo* after the type of raffia from which they were made, and were bought with beads from Owas on 16 June. A third was called *lilo* after the type of young rattan from which it was made, and a fourth was called *kambalaina* and was partly dyed red. This was also bought with beads from Owas on 15 June. The final two items were both called *kuwo* (or *kowo*), and these formed a 'bustle' for dances and were again partly dyed red using a flower. Skirts for daily or ceremonial wear required a constant amount of labour to replace them. Skirts for dancing would have been used once and thrown away; those for daily use were worn for somewhat longer. Part of the rhythm of each woman's life would have been collecting suitable grasses for skirts and the flowers and roots for dyeing them, cutting and tying the grasses into bundles. Each woman would probably have made her own skirts, but there may well have been sharing of the grasses and dyes on an informal basis. This represents a different rhythm to that of men, who rarely made their own barkcloth belts, which would in any case last for several years.

Women, and to a lesser extent men, wore a variety of armbands and leg ornaments, either locally made or obtained through trade.

Several kinds of arm-bands (generic term *u-un* coast dialect, *emis* bush dialect) are worn, often with leaves or flowers tucked into them. They also serve as holders for sticks of tobacco, etc. A black band (*anul*) plaited with the mid-rib of the elk-horn fern, often with strings left hanging from it. Sometimes interwoven with yellow strands from the skin of an orchid-stem. Several other grasses etc. are also plaited or woven into armbands. (ibid.)

Men and women might well have made arm and leg bands, but one area of production that was purely in the hands of women was the making of looped bags.

Baskets – or more properly bags – of different sizes and mesh, are made from the split stem of the bush creeper *alikuiyi*. This is women's work. The chief varieties are named as follows:-
pirpiri. A large bag of wide mesh for carrying and storing taro, sweet potatoes, etc. Loosely woven of rather wide material.
Lila. The same but slightly closer weave.
Aiyon. Smaller bag with more closely twisted weave and narrower rows, for carrying ingredients for chewing the betel mixture, etc. A smaller, very finely meshed bag used for keeping valuables, is also called *aiyon*.
Igur. A stronger bag with a double layer of weaving in narrow rows, usually with a handle about an inch wide of the same weave. These are all made of the stem of the *alikuiyi* creeper. (Blackwood n.d.: 'Netting and basketry').

Blackwood bought six of these looped vine bags (compared with the eighteen purchased by Todd and twelve by Lewis), and paid between one and three sticks of tobacco per bag, depending on its size and the fineness of the weave. Some were bought where they were made in the inland village of Alomos, but others were purchased in the Möwehafen area. The production of these bags in 1937 down to the present was undertaken predominantly, if not solely, in inland villages, and like barkcloth and shields was an important aspect of the inland–coastal trade. Large numbers of these bags appear to have been in circulation, and each would have represented many hours work, once gathering the raw materials, cutting and soaking them in water to make them supple and then knotting them was taken into account.

In these accounts of material culture we have concentrated on items of personal dress, ornaments and exchange, but excluded many more, and have not touched on larger objects, such as canoes, houses or larger nets for fish and pig catching. Within any one community there was a great range of skills and forms of labour being deployed at any one time, and the production of items was the site of creation of a complex of important social relations, which was extended through their exchange and use. Various areal specialities are obvious, with the movement of objects from the coast inland, and in the reverse direction, and along the coast

Figure 7.6. Two women knotting vine-string bags. Selua village, Kandrian district (Pitt Rivers Museum, University of Oxford)

from both east and west. In the next chapter we will look more closely at the chains of action which created objects and the flows of finished objects, and how each of these were embedded within colonial relationships.

Return to the Museum

We have seen that the major result of Blackwood's collection was the manuscript for the proposed publication of her work. However, as it remained unpublished it had little impact away from the museum and the collection's documentation. When Blackwood returned from the field, as was the case with Lewis and Speiser, the Arawe work made up only one part of her research and as she had the Anga and Ramu River fieldwork to write up as well, the Arawe material remained largely neglected until the 1950s. Blackwood, eventually published on the physical, medical and intellectual impact of the practice of head binding, working with a human anatomist (Blackwood and Danby 1955). The publication was reworked from an earlier version of the paper given at the Second International Congress of

Anthropological and Ethnological Sciences held in Copenhagen in 1938, where she spoke in a session with Speiser, who gave a paper on cultural connections across Melanesia.[19] For this paper she also consulted Todd, sending him a preview for comments, and discussing in more detail the areas she wished to publish on and promising to leave the rest to him.[20]

The collections when they arrived in the Pitt Rivers Museum were catalogued by Blackwood, and then the majority went into storage in the museum, a proportion (about 10 per cent) went into the display cases and drawers in the public galleries. Blackwood was a regular lecturer on the department's postgraduate anthropology course, and certain items (including barkcloth, pig's-tusk ornament, turtle-shell ornaments, gold-lip shell, string of shell discs, axes and adzes, bone knife, skirts, paddle, blowpipe and the fire-plough) were used annually in a lecture course on the peoples of Melanesia, dealing with the subjects of art, 'Melanesia' as a regional concept, and technology. Some of these items were kept separately as a 'teaching collection' and came out for use year after year, others were on display in the museum and students were directed to them (Bob Rivers personal communication). However, the majority of the collection remained in storage, although at times the interests of other academics or other institutions caused them to be examined.[21]

In 1948 the Pitt Rivers Museum exchanged ninety-four of their objects (thirty-nine of which came from the Pacific, the rest from Africa and South America) for sixty-three artefacts of Native American provenance with Denver Art Museum. Blackwood negotiated the exchange on behalf of the museum and included several items from her New Guinea fieldwork including one piece of barkcloth from the Arawe collection. This was the only item to be removed from the Arawe collection after its accessioning into the Pitt Rivers Museums collections. Having originally collected thirteen lengths of finished barkcloth, and having had them in the museum for two decades, perhaps Blackwood, saw more value in the deployment of one example as an exchange item than in its potential for future research. As a desirable item these objects, including the barkcloth specimen, could bring items of equal or more value into the museum, and she may have already considered this as an option while in the field. Like Speiser and Lewis, it was Blackwood who chose the items from her collection that were suitable for the exchange.

Blackwood is unique amongst our four collectors for having contacted each of the others during her lifetime and investigating their knowledge and understanding of the area. She did this for two reasons. First her academic sensibilities meant that she did not want to 'poach on the preserves' of others, which makes an interesting reflection on the sense of anthropology in New Guinea at the time.[22] Anthropologists wanted to be pioneers, and certainly did not expect others to encroach on their intellectual 'territory', nor was it worth while visiting a region that had been 'done' by someone else. However, collectors did duplicate work as each museum wanted its own example of a particular artefact, not a photograph of one held elsewhere. For Blackwood it was polite to get in touch with Todd, and also to clarify his areas of expertise; logical to contact Speiser as she knew him well by this time and had met him briefly just after he had visited New Britain; and fortuitous that while visiting the Field Museum in Chicago she met A.B. Lewis, who described his own activities in the region and spent an afternoon with her looking at and discussing his collection.

Blackwood provides the best insights into both the processes of producing items and of collection. Taken together with the other three collectors, each with their sets of interests and modes of fieldwork, this can provide varied insights into the colonial culture of New Guinea. None of our collectors felt that they were documenting themselves and their position in a colonial world that embraced white and black, but we are using their collections to throw light on them as historical subjects, as well as the people them went to study. It is only through a comparison of the four collectors that can we can gain a full picture of colonial culture and its changes, and it is to this comparison that we now turn.

Notes

1. Arthur Thomson was Professor of Human Anatomy at this time based in the University Museum (of Natural History) through which the Pitt Rivers Museum is entered. As part of his academic post he taught physical anthropology.
2. From Oxford Evans-Pritchard went to London, and from Cambridge went Gregory Bateson, Reo Fortune and Camilla Wedgwood among others (Stocking 1995: 294).
3. There were almost 2,000 women in the Territory in 1933 (Bulbeck 1992: 12)
4. *Rabaul Times*, 3 July 1936, Personal column.
5. *Melanesian Mission Annual Report* (1934), March, pp. 45–6.
6. See Blackwood's diary. Blackwood Papers 8/1/3. Pitt Rivers Museum (PRM) Archives.
7. Letter to Blackwood from Father J. Krutzenblicher, n.d. Blackwood Papers, PRM Archives.
8. Blackwood was worried about covering the same ground as Todd, and wrote to him apologizing for 'poaching on his preserves'. Letter from Blackwood to Todd, 31 October 1937. Blackwood Papers, PRM Archives.
9. Speiser wrote Magnin's name as Maknin, but both made genealogies for him and these confirm that this was the same man. Blackwood Papers, PRM Archives; Speiser Papers, Museum der Kulturen, Basel.

10. Blackwood diary, Monday 2 August 1937. Blackwood Papers 8/1/3, PRM Archives.
11. Letter from Blackwood to Balfour, 19 September 1937. Blackwood Papers, PRM Archives.
12. Blackwood Papers 8/1/3, PRM Archives.
13. Diary, Blackwood Papers 8/1/3, PRM Archives.
14. Letter to Balfour, 19 November 1937. Blackwood Papers, PRM Archives.
15. The manuscript, approximately thirty pages in length, is divided into sections on aspects of material culture, but remains unpaginated. The original is to be found in the Pitt Rivers Museum, reference RDF 1938.36.1050–1334.
16. Blackwood Papers 8/1/3, PRM Archives.
17. PRM Accession book Blackwood II 137, entry written by Blackwood 1938.
18. Blackwood diary June 8 1937, PRM Archives.
19. Blackwood took notes on the paper and incorporated some of the themes into her lectures on the region. Lecture Notes, Blackwood Papers, PRM Archives.
20. Letter from Blackwood to Todd, 24 June 1938, PRM Archives.
22. In the 1960s Philip Dark and his wife visited the museum, and Blackwood gave them access to her notes and the collection (Dark 1996: 131)
22. Letter from Blackwood to Todd, 31 October 1937. Blackwood Papers, PRM Archives.

—8—

Comparing the Collections:
Experiment, Social Relations and Agency

Colonial Culture in New Guinea was an historical product, or rather a series of historical products. Objects were central to these histories. However, to understand objects and their roles we need to embed them in the full range of social relations created by colonial culture. The four collections we have analysed allow us to produce a model of the working of colonial culture in western New Britain between 1910 and 1940 with some glances at later periods, and to see what sorts of insights we can gain into historical change. Crucial issues raised by colonial culture concerned the nature of the community in which people lived and the sorts of relationships they could and should enter into. Community was at issue in a number of ways. Settlement patterns changed radically in the earlier twentieth century from small, mobile hamlets to large, sedentary villages. Most able-bodied men on the coast served time in plantations or trading posts, and there was a vast expansion in the extent and frequency of exchange links between groups. Communities after 1900 in western New Britain included white people as well as local, causing us to think about the nature of links with whites and the motives lying behind these links, which formed the very structure of colonial culture. The motives in linking up with whites ranged from the desire to get in touch with ancestral forces controlling the sources of cargo to attempts to increase personal standing within the community, or simply to gain useful items like knives or tobacco. All these new sets of relationships and forms of community raised a series of social and moral problems for people, as we shall see.

Objects were central to new forms of community and relatedness in a number of ways. The production and use of objects is through a series of forms of practical action which have spatial extent in that they are distributed across the landscape in various ways, temporal pattern and social intensity. Patterns of action needed to make or use objects were not just about physical action in the world, but were means of provisioning and animating social relations. New chains of action by themselves create novel forms of communalism and views of the world. Thus the processes of making and exchanging objects are crucial to forms of community, and we shall analyse them in this light.

From at least 1900 onwards the types of relationships that local people could set up with each other vastly expanded, mainly as a result of the extension of the Siassi trading system, together with exchanges between the coast and inland. The social system in western New Britain, as in many other areas of Papua New Guinea, was characterized by the multiplicity of kin links that people could utilize to claim land or set up exchange partnerships. Both Freedman (1970) for Siassi, and Goodale (1995) for Sengseng note the strongly cognatic natures of groups ranging across the western end of New Britain. People were able to argue for attachment to land, exchange partners and places of origin through both mothers' and fathers' kin. Not only are kin connections complex, but also kinship is only relevant to a small set of social activities, with the village, the men's house and the household all also being crucial means of bringing people together in joint projects (Freedman 1970: 159). Any individual inhabited a social universe with far more attachments and connections to people and places open to them than they could ever take up in their lifetime. The attachments and connections they did make use of derive from their own patterns of action during their lives, allowing them to construct their own social universe through action, which was larger or smaller, more or less intense, depending on their own energy and ambition. From the late nineteenth century onwards there were important shifts in the construction of community through patterns of settlement. Goodale's (1995) account of the small shifting hamlets at Umbi in the early 1960s provides us with a glimpse of what life was probably like throughout western New Britain until the late nineteenth century. People lived a fairly mobile life in their gardens and in the bush, sleeping in small hamlets of twenty to thirty people, the composition of which changed constantly. On the coast, from the beginning of the twentieth century onwards hamlets coalesced into larger villages which were both larger and more permanent in their populations. This in itself totally restructured people's worlds, and we will explore whether the rather confused social arrangements that Freedman (1970) documents for Mandok are due to the continued existence of older forms of co-operations within these new larger villages.

A vital extra dimension to these attachments was provided by colonial society, creating a new set of arenas in which people could develop their social standing and worth. Links with white people and their institutions was a dangerous but potentially fruitful avenue for self-creation. As we have stressed, each new plantation, trading centre or mission became the centre of new webs of connected-ness linking people and things.

The nature of community is also a puzzle for us as analysts. The production and sale of material culture is an important diagnostic for us, but we need to think about the sets of motives that lay behind the sale and the acquisition of objects; these arise not only at the point of transactions, but from the deeper motivations of all parties including their social, intellectual and economic standing. Understanding the nature of collections is not a simple quantative matter of looking at the changing numbers of artefacts of different types in the collections on which we have worked, although numbers do have some role to play, as we shall see. Quantities of things only tell us so much, as we are viewing objects not as static entities, but rather as processes, which change constantly and create varying relationships over time. In order to elucidate change we will take a broad view of the processes through which objects are formed and moved around, looking at as many moments as possible from initial creation to their present resting place and how far all aspects of these processes call into being relationships of particularly marked sorts.

We shall also make a brief comparison with a body of information on material culture in one part of the south coast of New Britain in the 1980s and 1990s, the Arawe Islands, which was collected by Christina Pavlides (1988), as part of a broader project directed by Gosden. This more recent evidence adds an extra dimension to the comparison of the four collections and the changing sets of processes creating objects and created by them.

A Tale of Four Collections

The collections as a whole were made over a relatively short period of time, with only twenty-five years separating the time at which Lewis was collecting from the time at which Blackwood was in New Britain. However, these twenty-five years span some of the most important changes in the colonial history of the island. There were very few plantations on the island when Lewis was there (1910), and the impact of the German administration in the area was still fairly recent. By the time at which Todd was making his collection (1933) and Blackwood was making hers (1937) there had been major changes as a result of the take-over by the Australians in the First World War and the coming of the missions. Before comparing the collections we need to think again about the sorts of relations the collections represent.

The Collections

In total the collections comprise 901 items. These range from everyday items such as grass skirts, men's belts or woven pandanus mats to objects of wealth and prestige, such as pig's-tusk ornaments or gold-lip shells, as we have seen. In order to facilitate comparison we have not presented the items individually but have classified them into nine categories according to the context in which they were used, such as hunting and fishing, warfare, food preparation and eating (see Table 8.1). This is a necessary condensation of the information, but does mean that we have imposed a structure on the material which will of itself influence our conclusions. However, we see no way around this if we are to appreciate general patterns of change and difference. In reducing individual items to broad categories, 809 artefacts were used from the overall data set, leaving out roughly 100 miscellaneous items (toys, human skulls etc.). Not only have we categorized items as to type, but we have divided the material into categories of provenance and exchange, including local (made and used in the same village as far as we can tell), local exchange (moved 10–15 km) and long distance movement (material from further afield – most of which comes from the Siassi traders and the western end of New Britain). In putting items into these categories we have attempted to use actual evidence from the collectors of how far objects might have been moved, or the testimony of local people, and therefore the number of items is again reduced as some items could not be put into these categories. This is an attempt to look at patterns of distribution and exchange and their possible changes over time. Finally, each item was assigned a category according to its gender association. The categories were: mostly made and used by women; mostly made and used by men; and ungendered. We could potentially have created finer, more nuanced categories, dividing objects into whether they had been made, used and transacted by women, or made and used by women but transacted by men, or made by women, but used and transacted by men and so on. This would have given us a possible nine categories into which any item could have been placed (see Sillitoe 1988). Not only was information often lacking on exactly who made, used and transacted things, but also to divide our objects amongst so many categories would have placed very few objects in each category, again making the perception of patterns tricky. We lumped together rather than split up our objects in order to perceive general trends at the cost of some fine detail.

Our comparisons of the collections are partly influenced by their size, with Lewis's the biggest with over 300 items to Speiser's which contains just over 100 objects. Nevertheless comparisons can be made once size is taken into account. Some obvious emphases in collections stand out: Blackwood's penchant for axes, obsidian or items of craft production; or Lewis's emphases on valuables and ornaments. Some aspects of the collections are less expected. Todd collected more female items than any of the other three collectors, including Beatrice Blackwood, confounding any straightforward notion of how gender might structure collecting. Why this should be is hard to say; the number of female items may be partly because of Todd's initial interest in 'sex totemism' taking him close to what we would today call gender. It may also reflect the structure of Todd's local relations, which may have been very local (Gosden 2000). Changes are not just, or mainly, manifest in the shifting numbers of objects, but in the patterns of social action creating objects.

Table 8.1. Number of Items in the Four Collections Associated with Each Category of (a) Context in which it is Used, (b) Production and Exchange Sphere, and (c) Gender Association. For further explanation see test

	Lewis 1910	Speiser 1929	Todd 1933–4	Blackwood 1937	Totals
Context of Use					
Hunting/fishing	38	15	9	36	98
Warfare	42	12	8	5	67
Craft production	8	2	1	25	36
Axes/obsidian	7	8	1	89	105
Food prodn & eating	14	8	19	7	48
Containers	39	10	36	9	94
Ornaments & clothing	65	26	60	36	187
Valuables	59	8	31	16	114
Music	24	10	10	16	60
Totals	296	99	175	239	809
Exchange Sphere					
Local	83	33	62	45	223
Local exchange	121	50	72	101	344
Long-distance exchange	89	16	35	90	230
Totals	293	99	169	236	797
Gender Association					
Male – mostly	161	49	59	77	346
Female – mostly	44	17	74	21	156
Ungendered	88	33	36	138	295
Totals	293	99	169	236	797

Collected Objects as Process

We have argued from Chapter One onwards that a notion of the *chaîne opératoire* can help us understand not only the sequence of events needed to produce particular objects, but also the sets of relationships involved in acts of production and the social consequences of these enchained actions and relationships. People along the south coast of New Britain were and are linked by a mass of relationships, many of which surround objects, and we want to map out a number of the more important forms of relationship, their social consequences and their changes.

These are a number of changes that appear purely technical, but are in fact more than that. The shift from stone to steel occurred, with metal axes, bush knives and knives taking over a whole range of tasks from clearing gardens to more intricate types of wood carving. The gradual decline in the need for stone and obsidian meant there were considerable changes in exchange networks, plus a disappearance of skills of knapping and polishing stone. First of all we need to establish when these changes happened. Lewis collected five hafted axes, showing that handles were still relatively common early in the century even if axes were not still in use. By 1937 Blackwood, who acquired many axes had none which were hafted, and the last use of stone axes was probably nearer to Lewis's visit than to Blackwood's. Axes originated on the volcanic north coast of New Britain, and were traded both over land and round the coast in their finished state, to be hafted in their place of use. The end of a demand for axes would have had major repercussions for the north-coast producers, although we have no direct evidence of this (see Burton 1984 for a detailed account of what the end of axe quarrying meant to one Highland's group in the 1930s). The lack of movement of axes would also have had effects on trading systems, but this would have been more minor as other objects flowed through the same links. On the south coast, the need for cane for the handles, and the skills in hafting both disappeared. Also, patterns of co-operation in gardening changed. From the testimony of Arawe people in the 1980s it is clear that not everyone owned a stone axe, with those who did hiring them out for clearing garden plots and other heavy work, like making canoes. Patterns of relative advantage and dependency changed once steel axes were in general use, weakening social differentiation within communities. It was the efficiency of steel axes that made it possible to clear large areas of garden land, and this underwrote the provision of food for new, large villages, the supply of food to plantations, and coastal communities' ability to provide food for the trading system. Steel axes had far-reaching effects in changing social relationships.

Obsidian provides an excellent example of the *chaîne opératoire* as each block of obsidian reaching the south coast was quarried in the Talasea region, traded by land or sea, perhaps with further modification along the way, and then reduced further for use in each community along the south coast. Each piece of obsidian that eventually came into use had a mass of social and physical relations inherent in its creation. Obsidian was used mainly on the human body: for circumcision, scarification, shaving and blood letting, and might occasionally also been used for fine carving, such as that found on the front of shields. Obsidian occurs at five major sources in the Talasea region on the north coast of New Britain, plus sources at Mopir near present-day Hoskins (Summerhayes, Bird, Fullagar, Gosden, Specht and Torrence 1998). Each source is chemically distinct, so that it is possible to assign obsidian found on the south coast to specific sources on the north. One startling fact is that the obsidian found on the south coast came predominantly from one source over a period of 3,500 years or more, that of Kutao-Bao (Summerhayes *et al.* 1998). As there are no real differences between the sources in terms of the quality of obsidian, this long and specific link is difficult to explain, but appears to have some basis in long-term social connections. Obsidian was generally traded as blocks, the smallest being the same size as a coconut and the largest being some 70 x 50 cm. Each men's house had at least one of these blocks which could worked into smaller flakes by both men and women. Hammerstones, known as *epit*, were traded from villages inland from Möwehafen, as local hard stone was rare; three specimens were collected by Blackwood from a woman called Siar in exchange for beads. Working obsidian probably continued until the Second World War when razors became relatively common. Giving up obsidian would have been gradual, with bottle glass being an important item of trade by Europeans from the late nineteenth century onwards. Blackwood notes 'Obsidian (*eye*) is found in small pieces in the ground . . . Quantities of these small pieces are to be found on every village site, but larger pieces are rare. They are little used now-a-days as most natives have safety razors or bits of bottles' (Blackwood n.d.: 'Obsidian'). One of the reasons that people had razors was that Blackwood and other collectors used razors as an item of trade, so that collection had some influence on giving up obsidian. By the 1980s in the Arawe Islands there was one very old woman who could still knap obsidian, but she represented the end of a long and important tradition of skills.

Another major skill which must have declined rapidly early last century was shell working. Shell was used for fish hooks, knives and ornaments. Complex reduction sequences were needed to produce fishhooks (Smith 1991) which may have been important items of trade. As we have seen, shell ornaments like armbands are still made, and indeed the skills to make these may be more widely distributed than they were. Black-lip shells are also still important for peeling taro as metal knives cause discolouration of the root due to a chemical reaction, so each woman today still owns a shell knife.

The decline of stone and obsidian use would have created a demand for metal knives and axes met through a complex of colonial relations including paid employment and transactions with collectors of various kinds. All our collectors included knives amongst their trade goods, and Lewis, at least, also had axes, which were held in reserve for more important forms of transactions. It is likely also that knives and axes were traded between local trade partners. The rising demand for steel over stone meant that people were locked into relationships with Europeans, rather than their local trading partners.

When axes and obsidian dropped out of use this was much more than a technical matter. A whole series of bodily skills was employed in creating suitable tools for use, hafting them and deploying them to clear gardens or let blood. The creation of new, larger gardens saw a shift in the balance between wild and cultivated foods in favour of the latter, bringing about new relations to landscape and to food. From the beginning of twentieth century onwards, people created much larger gardens than before, partly to feed the larger, more permanent villages, partly to host exchange partners, and also to feed the demands of the plantations for food. These shifts in subsistence and settlement patterns represents an important alteration in a basic dimension of life in which all values shifted.

The Formal Qualities of Objects

One expectation we had at the start of this project is that we would see obvious changes in the formal qualities of objects. This has turned out not to be the case. As discussed in Chapter Three, we measured all the objects we looked at and took detailed notes on form and decoration. Important objects have not changed either in their sizes or forms. Pig's-tusk ornaments, Siassi bowls or barkcloth vary in size and complexity of decoration within and between collections, but there is no direction to that variation through time: these objects do not become bigger and more complicated as time goes by, nor do they become smaller and simpler, and there is as much variability within one collection as there is between collections. One exception to this is shields. Shields do not change in their length or width between 1910 and 1937 as far as we can tell, and all the examples we have are remarkably uniform in their dimensions (an average of 1,360 mm long and 330 mm wide is a reasonable summary statistic). They are always made in three parts and always decorated on the front in a variety of ways. However, what does drop out is the decoration of the rear side of the shield, the part nearest to the man holding it. Early shields, (see Fig. 8.1 for an example from Blackwood's collection) have complicated curvilinear decorations on the back which are similar to the decorations found on men's barkcloth belts. Each man had his own decoration on both belt and shield, and this was an important part of his persona, related to war and to male ceremony in which shields were used. As warfare was given up and forms of ceremony shifted (see below), a subtle alteration took place in the decoration of the shield, so that the back was no longer painted which would have been most obvious to the man holding it. Also, shields were a major item for collection, as the tripartite form is special to western New Britain and an indicator of regional difference. Shields were sold in large numbers, partly due to their declining importance as a marker of male identity, although the scale of collection may have contributed to new shields being made in large numbers, with simplification being a partial result of more rapid production.

As we shall discuss in more detail below, we feel that the change in the decoration of shields is part of a shift away from male separation from the rest of the community and of the decline in male-only rituals. The fact that formal qualities of shields change as part of this shift, indicates that there are links to be expected between the social values attached to objects and their formal qualities. The lack of change in many items becomes significant of important continuities in life, rather than a residual effect of innate conservatism.

Figure 8.1. Back view of shield (Pitt Rivers Museum, University of Oxford)

Changes in the Local Community

We need also to think about what can be said about the use of objects on the basis of the data presented in Table 8.2. As well as charting these earlier changes in material culture and colonial history, a comparison is made with information collected by Pavlides (1988) on Pililo and Kumbun Islands in the Arawe Islands group in the eight years up to 1992, reflecting the effects of the Second World War and the introduction of the cash economy over the thirty years prior to that. In Table 8.2 percentages are given, and these refer to the number of potential classes

Table 8.2. Changes in the Percentages of Artefact Types in Each Category Between the Five Collections

	Lewis 1910	Speiser 1929	Todd 1935	Blackwood 1937	Pavlides 1992	Decline
Hunting & fishing	69%	62%	23%	62%	54%	10%
Warfare	75%	100%	50%	75%	0%	100%
Craft production	50%	17%	17%	83%	83%	None
Axes & obsidian	33%	40%	10%	70%	0%	100%
Food prodn & eating	56%	44%	44%	33%	56%	None
Containers	100%	50%	83%	50%	30%	70%
Ornaments & clothes	68%	58%	42%	47%	32%	30%
Valuables	53%	35%	59%	53%	Increase	Increase
Music	44%	78%	11%	78%	22%	50%

of item in each collection which fall into each of the categories. For example, Lewis's collection has examples of all the types of containers that are known from the collections as a whole (100 per cent), while he has only 44 per cent of the different types of musical instruments.

Given that each collection represents a particular 'time-slice', we are attempting to look at change through time by focusing on the increases and decreases in the different types of object within each collection, bearing in mind the influences of the interests of the collectors. Let us compare Lewis's collection (1910) and Pavlides's observations which ended in 1992: over a period of eighty-two years little change is discernible in the categories of hunting and fishing, food preparation and craft production, showing some basic continuity to life. However, over the same period, a major decline can be seen in the availability and collection of objects associated with warfare, stone tools, containers and music. We have already dealt extensively with stone tools and obsidian, so let us turn our attention to other categories.

Warfare and music were linked, and the decline in the collected objects that are connected with both of these aspects of life was associated with the sharp decline in exclusively male artefacts collected since Lewis's visit in 1910 (see Table 8.1). Lewis arrived at end of the old order on the south coast of New Britain;

there was still much fighting, and although some large villages were to be found there were also smaller defended settlements located away from the coast (Fig. 2.2). In pre-colonial times male prestige depended partly on prowess in warfare, and there was a rigid separation of men from women and children. The men's house was the centre of male life and of active male-only cults. As colonial peace was imposed and more young men were removed from communities to work on plantations, the focus of male life shifted, and with it relations within the community as a whole. Warfare was not given up suddenly, but declined rather slowly and, as Goodale (1995) has shown, some rituals led to fighting, so that the division between war and peace is not marked in the manner we might imagine. Warfare was the basis of indigenous male prestige, and the enforced cessation of warfare by the colonial authorities became the basis of white prestige: pacification was how the regime took control.

The gradual cessation of warfare happened at a time when there were in any case massive changes in the nature of the community. The movement from hamlets to villages was a traumatic one, reordering and revaluing all relationships as previously separated groups were brought together. In some areas of the southern part of New Britain the change was such a difficult one that it was reversed after independence, with people going back to small hamlets in the 1970s (Maschio 1994), although all communities directly on the coast have maintained the larger units. The larger gardens needed to support these villages necessitated new forms of co-operation and distribution of produce. Going along with this were the extensions in the forms of exchange involving local people, Asians and whites, whereby much greater effort was being put into exchange. Last, and certainly not least, were the effects of labour recruitment, with large numbers of younger men leaving the community and coming back, together with a smaller number of women. Villages near the new plantations, like those in both the Arawes and Kandrian would have contacts with plantation workers from elsewhere in New Guinea, bringing in new customs, ceremonies and exchange links.

All these changes brought into question the nature of the community in which people lived, both at a village and a wider regional level. Ritual was a crucial arena in which change was made manifest and dealt with. The major shift was from male-only rituals to ceremonies involving the whole community. Circumcision, marriage and death reflect entry into the community, a change of state within it, and exit from it. Rituals surrounding these changes predominate today and probably have done since just after the First World War. The earliest collection, that of Lewis, is the only one in which masks relating to the male-only *warku* cult are found. Five examples were collected by Lewis, and derived from *warku* ceremonies, which were men-only and centred on the men's house, but these ceremonies might have been in decline even when Lewis was there. Speiser discussed *warku* with Aliwa. On 21 April 1929 Aliwa said that there were two *warku* masks, named *sala* and *einsparna*, left on Pililo, all the others had been destroyed by the missions or bought by whites (including Lewis presumably). *Warku* masks were used during circumcisions which were carried out in the men's house. Women were allowed to glimpse them under certain circumstances, unlike in Siassi or New Guinea, where *warku* were also found and where it was completely forbidden for women to see the masks. *Warku* masks are not found in any later collections, and this accords with the testimony of people in the Arawes, who said that *warku* ceremonies had not been run for most of the last century. *Warku* were also connected with bull-roarers, which were still present when Blackwood was collecting (she has two in her collection) but have subsequently disappeared.

Lattas (1998: 9) tells how in Kaliai the *tambaran Varku* is seen as the basis of male power and is linked in myth with male usurpation of what was originally women's power. The set of ceremonies surrounding *Varku* must be kept secret, so that women will not realize this original theft. The initiation of boys was an induction into the world of men's secrets and the material paraphenalia surrounding those secrets. In Arawe there has been a considerable change between the late 1920s when the circumcision of boys was a secret male-only matter and the more recent past when initiation ceremonies are attended by men and women alike and the circumcision is conducted in the open. Maschio (1994: 103) notes the ambivalence many feel towards the actions of men trying to enhance their own reputations. A big man with some regard for the social good is vital in ensuring the health of the community, while a self-aggrandizing violent man is one of the ultimate threats to the community. In this observation we see the history of the region manifest in the present, when the good and cohesion of the community has come to be paramount and the older order of male violence and ambition a threat to the community, and thus it must be curbed.

The origins of the *warku* ceremony in the Arawe Islands are of interest. Aliwa told Speiser[1] that *warku* masks and the ceremony came from Siassi but they were also known from the coast of New Guinea. However, it seems likely that there was also a connection with Kilenge. Dark (1979: 149) noted that the five masks Lewis collected were Kilenge in style, and Lewis records their Kilenge origins. People in the Arawe Islands felt that the *warku* ceremonies were not ancient, having only come into the region a few generations before they were given up early in the twentieth century, although the bull-roarer and the practice of circumcision were much older. Aliwa's father had told him that the Arawe Islanders had taken *warku* to Möwehafen some two generations previously, so that the Arawe Islands represented an important intermediary between west and east.

The sale of the *warku* masks and ceremony is part of a much larger movement of objects and ritual between areas in New Britain that were earlier distinct in their material culture and ritual. There are complicated reasons behind these movements of ideas and rituals, partly to do with the opening up of exchange networks and partly with the mixing of people on plantations and missions which enabled people from one area to learn about life in another (Chowning 1969: 29). The earlier importation of male-only ceremonies shifted to an emphasis on, and acquisition of, community-wide ceremony.

Other sets of distinction which broke down were those within the local communities relating to the ownership or control of objects. At the beginning of the twentieth century on the coast and later in inland areas, only big men and women could own and control ritually powerful objects, such as *mokmok, singa* and named pearl shells. Such items were dangerous and could have ill effects on the community at large if in the hands of the inexperienced or unskilled individual (Goodale 1995: 89). Now all men and women own such stones, although it may be true that the most powerful objects are restricted to the most powerful individuals. The same was also true of certain forms of taro and other plants, which at one time could only be planted by people with sufficient personal power to control the magic associated with their growth. Communities in western New Britain have allowed the erosion of such distinctions over the last century, which has opened exchange networks still further. Although the evidence is not clear, it seems that people of Aliwa's standing and generation were the last who had the power to enforce such distinctions in ownership and use. Arawe communities were much more internally fractured and distinct from each other a century ago, but the breakdown of a series of differences has led to a massive expansion of the social universe that people now inhabit.

One indication of the greater size and intensity of links between people has been an inflation in payments of various kinds, especially marriage payments. The one category of items which shows an increase in Table 8.2 is that of valuables. This increase is made up of both a greater number of different objects exchanged and a greater frequency of exchanges for existing objects. These increases are difficult to quantify, but it is certain that there has been an inflation in certain types of payment, such as bride price, with far more objects needed to complete a bride price now than earlier in the century (Gosden and Pavlides 1994: Table 2). Many objects are used in a variety of forms of ritual, such as initiation or death rituals, and it is likely that payments of all types have increased. Such rituals and forms of exchange, involving the kin group as a whole, are now central to peoples' lives and have replaced the male-centred rituals of the nineteenth century. We feel that it is no coincidence that most such rituals concern life cycles and initiation of children into the group. Such an emphasis on the group is partly as a result of the many changes to the nature of group life, through alterations of settlements patterns and movements of people as a result of labour recruitment, as well as shifts in the relationships between men and women. The group as a whole was re-thought, and people have used existing cultural means, constructed in novel ways, to carry out this re-thinking.

Not everything changed, and at the heart of the system there is a marked conservatism associated with the formal qualities of objects, as we have seen. This conservativism was not a perverse reaction on the part of the Arawe, but was rooted in deep cultural values. The Rauto give names to people that are also the names of objects. A child's name 'might be the name of an important cultural object, such as a part of a sacred spirit mask (*uakuakio*), or a section of the men's ceremonial house (*molokio*)' (Maschio 1994: 47). Objects are treated with reverence because they are infused with human spirit and link people to the world. The distinctions between people and things at the centre of Western Cartesian views of the world do not exist here, so that people's identities are made up partly, but fundamentally, through connections to things. Such naming practices are common throughout Arawe. If objects changed continuously in their forms and the names given to their forms, the links between people and things would be difficult to draw. As it is, even someone who lived through most of the twentieth century would find many objects that they knew as a child unchanged at the time of their death. People are created as personalities partly through their links to objects and the uses to which these can be put. The social universe in which people and objects now exist is vastly larger than it was a century ago, obliging people to remember an immense amount of information. This effort of memory is possible and effective because the objects themselves have not changed, even though the uses to which they can be put have.

Community at a Broader Scale

Through the last century that was continuous change in how people conceived of themselves and the sorts of communities in which they lived. We have seen how the collections can guide us in thinking about community at the local scale, but we need also to be aware that a major change occurred at the broader spatial scale, which set each individual and group within a hugely expanded social system created through the movement of people and objects over large areas.

A crucial area of change is that of exchange. Two main changes appear to have occurred: the geographical extension of exchange links of various kinds; a greater frequency and intensity of trade between those already linked. The geographical extension of links took place in a number of ways. At the end of the nineteenth century, before the period we are directly concerned with here, the Tami traders contracted their sphere of activities of production and exchange, in large part due to the new missionary activity on Tami and in the Huon Gulf (Harding 1967; Welsch 1998). The Siassi islanders swiftly moved to fill this vacuum and started producing bowls and canoes of Tami type (probably taught by Tamis), and they set up greater links with both the north coast of New Guinea and the south coast of New Britain than they had enjoyed earlier, so that they had a monopoly on the movement of many items where previously they had had to compete with the Tami. This shift had taken place certainly by the time Lewis visited the area, and he was one of the few people to collect from the Tami area and the south coast of New Britain.

The system of trade and exchange centred on the Siassi islands of the Vitiaz Strait linked some 150,000 people in several hundred different communities between the north coast of New Guinea, the Vitiaz Strait and New Britain (Map 1) (these figures were gathered by Harding [1967] who carried out fieldwork in the area in 1963–4 and are relevant to that period). Within this exchange system some communities were specialist traders (such as the Tuam and Malai islanders in Siassi); some were specialist producers (such as the potting villages of Sio and Gitua on the north New Guinea coast); and some supplied raw materials and food (as did the communities on the south coast of New Britain). Pavlides (1988) documented the exchange partnerships for the Arawe Islanders, and she noted that an individual might have as many as 3,000 exchange partners, known as *saunga* locally, found in an arc around the western end of New Britain and Siassi and back to Kandrian in the east. Similar documentation in Kandrian would reveal a series of coastal links, but also many connections inland to the Kaulong and Sengseng areas. A similar institution of trade friendships exists in Siassi, this time linking the north coast of New Guinea, Umboi and Long Islands, and New Britain (Harding 1967: 165–8). An individual is obliged to act as a host and protector to a visiting friend, to graciously receive any gift given by them, and can request specific objects in exchange. Friends may visit by prior arrangement or simply drop in, and people may be invited to marriage feasts, funerals or initiations in which their trade friend is a principal. Trade friends are inherited and represent continuing links between kin groups. Not all necessarily runs smoothly between friends, and the Siassis are particularly notorious for defaulting (Harding 1967: 168), which can lead to the end of the relationship in severe cases.

The basic geography of these links has probably stayed much the same from the late nineteenth century onwards, so that each area in contact now was in contact then. What has changed is the number of people linked to each other and the frequency with which they visit each other. It seems likely at the beginning of the last century that the longest-distance and most important exchanges were between those of high social rank only, who had privileged access to items of long-distance exchange. Given the danger of attack, it might only have been those who could command war parties who could engage in long-distance exchange with any safety. Peace brought democratization, so that small parties or even individuals could journey for trade without danger of attack. Also, the movement of people through labour recruitment and work, provided avenues for travel and inter-group links which would not have existed previously, and an Arawe man going to work at Iboki plantation on the north coast of New Britain, for instance, could have made a series of trading contacts previously impossible.

Table 8.3 shows the main balance of production of items, which are then exchanged. There are three main sets of exchanges, which are vital to obtaining important objects. The Kaulong area inland from Kandrian, plus an area of inland villages in a band across to villages on the Pulie, were the sites of production of shields, barkcloth and vine bags. For instance, the Sengseng received shells, coconuts, lizard skins and salt from the coast and gave shields, barkcloth, minerals, tobacco and betel nut in return (Chowning 1978: 297). The same was true of the Kaulong and, to a lesser extent, the Lamogai speakers to the west. The other major items were those exchanged, but not produced, and these were *mokmok* and *singa*. The origins of these stones is obscure, but it seems very likely that these were prehistoric items, now found in streams and old settlement sites in the Kaulong area and exchanged widely throughout southwest New Britain.

Table 8.3. The Items Used in Exchanges over Varying Distances and Between Different Areas

Inland (from Kaulong/Sengseng to Lamogai) – shields, barkcloth, *mokmok, singa*, vine bags, blow guns.

South coast (Arawes to Kandrian) – gold lip, salt, pigs, dogs, Siassi items

North coast (Kilenge to Talasea) – axes, obsidian, drums, baskets, masks, pigments

Siassi – 'Tami' bowls, wooden mortar and pestles, spoons/paddles, bull-roarers, pottery, lime gourds, shell and turtle-shell armbands and earrings, woven arm and leg bands, dog's-teeth head bands and belts, pig's-tusk ornaments

Local (all areas) – nets, slings, pandanus mats and rain capes, skirts, shell knives, woven arm and leg bands, flutes, panpipes, shell knives, coconut-leaf baskets, betel nut and food.

The great expansion in the range of contacts has made for many greater links between the inland areas and the coast. There was some movement inland of collectors, recruiters and patrol officers from just before 1914 and onwards. However, the communities further inland contacted the outside world, rather than *vice versa*, with people from inland Kaulong and Sengseng communities going to work in Rabaul and on plantations from the 1930s onwards. The setting up of the government station in Kandrian by Horace Niall in 1930 meant far more government influence in the area.[2] The first government patrols did not enter inland Kaulong or Sengseng areas until the late 1950s, making these some of the last areas in Papua New Guinea to be brought within the administration, but by which time local people had a reasonable knowledge of the colonial world at second hand at least (Goodale 1995).

Nowadays items from the Siassi trading system and gold-lip shells are found in the most inland communities, but this has happened progressively over the

Figure 8.2. Alip, Luluai of Alu'u, seated with his wife Owas, displaying their wealth in gold-lip shells (Pitt Rivers Museum, University of Oxford)

second half of the twentieth century, so that now gold-lip shells are used for a range of basic transactions where once they were in extremely short supply (Fig. 8.2). The old divisions between inland and coast have been rearranged, so that the old marked differences are no longer as evident.

People's motivation to engage in exchange expanded as other opportunities for social advancement declined. For men, exchanges helped compensate for the lack of opportunities once found in warfare and which for women had existed in much more restricted form while warfare was constant. Today throughout the region peoples' social reputations, their names, are associated with the ability to host song festivals, feasts and ceremonies and to engage in exchanges. Both Maschio (1994) and Goodale (1995) emphasize the two-way process whereby people in western New Britain develop their individuality through social links with others. Relations with other people and groups necessitates the husbanding of material resources, trade objects, the creation and maintenance of links with others, and the retention of knowledge about the social world in general. Knowledge about objects and people and the ability to use this knowledge constructively was the basis for social success, and this is brought about by both travel and a wide circle of friends.

Gifts and Commodities

Anthropology, in only concentrating on the trading systems seen as indigenous, has only given us part of the story of expanding links. It is impossible to understand the growth of such trading systems without looking at the broader historical forces of which they were a part. Harding's (1967: chap 9) documentation of the effects of European contact is an honourable exception to this, in that he sets the recent history of the trading system within the context of wage labour and the exchanges of Western goods, but even here he sees the trading system as being in decline and New Guineans as faced with a choice between indigenous and Western economic values. However, when we consider Lilley's conclusion on the basis of archaeology in the Vitiaz Strait, that the present trading system may be less than 300 years old (Lilley 1986: 471–2), the colonial period represents about half the total existence of the system as a whole and is integral to its recent operation. Our argument is essentially against the notion of a dual economy, whereby Western economic values are seen to confront indigenous social values with the former inevitably winning out. We are concerned rather with the sets of relations that are set up through objects (irrespective of whether these might be deemed Western or local), the patterns of social effort to create, circulate and use objects, and the meanings attached to both people and things. Having stressed the need to consider all relationships together, we need to emphasize that not all relationships had the same value. There would have been a marked contrast between the exchange partnerships inherited from one generation to the next which sustained the Siassi trading system and the more or less temporary relationships with whites.

European goods were freely exchanged, but never became socially marked. Today all European items and money are excluded from brideprice and all forms of customary payments, where the same items are used as were used a century ago. Figure 8.3, taken in the late 1980s, shows a good selection of the wealth items then in use. Comparison with other illustrations throughout this book will show the lack of change in the types and forms of objects over the twentieth century, and this lack of change is itself an important historical fact to which we shall return below. This is in contrast to the Highlands, where money and European objects often supplement locally made objects in customary payments of many kinds (Strathern 1984) and we will explore this difference further in the next chapter. In New Britain European goods represented a supply of use values, which might produce socially valued objects, but could not of themselves sustain important relationships. A big man was looking at a very different form of control through attempting to monopolize the movement of store-bought goods, and the

Figure 8.3. Arawe elder Peter Kameklung setting out his wealth. Paligmete Village, Pililo Island (Chris Gosden)

limits of this control might have been insisted on by the rest of the community. Within the system of exchange partners through which gifts flowed, it was the relationship which was important. It is not clear how far relations with Europeans and Asians were important as relationships or merely as conduits for useful objects. It may well be that length of residence and depth of sympathy with local people did make a difference. As noted above, Blackwood felt that Koch could get items at more reasonable prices than she was able, and this may have been due to the fact that people valued a relationship with him too much to either ask too much or to refuse him. We are led to wonder about whether our longer-term fieldworkers like Todd and Blackwood were seen any differently from transients, such as Lewis and Speiser, who would have fitted within the normal run of white travellers in the area and whom local people would have known were likely to disappear for ever. As the first long-term anthropological fieldworker in the area, Todd might have been treated like a plantation manager, as a semi-permanent resident, and his collection hints at this as he was able to collect the valuable dogs'-teeth ornaments that others could not. Goodale (1995: 130) notes how the Kaulong big man Maklun had an exchange network which included Europeans (Goodale herself became part of it), and this helped mark him out as having exceptional status. It is quite possible that exceptional individuals were able to do the same in earlier periods with white residents.

An undeniable effect of the mass of white and Asian contacts was to take items out of circulation. Blackwood notes the number of visitors passing through the Kandrian area in the time she is there, and there is no reason to believe the period of her stay is atypical. Our collectors removed over 1,000 objects from the area, and this is obviously the tip of an iceberg which would have had a considerable effect on the production of objects, and which would have had to have been reorganized to take account of these new demands. Specht (in press) estimates that 50,000 or more objects must have left the Bismarck Archipelago between 1875 and 1914. Such levels of collection continued until the Second World War and probably beyond. It is ironic that an anthropological interest in gift exchange came about at the same time that colonial culture was helping to promote and heighten the very gift-exchange systems that they studied. And it is the final irony of the salvage paradigm of collecting that collections made to record a vanishing material culture helped stimulate unprecendented levels of production.

Conclusions

The complex historical changes we have charted here are not the result of a series of impositions by the colonial power, but rather the result of new sets of relation-ships being created and negotiated. The agents of change were everywhere, and it makes no sense to pick out some groups or individuals as prime-movers and others as passive victims of change. Communities were radically altered to the point at which it might not have been clear what the nature of the community was. The role of individuals, partly formed by the workings of the social matrix, was radically altered. Everything got bigger. Small hamlets coalesced into large villages and garden plots became large and productive. Exchange networks expanded in scale and intensity, so that larger areas were linked and the movement of people and objects became more frequent. The exchange networks also embraced European people and goods, with plantations and trading stations important new nodes in linking people and places. Harding (1967) saw the Siassi-centred exchange system as being in decline in the post-war period. However, this is not an accurate diagnosis as there never was *an* exchange system. It was always changing, with new sets of relationships to be negotiated between people and objects. The introduction of Western trade goods into exchanges was limited by the fact that commodities never really became gifts in any socially important sense, although gifts could become commodities if sold on the open market.

It is ironic that what we thought initially might be major indicators of change, the forms of material culture, were relatively stable. This stability is historically embedded and a means of dealing with changes. People are linked closely to objects through the sharing of names, such that there is a close emotional attachment between people and things. As all people's crucial relationships to other people changed, relationships to objects formed a stubbornly enduring element of continuity. The objects that have dropped out of use and circulation, apart from stone tools, are mainly to do with war and male-only ritual. As the nature of community became an increasing issue, rituals concerning the community as a whole increased, and things like circumcision, previously only the realm of men, came to be conducted in the open spaces in the middle of villages, rather than hidden in the men's house. Individuals were linked to the community, and as a man's ability to define himself through war vanished the skills of the big man and woman, who could create and maintain large personal networks, came to be valued. Both individual and community are, of course, difficult terms, but people were individuated in new ways through the existence of larger communities, and forms of communalism were made anew to include whites, but also those locals who could operate successfully in the wider social world.

Life became saturated with new meanings of time, space and the values attached to people and things. Colonial culture in Arawe shared similarities with the rest of colonial New Guinea, but also exhibited differences. It is the balance between difference and similarity in colonial cultures to which we now turn.

Notes

1. Fieldnotes, Aliwa, 21 April 1929. Speiser Papers, Museum der Kulturen, Basel.
2. Niall Archive, National Library of Australia.

—9—

Varieties of Colonialism

We have so far tended to write of colonial culture in New Guinea in the singular. Colonial culture in the Arawe area was just one of many different types of colonialism found throughout New Guinea. We shall sketch here some of the various forms of colonialism in New Guinea and lay out some of the possible reasons that life was so different across time and space. There was superficial variability and deep variability. Superficial variety derived from the chance meeting of personalities and the intersections of events. Without Aliwa the history of colonial society in the Arawe Islands would have been different, just as Harry Bond left multiple and slightly disorderly traces through his actions. As we pointed out in the last chapter, collections can provide a wonderful window on personalities and events, as well as on broader processes. On the other hand, the long-term history of an area created forms of sociability, ritual and personality particular to a region, and we need to turn from anthropology to archaeology in order to understand continuity and change over the *longue durée*. Different parts of Papua New Guinea have their own long-term histories going back several thousand years, which have created regionally specific cultural logics: the emphasis on intensive agriculture to fund large-scale pig production is found in more pronounced form in the Highlands than elsewhere, for instance, and seems to have been a developing trend over the last 6,000 years or more (Golson and Gardner 1990). Superimposed on these long-lasting trajectories are more recent developments that seem to have brought about greater intensifications of the social process in many places over the last few centuries.

A further factor, somewhere between the long and the short term, has been the exact form and date of the incoming colonialists, varying from the earlier nineteenth century to the 1950s in different parts of the country. Nineteenth-century forms of colonial encounter were brutal and random, when the actions of recruiters and traders operated beyond many of the restraints found in the liberal Western societies from which these people came. By the 1930s, when colonial culture swept through the Highlands, violence and death occurred but were generally due to the shock of new encounters, rather than being a standard mode of interaction. Colonial cultures on the coast, in contrast to those in the Highlands, might have retained a greater wariness, certainly on the part of local people, due to their early history colouring various forms of transaction and encounter.

More surprising than variety is the existence of broad similarities throughout Papua New Guinea. Given the varying histories of the regions, the complicated incursions of colonists and the random nature of personalities and events, we might expect that variety is all we would see once we started to consider New Guinea more broadly. This is not the case. All New Guineans seem to have taken whites to be ancestral or spirit figures on first encounter (Schieffelin and Crittenden 1991), all subsequently engaged in exchange with whites, and in most parts of the country cargo cults sprung up as a means to deal with these new people and the riches they appeared to possess. At the core of these similarities in response were moral issues. For New Guineans these moral issues were not abstract ones, but had to do with how people should best relate to each other and to the material world. Unsurprisingly, the ways in which New Guineans created colonial relationships with whites was through the same means that they created relationships with each other, and we shall look first at how this was done.

Cultures for Sale

Over the years there have been many attempts to understand the diversity of Papua New Guinean societies by creating social typologies which divide groups into different types with common characteristics. A recent influential typology is that which divides societies deriving their power from the creation and exchange of wealth from those in which power resides in the ability to control knowledge and ritual. For instance, Errington (1988) has distinguished the 'knowledge cultures' of the Sepik region, which stress esoteric knowledge, from the 'thing cultures' of the New Guinea Highlands, which emphasize control over the exchange of pearl shells and pigs. The most influential version of this dichotomy is that of Godelier (1986) who sees a basic difference between the entrepeneurial big men of the central Highlands whose control of wealth is central to social reproduction, from great men found in many other areas of Melanesia whose power was based on control of ritual and particularly initiation. However, no sooner is such a distinction set up, than it starts to be undermined. Harrison (1993) feels that the distinction between wealth-based and knowledge-based groups is false, due to the fact that ritual and knowledge is regularly traded in Papua New Guinea against valuables such as pigs and pearl shells. This he sees as the movement of economic capital against symbolic capital (Harrison 1993: 147). The aspect which unites these two forms of capital is that ritual and knowledge can be seen as a prestige good, in the just the same way as pigs and pearl shells. Harrison picks up an old distinction between 'importing cultures' such as the Mountain Arapesh who regularly purchased masked dance-complexes from the exporters of the Coastal Arapesh, drawing on Mead's (1938) account. 'Each dance brought with it new styles of body-decoration, songs and techniques of magic and divination. The purchase included physical objects such as masks and ornaments, but it was not simply the objects alone that were purchased but the rights to copy them' (Harrison 1993: 146). When new dances were offered by coastal villagers, the Mountain Arapesh would sell the old ones off to people further inland along their trade routes. The coastal people constantly developed new dance-complexes for sale and '(t)he results were, on the one hand, the constant production or supply of novel dance-complexes by the maritime and coastal peoples; on the other, the perpetual striving by the hinterland peoples to emulate the perceived elegance and sophistication of the coastal cultures' (Harrison 1993: 147). Of course, the exporters rarely gave the full story of how to deploy ritual, as this would involve handing over a dangerous amount of their intellectual copyright.

The flow of cultural property led to a mutual ranking of the two groups where the coastal groups were seen to be the mothers of the daughter inland communities, and sustaining this hierarchy was a flow of wealth from the inland to the coast. Dances were not seen as traditions to be handed down to the next generation, but as prestige goods moving along paths of exchange. In this and many other areas the emphasis was on acquiring rituals that were effective for initiating the young or maintaining the fertility of land and people. Ritual was a crucial element in the necessary link between people and the cosmological forces of their universe; there was thus a need for ritual that did the right job. The constant movement of ritual has meant that no group has a unique culture, but holds a particular portfolio of property rights in its own special combination of ritual complexes, in which its neighbours own a different combination of shares. As we have seen, there are numerous New Britain examples of such sales, such as the widespread purchase of the dance Sia from Siassis, who acquired it from the New Guinea mainland, and the movement of the *warku* initiation ceremony from New Guinea to Siassi, whence it went to the Arawe Islanders who sold it on to Kandrian groups.

Just as other rituals could be bought and sold, so could cargo cults:

> In Mount Hagen in the 1940s, a traffic in cargo rituals arose in response to the massive influx of shell valuables and other wealth brought by Europeans. Big Men in outlying areas sought access to the greatly expanded pool of wealth by creating cargo cult rituals and selling them to groups closer to the centre of European influence. (Harrison 1993: 153, drawing on Strathern 1971: 263–4)

The constant movement of ideas, material culture and performance might have led to a break-down of cultural difference between groups (a state of affairs which is patently not the case in the highly varied social world of Papua New Guinea) if it were not for the need to maintain differences between groups in order to have cultural forms for exchange. The movement of rituals between exchange partners across group boundaries has led to an emphasis on innovation to create newly efficacious rituals desired by neighbours.

Harrison's views allow us to understand difference and similarity not as static properties of people's lives, but as a cultural topography that needs to be maintained. The production, acceptance or rejection of new cultural forms is the real stuff of history, and a fast-changing history at that, alerting us to the dangers of seeing any one period of time as anything more than a temporary moment within the overall flux of cultural forms. We can also see how a hierarchy between groups can rest partly on the flow of efficacious rituals against material wealth, taking advantage of the general need for rituals which work. Harrison (1993: 155) outlines a spectrum of cultural forms ranging from the introverted Baruya, whose leaders wish to maintain control of knowledge within the group, to others, such as the Coastal Arapesh who are constantly and actively seeking to transform intellectual property into material wealth. Although the sale of cultural property does not happen in the same manner everywhere, it does appear to be a general aspect of Papua New Guinean life, leading us to wonder what impact these widespread attitudes to intellectual and material property might have had on the creation of colonial culture.

Buying Colonialism

Two aspects of Harrison's argument are particularly salient: the need for people to buy effective rituals and the relationships of inequality that are set up between those buying and those selling the ritual. Throughout Papua New Guinea there were two responses to the arrival of whites: the setting up of exchange relationships with white people and the creation of cargo cults which are found generally in Papua New Guinea (Lawrence 1964) and are very prevalent in New Britain (Lattas 1998). Until now people's willingness to exchange with whites and their propensity to set up cargo cults have never been linked, but by reworking Harrison's argument we can see how they might be. Cargo cults were not so much about the acquisition of European goods, but were rather a continuing search for access to the sources of power through which whites gained such goods. Lawrence and Meggitt (1972: 22) pointed out that 'Everywhere religion is regarded as a means to or a guarantee of material welfare,' and this is as true of cargo cults as of any other expression of religious belief. People, especially on the coast, did not want to rely on whites, but desired their own access to white sources of power, which would make such reliance unnecessary. Cargo cults created new forms of ritual, generally through reworking christian forms and doctrines designed to remove some of the blocks thought to exist between people and their ancestors, which whites had set up in order to gain privileged access to wealth. The misrepresentations of whites had to be exposed to make this process effective. 'The Garia claimed that they had not been taught the Christian equivalent of their own ritual formulae and hence had no way of actuating God to send them goods. The Ngaing accused their missionaries of hiding secrets about human origins by persuading the natives to accept Adam and Eve as the only totemic forebears of all mankind' (Lawrence and Meggitt 1972: 25). Such suspicions of whites account for the enthusiastic acceptance of christianity as the ritual road to the sources of white power, which was generally followed by people not becoming christian in the manner which the missionaries had hoped.

Like cargo cults, exchange relations are an attempt to set up beneficial relations with others, and are surrounded by moral questions about what should be exchanged, where and how. The transfer of objects between people is always bound up with material, moral and social questions about the transformations in relations that the movements of objects might entail. Exchange relationships might also have been set up to gain access not just to white goods, but to the sources of white goods. The large amounts of material offered for sale to whites were not only or mainly for economic purposes, the acquisition of use values. Rather they were partly designed to set up relationships with specific whites or the white community in general that would have general benefits. The qualities of objects exchanged by local people and the uses of Western objects, once acquired, are key indicators of motives and relationships. It was not just objects that were important, but also forms of relationship with whites. In discussing the island of Ponam in Manus, the Carriers (1991: 68) felt that the transfer of labour on plantations was analogous to brideprice – 'Joseph Karin asserted that fathers forced their unwilling sons into labour contracts in order to get wealth out of Europeans, just as they forced their unwilling daughters into marriage in order to get wealth out of their affines.' Joseph Karin was speaking from slightly bitter personal experience, having been recruited around 1914 (Carrier and Carrier 1991: 68).

The widespread nature of cargo cults throughout Papua New Guinea indicate that there was a common baseline in response to the material culture of Europeans and Asians. Cargo-culting activity derived from the general New Guinean template of the exchange of ritual, with local people taking the foreign rituals of christianity and adapting these in manners they hoped would be efficacious. New Guineans exchange constantly with each other, and this helps explain the universal occurrence of exchange with whites, as attempts to create relationships of benefit in social and spiritual terms. Lattas (1998) sees cargo cults primarily as resistance. This is not quite the right term. Cargo cults and forms of exchange were attempts to incorporate, enfold and make use of the forms of cosmological power possessed by whites. Enfolding European ways within local cultures was part of the means through which colonial culture was created, and this creation took place in this important instance on Papua New Guinean terms.

Varieties of Exchange with Whites and the Incorporation of European Goods

Everywhere there was exchange with Europeans, but everywhere exchanges varied. We can construct a rough spectrum of forms of exchange with whites that does not represent a series of fixed pigeon holes into which different cases can be slotted, but rather forms an initial means to understand variety. Our spectrum is graded from lesser to a greater intensities of links with whites, which could itself indicate an increasing wish to influence the relationships which made up colonial culture. We start with a theoretical possibility which is not, as far as we know, demonstrated to exist in actuality: the absence of any exchange with white people. As we have seen, not all objects will be exchanged, and individuals can on occasions refuse to transact, but we know of no group who, as a whole, prohibited exchange with whites, and this in itself is significant. Then there are those who exchanged regularly with whites, but did not produce items especially for exchange or alter the formal qualities of their objects. This is what we have found in Arawe. A further form is the deliberate production of objects for exchange with whites, but where these objects are substantially the same as those previously used and exchanged solely between local people. Firth (1986: 45) notes that the Tolai of east New Britain were making artefacts for sale to passing naval vessels by the later nineteenth century, and Gray (1999: 31) thought that the whalers in the Bismarck Archipelago brought about the 'rapid expansion in the making of handicrafts, with the sale of baskets, clubs, spears, bows and arrows, shells and fishhooks', some of which were useful items for the crew and others viewed as curios. Neumann (1992: 189) notes that *tabu* shell money was commonly traded with Europeans on the Gazelle Peninsula in the early days of contact when it 'had an important spiritual significance because its distribution in mortuary ceremonies established relations with ancestral spirits', opening up the possibility that relations with Europeans were seen to be analogous to connections to the ancestors. Kuchler sees the *malanggan* of northern New Ireland as part of a class of sacrificial objects, and discusses their sale to Europeans in the following terms: 'In Melanesia, sacrificial economies developed alongside millenarian and cargo cult movements as the sale of sacrificial remains to western collectors proved early on to be a successful means to open the road to the ancestors that was thought to be blocked by the white man' (Kuchler 1997: 49), a point also made by Kaplan (1990) and Kaplan and Kelly (1994) for Fiji. The last of our categories is where people deliberately produced objects which would have been attractive to whites. The best documented case of production for sale to whites comes from Manus and it is worth discussing in some detail.

In two articles Torrence (1993, 2000) has laid out a clear and convincing argument that, between the nineteenth century and 1990, Admiralty Islanders shifted the production of obsidian daggers and spears from local exchange and consumption to production chiefly for sale to Europeans. Torrence quotes Moseley (1892: 231) who says that all sorts of badly made objects were offered to the people on the *Challenger* expedition. Torrence analysed some 1,500 specimens in various museums around the world and based her results on a sample of these. Over time Manus people modified the form and decoration on daggers and spears both to please European taste (collectible items were made attractive on the basis of European notions of savagery) and to allow greater efficiency of production. Less effort was put into the production of the obsidian blades until their production ceased altogether and only recycled blades were used (Torrence 1993: 476) and decoration was simplified (Torrence 1993: 475). From 1940 onwards daggers are mainly mass-produced, and 'It seems the producers diversified into two classes: a cheap momento or small ornament for the tourist or low-income collector and a large, elaborate, expensive object for the serious collector' (Torrence 1993: 477). Here the impact of the enormous numbers of troops passing through Manus in the Second World War can be seen. It would be interesting to extend the scope of Torrence's analysis to include changes in other items over the same period of time. Carrier and Carrier (1991: 71) note that the level of labour recruitment in Manus generally meant those left in the villages had to devote more of their time to food production, with the result that the production of valuables began to decline and trade systems throughout the province started to decay. Mead (1963 [1930]:231) noted that by the late 1920s less labour was devoted to carved beds and bowls, breaking up exchange networks and accelerating the up-take of Western manu-factures. How daggers and spears fit into these broader changes in material culture (see Ohnemus 1998) might tell us much about the motives for producing them.

Other well-documented examples of production for sale to Europeans are few. A further possible example of an object produced for sale to Europeans is the 'man-catcher' so finely analysed by O'Hanlon (1999). The whole point of O'Hanlon's article is to show the multiple roles and contexts that objects can have, but he does raise the possibility that 'man-catchers' might have been deliberate fabrications by those on the Papuan Gulf to provide objects that would attract the recognition of early colonial agents who thought themselves to be in cannibal country (O'Hanlon 1999: 394). However, there is no direct evidence in this case for the large-scale production of these objects specifically for sale to whites. Campbell (1984: 62–5) on the other hand does document how Trobriand crafts-people started to produce carvings for Europeans using the missionaries as intermediaries. Kiriwinans not only made a variety of carvings, but also produced small tables for Europeans to put these carvings on. In the early 1920s such forms were promoted by Mrs A.C. Lumley, the wife of a trader on Kiriwina Island, who encouraged to carve people who had not done so previously; 'In so doing, she cut across the indigenous boundary separating carver from non-carver and craftsman from artist' (Campbell 1984: 64). The occupation of the Trobriands by Allied troops during the Second World War provided further outlets for carving, and in the 1950s the Kuboma Progress Society was formed to market the art and channel the money earned from it into local projects (Campbell 1984: 65).

In all our cases except the first, white collection would have increased the level of production. Colonial collection represented a new level of demand and was part of the often-recognized effloresence of trading systems within Papua New Guinea. Kuchler (1997) estimates that there are over 10,000 *malanggan* in museum collections and another 5,000 in private hands (Kuchler 1997: 40). It is ironic that so much of the anthropological literature on New Guinea in the twentieth century concerns gift exchange, and yet it contains so little recognition of the effects of anthropologists and other white people on the level of exchange of objects.

We have dwelt so far on varieties of forms of production for exchange with whites. There was also much variety in the use of European objects within local systems. Very often European goods, because they were obtained through short-term contacts with traders or collectors, could provide the basis for individual (and individualizing) strategies of exchange and could be lent or sold to other local people at will. As far as we can tell, this was the case in the Arawe area, and European goods never became incorporated into socially marked exchanges to do with community rituals. Foster (1995: 243–4) shows that in the island of Tanga, off New Ireland, in the 1920s and 1930s local big men fed money and trade goods obtained by younger men into competitive exchange networks, which was thought to be destabilizing the whole system. The Tangan community then decided to exclude Western goods from exchanges and defined an area of *Kastam*, the province of a newly recognized traditional forum for exchanges, which was the province of the lineage, as against the commercial transactions of *bisnis* linked with households. *Kastam* was not so much an invention of tradition as a sharper definition of internal community relations, as opposed to links to the wider colonial society which were more difficult to control. The exclusion of Western goods from socially important exchanges contrasts with the Highlands where Toyota Landcruisers and money have been incorporated into brideprice and ceremonial exchange, as we shall see below. We wonder whether the more traumatic circumstances of nineteenth-century forms of colonialism, compared with that in the Mandated Territory of New Guinea under the watchful eye of the League of Nations, led people to be wary of whites and the goods they brought. Exchanges in coastal regions passed through semi-permeable membranes, which let white goods into some areas of society and not others, as opposed to the more open circumstances in the Highlands. Such a distinction does not quite hold good of course, as Counts and Counts (1970) note for Kaliai on the north coast of New Britain where money was allowed as part of brideprice, in marked contrast to the situation in Arawe.

What disrupts our embryonic typology is the feeling that none of these strategies was fixed in time or necessarily confined in space. Exchanges and ritual links with Europeans were more in the nature of a social experiment. It was difficult to tell what forms of relationship were possible or desirable with whites and what the outcomes of relationships would be. We have the impression that each of our four collectors had rather varying social skills when it came to local people, and whereas Blackwood might have had good relationships with people in the main, perhaps those of Todd were rather more nervous and restricted. In setting up varying relations, Lewis, Speiser, Todd and Blackwood represented only a small portion of the relationships that made up colonial New Guinea. All parties to exchanges were trying to realize some goal, without often being clear what that goal was, or how it might be attained. The lack of a clear sense of future outcomes and the absence of well-defined patterns of interaction gave meetings a trial-and-error feel, which of itself generated variety.

We have noted both similarities and differences in the sorts of relationships set up within colonial culture in New Guinea. We have yet to look at a more profound set of origins of regional difference deriving from ancient regional traditions. As a means of establishing, rather than exhausting, the point that there is considerable diversity in Papua New Guinea dating back to early periods, we will contrast the prehistory of western New Britain and the Vitiaz Strait on the one hand with that of the Highlands on the other. Quite different histories could be found by concentrating on the other areas. For instance, the Sepik has a special trajectory of its own in both prehistoric and colonial times, which can be glimpsed in the archaeological work of Swadling (1997) and her team and the historical ethnography of Gewertz (1983).

The *longue durée* in Papua New Guinea

Papua New Guinea has been occupied by people for at least 35,000 years, and the island of New Britain was also settled around that time (Pavlides and Gosden 1994). Right from the start there appear to have been regional variations in the way people lived, with island life being based around sea-faring from an early stage (Gosden 1994b). Certainly for the last 10,000 years there is quite marked regional diversity and evidence that intensive systems of food production started in the Highlands not long after this date, in contrast to the evidence from elsewhere. Given such a long history, with diversity evident for much of it, we want to make the point that there was no single originary state of human affairs in Melanesia from which diversity developed; rather it is diversity all the way down.

Due to our western New Britain focus, we will start with the prehistory of the region, before looking at other coastal regions and then a much broader contrast between the Highlands and coastal regions, before returning to New Britain again with a new appreciation of variability.

The Prehistory of Western New Britain and the Vitiaz Strait

As we mentioned above, New Britain was occupied by people for the first time at least 35,000 years ago, a history it shared with the neighbouring islands of New Ireland and Bougainville (Gosden 1994b; Pavlides and Gosden 1994). Although people utilized inland resources, they were adept at travelling by sea from an early stage, and island life was as much sea-based as restricted to the land (Gosden and Robertson 1991). Right from the start of human occupation the ability to travel by sea was a central feature of people's lives.

The main evidence we have of the long-term occupation of New Britain comes from the interior rainforest area. Here work by Pavlides (1999) has revealed a series of archaeological sites stretching back 35,000 years which are stratified between a series of volcanic ashes. An analysis of the form of the stone-tool technologies leads Pavlides to the opinion that a highly mobile and low-density population occupied the rainforests of New Britain for most of this period, although the degree of mobility gradually declines through time. In the last 1,000 years a settlement pattern of scattered hamlets and some gardening seems to have been set up, which was essentially the same as that found by Chowning and Goodale during their fieldwork in the 1960s (Pavlides 1999: 407). At no point in this history is there evidence of intensive food production.

On the coasts of western New Britain there is evidence of continuous and fundamental change. There is little very early evidence from the coast as compared to the inland. From just over 3,500 years ago, the prehistory of the coast comes into much sharper focus compared with earlier periods.

Let us follow the history of Arawe life back to the Lapita period (Gosden and Webb [1994] give a summary account of the evidence from Lapita and later periods). Lapita sites are found from Manus in Papua New Guinea out to Tonga and Samoa in the east and are characterized by similar forms of pottery (Fig. 9.1), worked shell and stone (including obsidian and polished axes) together with a range of other portable artefacts, plus animals such as the pig, dog and chicken. There is much debate about the nature of the Lapita phenomenon. We feel that that Lapita distributions do not represent a series of land-based communities linked by exchange, rather the Lapita phenomenon may provide evidence of one super-community of immense scope stretching from island Papua New Guinea out to Tonga and Samoa, and this was made a community through continual sea movements. Our reasons for putting forward this idea come from the archaeological data, in which the locus of change in material culture is in the whole rather than the parts. From the Bismarck Archipelago to Tonga and Samoa 3,500 years ago

Figure 9.1. Lapita pottery excavated in the Arawe Islands in 1989 (La Trobe University, Melbourne)

there was a design suite with marked regularity both in the elements of decoration and their means of layout on the pot (see articles in Spriggs 1990). This suite of designs was combined with a limited set of forms. The most striking aspect of the pottery assemblages is not simply their widespread nature, but the fact that similarities are maintained through time by contemporary changes in widely spread regions. The initially complex forms of dentate stamping found over 3,500 years ago become simpler with the passage of time and eventually give way to incised and applied decorations. This happens not at single sites but throughout the area from the Bismarck Archipelago to Vanuatu and maybe beyond to Tonga and Samoa. The locus of larger cause within the area resides at the level of the Lapita phenomenon as a whole, with continual contact leading to co-ordinated changes.

In western New Britain, and focusing mainly on pottery assemblages from the Arawe Islands, Summerhayes (2000) has analysed the raw materials used to make Lapita pots, together with their form and decoration, to show that each local area has a slightly different suite of pots made from local raw materials and with minor differences of decoration. There was very little exchange of pottery, and he feels that pottery was made by intinerant potters, moving between communities which themselves may have had some degree of mobility (Summerhayes 2000: 234–5).

The lack of trade, despite basic similarities of pottery forms and decorations, signals the movement of information and the commonality of custom in the area as a whole. Although pottery did not move very much, the volcanic glass, obsidian, did, with one source in the Talasea region (Kutao-Bao) furnishing the majority of the obsidian found in the Arawes, not just in the Laipta period but through to the start of the twentieth century (Summerhayes 2000: 234). We can only wonder what sort of social connections were involved to maintain the Arawe's links to one particular obsidian source for over 3,500 years, when there were other sources available which yielded obsidian of similar quality.

The Lapita period came to a gradual end around 2,000 years ago. Paradoxically, the more recent prehistoric periods are less easy to recognize archaeologically and are not so well understood. The situation in the post-Lapita period is dominated by the eventual rise of specialized exchange systems known in the present, which means for this region the system of exchange organized by the Siassi Islanders (Harding 1967; Lilley 1988), although it must be noted that recent exchange systems may be linked into systems of exchange linking New Guinea with south-east Asia (Swadling 1996).

Lilley carried out a programme of archaeological research in Siassi and on the north coast of New Guinea, and his findings were complex. However, a number of points stand out. The first demonstrated occupation of the Siassi islands occurred within the Lapita period, with a site on Tuam dating to c. 2,800 BP. There is then a break in the sequence until c. 1,600 BP when there is evidence of the movement of pottery, obsidian and probably chert across the Vitiaz Strait, although this is likely to have been at much lower volumes than in the historically known period. Lilley (1986: 470–1) speculates that this could have been because the social structure within which trade was embedded was different. The modern system as documented by Harding may only have an antiquity of 200–300 years, with a maximum of 500 years. The real efflorescence of the system may only have occurred within the colonial period. These results are important as they necessitate caution in projecting the ethnographically known situation too far back into the past. It is interesting to note in passing that many of the specialist trading systems of coastal Papua New Guinea seem to have grown up in the last 500 years (Allen 1984).

There are two forms of prehistory in western New Britain. Inland areas always seem to have been inhabited by small mobile groups moving amongst the dispersed resources of the rainforest. They do not seem to have been involved in the Lapita forms of interaction or the specialist trade of later periods, although they did receive obsidian from the north coast from an early date. Communication and later trade has, by contrast, been the key to the history of the coast. During the Lapita period New Britain was part of a network of connections covering the whole of the western Pacific, and these gradually declined in scope. During the last 500 years there has been the rise of specialist traders, bringing about more localized and possibly more intense forms of interaction, and here the Siassi Islanders were just one of a series of specialist trading systems found throughout coastal Papua New Guinea. However, there are similarities found also between the coast and the inland. In neither part of New Britain was there ever any emphasis on intensifying agriculture or the large-scale production of pigs. In fact, for much of prehistory people may have been closer to a hunter–gatherer lifestyle with cultivated food acting as a supplement to the wild. Over the last 1,000 years in both coast and inland has grown up a settlement pattern based on small hamlets, which only ended with the colonial period in some areas. In the absence of the intensification of a wealth economy, the emphasis in New Britain has been on widespread, flexible contacts and perhaps control over information and knowledge (see Goodale's 1995 discussion of the importance of knowledge to the Kaulong). This lack of emphasis on the large-scale production of wealth created a very different past and present to that of the Highlands.

Prehistory in western New Britain provides the key to the creation of colonial culture. Connections between different areas and flexibility in social networks is inherent in ways of life from the Lapita period onwards. These were given new form over the last 500 years with the rise of specialist trading systems based on Siassi and Tami. From at least this period onwards there is a marked regional division of labour, with various parts of the region producing different items, be they pots, obsidian, dog's teeth or forms of ceremony. Variability in production provided reasons for exchange, although exchanges did not take place through the massive ceremonial transactions of the Highlands. Exchange would have broken down without regional differences in production, and this may help to explain why objects change so little in the colonial period: each object that dropped out of exchanges disadvantaged the communities which produced it and jeopardized the network as a whole. Similarly, allowing Western goods into socially marked exchanges to any great extent could have eroded vital regional differences. The exchange networks have been preserved and expanded, becoming the means through which objects and people have flowed, which have supplied the community-based forms of ritual vital to working through the puzzles about community posed by colonial culture.

The Highlands

The long-term history of the Highlands concerns people's relationship with land and intensive food production. The Highlands can mean different things to different people, but here we concentrate on the inter-montane valleys between 1,200 and 1,800 m which have the densest populations in Papua New Guinea and some of the most intense agricultural and exchange systems. Feil (1987) has demonstrated the variability within Highlands societies, concentrating especially on the differences between the eastern and the western Highlands. People have been in the Highlands for at least 30,000 years, and from 20,000 years ago there are indications of human burning to alter the structure of the vegetation (Haberle 1994: Table 8.1). The key to understanding the prehistory of agriculture and exchange in the Highlands is the site of Kuk in the Wahgi valley, excavated by Jack Golson since the 1970s (Golson 1977). The site is an important one in itself, but Golson has also argued that developments evidenced at Kuk are found more generally throughout the Highlands zone (see discussion in Bayliss-Smith 1996). In Kuk swamp there is evidence of agriculture by 9,000 BP, probably based on the cultivation of indigenous crops, such as taro, sugar cane and *Australimusa* bananas. Phases 2 (?6,000–5,500 BP) and 3 (?4,000–2,500 BP) show more organized and intensive use of the swamp, but real intensification occurs after 2,000 BP (Bayliss-Smith 1996: 509–10). Wetland cultivation is the most visible element of a broader agricultural system which also sees intensification of agriculture on the dry-land slopes above the swamps. Agricultural change is paralleled by, and probably linked to, evidence of trade and exchange. Axes and marine shells, both vital elements of exchange systems on contact, are found from 9,000 BP onwards. It is uncertain when pigs were introduced, with dates varying between about 6,000 BP to possibly only within the last 500 years (Bayliss-Smith 1996: 500). Intensive agricultural systems have a long and complex history in the Highlands and were developed not to supply greater numbers of calories for human consumption, but rather to provide the basis for pig herds, with pigs being important in all exchange ceremonies and marriage payments in the present and past. People were willing to work hard in the agricultural sphere because it was the basis for success in the exchange networks found throughout the Highlands. Another vital introduction is the sweet potato, which might have arrived at 1,200 BP, but is more likely to have come in the last few hundred years, as we shall see.

Sweet potato is vital as it brought about revolutionary change. Being more resistant to cold and poor soils, sweet potato can be grown at higher altitudes and in less favoured soils than taro. Sweet potato is important not in itself, but because it can support pigs. The extension in the areas on which sweet potato could be grown meant that higher areas and those without access to high-yielding wetlands were better able to support pig herds and to engage in exchange.

Golson (1982) has combined historical ethnography and archaeology in looking at the intersection of agricultural intensification and white contact in the Wahgi valley in the Highlands. Drawing on accounts of missionaries who entered the Wahgi soon after the first European contact in 1934, Golson describes a society with inherited, not achieved, status. Vital in creating and maintaining status were marine shells, exchanged from group to group between the coast and the Highlands. In the pre-contact period, links were so attenuated and difficult that few shells made it through into the western Highlands, and only people with high rank had the trade connections necessary to achieve a steady supply. Shells were vital to wealth payments in many areas of life, including initiation, marriage and mortuary ceremonies, and the bulk of the population was dependent on those with access to shells in order to make the right types and amounts of payments.

When the first gold miners entered the area after 1934 they flew in several million shells from the coast in order to pay their workers. Suddenly all ranks of people had direct access to shells in some number, causing the collapse of the hierarchical social structure and its replacement by a set of exchange relations between relative equals. Change is not a product of colonialism alone, and Golson goes on to show that the introduction of the sweet potato, either 1,200 years ago or in the last few centuries, may have caused a similar democratization to that brought about by the introduction of large numbers of shells in the 1930s.

A complement to this argument is contained in Wiessner and Tumu's (1998) massive treatment of Engan oral history. Some eight to ten generations ago, the Enga started consciously compiling a body of historical traditions to understand the history of each tribe and their inter-connections (Wiessner and Tumu 1998: 2). Wiessner and Tumu's work, which draws on interviews from people in all one hundred tribes of Enga speakers, lays out a structure to Engan history spanning at least the last 400 years. Within that time the sweet potato was introduced, and this brought complex changes in different parts of Enga, but overall caused a population explosion from some 10,000–20,000 people some 400 years ago to over 100,000 some 220 years later (Wiessner and Tumu 1998: 355) with continued growth to some 200,000 people today. This saw a shift from agriculture, complemented by hunting and gathering, which took place in a sparsely populated landscape, to the intensive forms of agriculture in a densely packed landscape, as is found today (Wiessner and Tumu 1998: 1). Inter-group dynamics became much more complex, but there is little evidence of greatly increased warfare over the last 400 years. Instead, the stresses of inter-group competition were mediated through exchange networks, especially the *Tee* exchanges, which started in eastern Enga and spread throughout the region. The changes precipitated by the introduction of the sweet potato were so great that the networks along which wealth and knowledge flowed needed to be restructured each generation (Wiessner and Tumu 1998: 3). In all areas, however, the greatest changes occurred in the raising of pigs, whose social and symbolic value rose throughout the last 400 years (Wiessner and Tumu 1998: 360). This increased intensification led to the rise of leaders who could organize agricultural production, finance exchange events and the theatre involved in their staging, and who could keep up with the flows of knowledge throughout the region. Constant change has made Engan society open to change, experiment and the import of cults and ideas. Rituals were regularly purchased from neighbouring groups and these were very important historically in providing new values attached to relations between people and things and novel emotional and intellectual environments relevant to changed circumstances (Wiessner and Tumu 1998: 361–3). By contact with the first patrol, that of the Sepik-Hagen patrol (Gammage 1998), the fabric of Engan society was strained by pressure on land, the levels of work needed to support pig herds and put on ceremonial events, and competition between groups.

Amongst the Huli, the southernmost Enga speakers, the work of Ballard (1995), which can be characterized as historical ethnography, has revealed a picture in which people have a very definite attachment to land. This attachment is anchored in genealogies which are remarkable in their time-depth, going back some twenty-four generations, telling a consistent story which can be traced over large areas of the Tari Basin. Ballard collected a huge amount of genealogical information, which became the basis for a history of the Huli. Over a maximum period of 500 years the genealogies outline rights to the ditches which are used to drain the swamps of the Tari Basin, plus the ability of individuals to participate in ritual and trade. Individual ditches are named after known individuals, often the people who dug them, so that a map of the ditches also forms a map of the historical social landscape. These ditches were used for growing taro, which only in the last two centuries has been supplemented by sweet potato, and this forms the basis for pig herds, which are central to exchange systems in Tari. Again, sweet potato has brought about massive changes in Huli society since its introduction around 250 years ago. At this time, people were already engaged in intensive agriculture, and the pig was the principal valuable (Ballard 1995: 246). But again the sweet potato brought about rapid population increase and a greater concentration on intensive wetland agriculture than previously, with the main use of the swamp in the Tari basin dating to the 1840s and 1850s (Ballard 1995: 175). The changes in the wealth economy encouraged new forms of leadership and ritual, especially the *tege pulu* which involved the exchange of much larger numbers of pigs than in any previous form of ritual and was controlled by secular leaders, unlike the older ritual forms which could only be conducted by hereditary specialists (Ballard 1995: 241–6).

These examples show that in many areas of the Highlands society was totally reordered in the few hundred years before contact with Europeans and that many of the features of Highlands with which we are familiar from ethnographies, such as massive pig production, large staged exchanged events and charismatic male leaders, may be relatively recent. The Highlands had one of the shortest colonial periods of anywhere in the world, lasting from the mid-1930s (or later) until 1975. Nevertheless, considerable changes took place (see Strathern 1984). Of interest to us is the instability of exchange media, which, with the major exception of pigs, have altered continuously since the 1930s. As Wiessner and Tumu (1998: 375) point out, the predominance of pigs as the dominant means of providing war reparations and marriage payments is relatively recent. 'In the early generations of Enga oral history, trade goods and valuables, land and the products of the hunt filled this need. Pigs began as a supplementary component and gradually moved into a prominent position' (Wiessner and Tumu 1998: 375). All other valuables and objects must have been revalued by comparison with pigs. However, over the last few centuries pigs have been central to all other forms of exchange.

In looking at the axe-making activities of the Tungei group in the Wahgi valley to the east of Enga, Burton (1984: 139) noted the importance of axes in the wealth economy. The Tungei were axe makers until 1934, and prior to that period were able to contract a range of marriages with their neighbours, partly because they could supply axes for marriage payments. On average, five finished axes and eight rough-outs were given in each marriage payment before the Second World War (Burton 1984: 139). As the Tungei were able to produce up to 20,000 axes and rough-outs in a single quarrying expedition they were well-placed to attract marriage partners from other groups. By around 1940 axes had been replaced by shells in bride-price payments, due to the influx of shells brought by miners, discussed by Golson. Between 1940 and 1960 the Tungei's ability to attract marriage partners from outside the group declined, and Burton ties this decline to the cessation of the demand for axes. The relative advantages of other axe-making groups, such as the Jimi and Dom Gaima quarriers, also disappeared as axes were no longer needed. The disappearance of axes had little to do with replacement of stone by steel, but rather was connected with shifts in the wealth economy.

The shells, which replaced axes and other exchange media, did not retain their attractiveness for that long. In the Mount Hagen area, immediately west of the Tungei, the shells used in bride-price rose during the 1950s 'from just a few to as many as fifty' (Strathern 1984: 94). By the 1970s money began to figure more prominently in both marriage payments and *moka*, the ceremonial exchange system, with money gradually displacing shells. 'The last occasion I saw pearl shells given in Dei was in November–December 1973 when the leader Ndamba used them to pay Kaugel experts for their ritual services in a Female Spirit cult performance' (Strathern 1984: 92). For some thirty years, shells were vital in the most important exchange contexts, and many strove to convert pigs into shells, but from the 1970s onwards money and mass-produced items, such as Toyota Landcruisers, became central to prestigious forms of exchange, as they remain until today. The main source of money is from cash crops such as coffee. The emergence of money as an important element in the exchange system, has brought about something of a return to the intensive agricultural production characteristic of the longer-term history of the Highlands, but within a new context.

Varieties of Colonialism

The Highlands provide the best-documented examples of changes in wealth items, and this is only partly because so much changed since the 1930s when it could be documented by anthropologists. The relative instability of exchange media is due to the centrality that pigs have come to have over the last few centuries, so that pigs form the major item at all ceremonial exchange systems. As many have pointed out, the central historical nexus in Highlands society is intensive agricultural production for the support of large pig herds. While this remains central, other forms of wealth can come and go, as dictated by social and historical forces. Western goods and money have entered exchange networks and bride-prices in the same way that shells became central earlier last century. The introduction of new forms of wealth is not without its problems (see Strathern 1984), but does not threaten the logic of the system as a whole. The lack of intensive forms of agriculture to fund high levels of pig production in New Britain means that although pigs are important, so are lots of other forms of wealth. The regional production for exchange found throughout the area over which the Siassi move encourages stability in the forms of objects to be exchanged, a desire for conservatism increased by so many other basic challenges to the nature of community.

Foster (1995: 233) feels that Tangan society now operates through replication, whilst many Highlands societies are dominated by multiplication in which returns on exchange transactions always involve some increment or increase on the original amount given. In sketching out the general logic of Highland's multiplication, he agrees with Strathern (1982: 551): 'Highlands systems of prestige gift-giving do map themselves on to an introduced capitalist system in a remarkable fashion.' In the Highlands, commodity relations are put to the service of developing indigenous forms of circulation, whereas in Tanga the two are kept at arms length. These distinctions help explain why Highlanders are happy to incorporate initially foreign objects into their exchange systems, whereas others are not. In western New Britain the distinction between *kastam* and *bisnis* is not drawn in the same manner as in Tanga, although the exclusion of Western items and money from the exchange system is marked in both cases. In addition, there are other differences to be drawn between areas of Papua New Guinea, and these involve not how Western objects are incorporated into local systems of exchange, but the manner of exchange of local items to Westerners, which might be seen as the manner in which Westerners are incorporated into local systems.

What comes out of a consideration of prehistory in New Guinea is the need to embed the production and exchange of objects and the forms of sociability they can create within the longer-term histories of various regions. Each region has its own canons of acceptable behaviour and means of transforming objects into social relations. Faced with the shock of the new when colonial regimes were set up, each area drew on its own stock of traditions in creating guidelines for new forms of sociability with whites. Each tried to enfold whites and white power into local social forms, or set limits on the closeness of these relationships. Cargo cults and forms of exchange represent a huge series of social experiments in setting up novel colonial relationships, with all the courage that is involved in putting at risk values and objects that one holds dear.

Cargo cults and forms of exchange created arenas in which New Guineans could deal with Europeans on their own terms, and this created overall similarities of response across the region. The exact terms on which they dealt with whites were constructed though the long-term histories of different regions, and this made for diversity in colonial cultures. Running through all of these relations were problems of morality, and it is to these we finally turn.

−10−

The Morality of Colonialism

Moral issues are key to any consideration of colonialism. By what right one group of people attempts to control and govern another is a crucial question in recent world history, but it is not the moral dimension we highlight here. Rather the creation of a colonial culture in New Guinea reordered the moral universe for New Guineans, causing people to wrestle in thought and practice with problems of relationships. What sorts of relationship were proper and satisfying, and how did these relationships create the self on the one hand and community on the other? Furthermore, the arrival of newcomers with access to vast amounts of material wealth made local people feel excluded from the sources of this wealth. Access to wealth was a moral and ritual issue, being a question of occupying the right position in relation to ancestral and spiritual forces. These were philosophical issues concerning persons, property and social being, and caused the revaluation of all previous values.

There has been a long discussion about the uses of things in New Guinea, partly about the morality of exchange and the forms of sociability that can be set up through objects. Much of this discussion has concerned the nature of the split between gifts and commodities. The thought that New Guineans have gifts and Europeans commodities comes straight out of the old notion of a bipartite and divided colonial culture. Even if we allow that objects can change in their significances when they pass through different contexts (Thomas 1991), this does not allow us to think about the fluidity and flexibility of objects and their implications. Things in New Guinea were tools to create a series of complex social experiments whose outcomes were unknown. People, both black and white, were trying to see what qualities of things would appeal to others and what sorts of relationships could be built around objects. Questioning, probing and imagining were all central aspects of colonial social practice, so that it was hard to be satisfied or disappointed with any outcome as there were no fixed measures of expectation. Colonial culture was unstable, as well as experimental, as people tried to make real various desired outcomes, such as a link into the sources of power lying behind white wealth. But they were not quite sure what these outcomes might be or in fact how desirable they were. Far more experiment took place amongst New Guineans than amongst whites and New Guineans learnt much more deeply about all parties as a consequence. Here were the true anthropologists for whom the need to understand social relations and mores was most urgent and pressing. Things did not have fixed values attached within the colonial arena, but oscillated in a manner that threw all values into doubt.

Such oscillations happened within a specturm determined by local values, which set up the distinction between *kastam* and *bisnis* in Tanga, incorporated European goods into ceremonial exchange in the Highlands, brought about production of new objects for sale to Europeans in Manus, or maintained the stability of objects in the Arawe. To approach New Guinean gift exchange now as if up to 150 years of experiment had never happened is to miss too much.

People at the western end of New Britain have since the late nineteenth century undergone massive population decline, basic changes in settlement patterns and forms of subsistence, the constant movement of able-bodied men out of the community to work in towns and on plantations (and who return bringing Western goods), the expansion of exchange relations, and the re-orientation of forms of ritual. Change on such a scale has only happened in Europe with the Black Death or the Industrial Revolution. The predictions of the salvage paradigm seemed plausible a century ago: people might have lost the will to live altogether or embraced Western values as a road to social salvation. Instead, a much more remarkable thing happened. People drew on their local cultural resources to fashion a new way of life. In the Arawe region the strongly cognatic kinship system provided a flexible network through which people, objects and ideas moved. New forms of ceremony and expanded exchange relations created new arenas of social practice through trade and ceremony. These regional contacts formed not one network but several, through which ceremony, language and material culture all moved in slightly different ways and at slightly different times.

A Western view of history is often inclined to see settlement, subsistence and technology as our most basic element of life. In the Arawe region these things changed first and most easily, although people do now revert to smaller hamlets when possible. Material culture connected with ritual and trade was more stubborn, as both of these were to do with the values attached to relationships of all kinds and both of which were used to deal with whites, in all senses of the word 'deal'. Objects connected with ritual and trade lie at the heart of continuities, through which change was dealt with. Many objects have not altered in their formal characteristics, but as life has been restructured around them their significances have shifted. As we have pointed out, the Arawe responses created just one of numerous colonial cultures around New Guinea, as people constructed new forms of life consonant with their histories and in tune with new circumstances.

Colonialism opened up new sets of possibilities and constraints, necessitating novel strategies. Neither acculturation nor stasis were possibilities, so that new social forms arose when local social logics were put to the test in the social arena of colonial relations. This has led to unexpected outcomes for us the analysts who have found both more and less change than we thought. Colonialism in the Arawes brought about massive change around a kernel of continuity. Continuity was provided by the material things that we thought would be the main markers of change, whereas pretty well all other aspects of life shifted. This meant that the unaltered objects took on new values and operated in a much larger social arena. The embeddedness of objects in other aspects of life is vital, and we need not only to understand change in the objects themselves, where this occurs, but also to link stasis and change to life in general.

Things did not fall apart for New Guineans when whites arrived, but rather life was worked into new configurations, work that continues until today. NEW Guinea indeed.

Appendix

The following is a list of all objects examined in the four collections, counted and divided up into type of object and then grouped by category. The descriptions of all objects in the four collections we have analysed are available as four catalogues with photographs of some of the objects. These catalogues are available through the museums at which the collections are held and the Pitt Rivers Museum.

CATEGORY/OBJECT	LEWIS 1910	SPEISER 1930	TODD 1935	BLACKWOOD 1937	Totals
HUNTING/FISHING					
Fish spear	6	1		2	9
Pig spear	3	1			4
Bow and arrow				4	4
Blowpipe	3	4		4	11
Blowpipe darts	10	3		18	31
Blowpipe related specimens				4	4
Sling	9	1		2	12
Net (for birds)	2			1	3
Net (for pigs)		1	2		3
Net (for fish)	3	1	6		10
Net (no specified use)	1				1
Fishing float	1	3	1		5
Fish poison				1	1
Totals	38	15	9	36	98
WARFARE					
Shield	13	2	6	2	23
Club		2			2
Spear	28	5		2	35
Cassowary-bone knife/dagger	1	3	2	1	7
Totals	42	12	8	5	67
CRAFT PRODUCTION					
Child's head binding				1	1

CATEGORY/OBJECT	LEWIS 1910	SPEISER 1930	TODD 1935	BLACKWOOD 1937	Totals
Barkcloth beater	1	1		9	11
Barkcloth related specimens				13	13
Totals	8	2	1	25	36
AXES/OBSIDIAN					
Stone axe (unhafted)		2		19	21
Stone axe (hafted)	5	2	1		8
Stone adze (unhafted)				40	40
Stone adze (hafted)					0
Other stone tools				4	4
Haft for stone tool				1	1
Core	1			4	5
Obsidian flakes	1	2		15	18
Hammer stone				4	4
Pestle (stone)		2		2	4
Totals	7	8	1	89	105
FOOD PRODN & EATING					
Pestle (wood)	1	1			2
Mortar (wood)	1	1	1		3
Wooden spoon	4		2		6
Pottery vessels	6				6
Cassowary-bone spoon		3		2	5
Pig-bone spoon				2	2
Shell knife		3	15	3	21
Coconut scraper			1		1
Cooking accessories	2				2
Totals	14	8	19	7	48
CONTAINERS					
Lime gourd	2		1	1	4
Lime accessory	2		1		3
Knotted vine bag	12	5	18	6	41
Bilum			1		1
Coconut-leaf bag/basket	5	4	7	2	18
Coiled cane basket	17	1	8		26
Rattan basket	1				1
Totals	39	10	36	9	94

CATEGORY/OBJECT	LEWIS 1910	SPEISER 1930	TODD 1935	BLACKWOOD 1937	Totals
ORNAMENT & CLOTHING					
Skirt	7	4	27	6	44
Raincape	4	1	1		6
Pandanus mat			2		2
Barkcloth (decorated)	13	3	13	15	44
Barkcloth (undecorated)				1	1
Fibre waistband			1		1
Leg band				2	2
Neck ornament (various)	3	3	2		8
Filed-off shell neck ornament		1		2	3
Earrings (turtleshell)	5			2	7
Earrings (other)	1				1
Comb	1	1	4		6
Feather comb head ornament	4	6		3	13
Feather head ornament (no comb)	7	2		1	10
Headdress	6				6
Other head ornaments	2				2
Other hair ornaments	1				1
Snail-shell hair ornament		2			2
Woven armband	11	2	10	4	27
Other ornaments		1			1
Totals	65	26	60	36	187
VALUABLES					
Shell armband	4		1		5
Turtle-shell armband	2	1	1	1	5
Partly worked turtle-shell armband				1	1
Dog's-teeth headband			2		2
Dog's-teeth ornament			4		4
Nassa-shell ornaments			5		5
Cassowary-quill string	9		3	1	13
Pig's-tusk ornament	11	2		1	14
Cowry-shell mouth ornament	7	2	3		12
Mokmok	1	1		2	4
Singa			2	3	5
Gold-lip shell (decorated)	3	1	2	1	7
Gold-lip shell (undecorated)				2	2
Gold-lip shell (polished and cut)		1			1
Shell currency (various types)			1	4	5

CATEGORY/OBJECT	LEWIS 1910	SPEISER 1930	TODD 1935	BLACKWOOD 1937	Totals
'Tami' bowls	17		7		24
Mask (Kilenge type)	5				5
Totals	59	8	31	16	114
MUSICAL INSTRUMENTS					
Panpipes	7	2	10	5	24
Rattles	2	1		1	4
Bullroarer	4	2		2	8
Flute				2	2
Water flute		1		2	3
Bamboo whistle		3		2	5
Leaf whistle		1		2	3
Drum	11				11
Totals	24	10	10	16	60
MISCELLANEOUS					
Human skulls		2		12	14
Teeth-blackening substance	1	1		1	3
Dance stick (human bone)				1	1
Paddle	17	2	7	2	28
Paddle (toy)				1	1
Paddle related specimens				1	1
Canoe baler	1	1			2
Toy				6	6
Wooden model for canoe				1	1
Figure		1			1
Model snake				1	1
Mask (Kuiunke type)		3			3
Native salt				1	1
Paint	2			5	7
Paint brush/pen	2			3	5
Cosmetic	3	1			4
Medicine	2				2
Cooking accessories	2				2
Coconut water bottle	1		4		5
Pipe	3				3
Fire-making equipment				1	1
Totals	34	11	11	36	92
GRAND TOTAL	330	110	186	275	901

Bibliography

Archival Material

Australian Archives, Canberra
Australian Museum, Sydney
Australian War Memorial, Canberra
Cambridge University Library, Department of Manuscripts and Archives.
Field Museum of Natural History, Chicago
Museum der Kulturen, Basel
National Library of Australia, Canberra
Pitt Rivers Museum Photograph and Manuscript Collections, Oxford
SOAS Library and Archives, London

Secondary Sources

Allen, J. (1984), 'Pots and poor princes: a multidimensional approach to the role of pottery trading in coastal Papua', in S. van der Leeuw and A.C. Pritchard (eds), *The Many Dimensions of Pottery: ceramics in archaeology and anthropology*: 409–63 Amsterdam: University of Amsterdam Albert Egges van Gifford voor Pre- en Protohistorie.

Ballard, C. (1995), *The Death of a Great Land: ritual, history and subsistence revolution in the Southern Highlands of Papua New Guinea*, unpublished PhD dissertation, Division of Archaeology and Natural History, Australian National University, Canberra.

Bayliss-Smith, T. (1996), 'People–plant interactions in the New Guinea Highlands: agricultural hearthland or horticultural backwater?', in D.R. Harris (ed.), *The Origins and Spread of Agriculture and Pastoralism in Eurasia*: 499–523, London: UCL Press.

Blackwood, B.M. (1935), *Both Sides of Buka Passage*, Oxford: Clarendon Press.

—— (1950), *The Technology of a Modern Stone Age People in New Guinea*, Occasional Papers on Technology 3, Oxford: Pitt Rivers Museum, University of Oxford.

—— (1970), *The Classification of Artefacts in the Pitt Rivers Museum, Oxford*, Occasional Papers on Technology 11, Oxford: Pitt Rivers Museum, University of Oxford.

—— (n.d.), *Notes on Arawe Material Culture*, unpublished manuscript [PRM RDF 1938.36.1050–1334], Oxford: Pitt Rivers Museum, University of Oxford.

—— and P.M. Danby (1955), 'A study of artificial cranial deformation in New Guinea', *Journal of the Royal Anthropological Institute*, 85: 173–92.

Bulbeck, C. (1992), *Australian Women in Papua New Guinea*, Cambridge: Cambridge University Press.

Burton, J. (1984), *Axe Makers of the Wahgi: precolonial industrialists of the Papua New Guinea Highlands*, unpublished PhD thesis, Australian National University, Canberra.

Buschmann, R. (1996), 'Tobi Captured: converging ethnographic and colonial visions on a Caroline Island', *A Journal of Micronesian Studies*, 4, 317–40.

—— (1999), *The Ethnographic Frontier in German New Guinea (1870–1914)*, unpublished DPhil thesis, Department of History, University of Hawai'i.

Butler, J. (1993), *Bodies that Matter: on the discursive limits of 'sex'*. London: Routledge.

—— (1997), *Excitable Speech: a politics of the performative*. London: Routledge.

Campbell, I.C. (1998), 'Anthropology and the professionalisation of colonial administration in Papua and New Guinea', *The Journal of Pacific History*, 33: 69–90.

Campbell, S. (1984), *The Art of Kula: an analysis of the Vakutan artistic system and the rituals of Kula*, unpublished thesis, Australian National University, Canberra.

Carrier, A.H. and J.G. Carrier (1991), *Structure and Process in a Melanesian Society: Ponam's progress in the twentieth century*. Chur: Harwood Academic Publishers.

Chinnery, E.W.P. (1925), 'Notes on the natives of certain villages of the Mandated Territory of New Guinea', *Territory of New Guinea, Anthropological Reports Nos. 1 and 2*, Melbourne: Government Printer.

—— (1926), 'Certain natives of south New Britain and Dampier Straits', *Territory of New Guinea, Anthropological Reports No 3*, Melbourne: Government Printer.

—— (1927), 'The blow-gun in New Britain', *Man*, 27: 208.

Chinnery, S. (1998), *Malaguna Road: the Papua and New Guinea diaries of Sarah Chinnery*, Kate Fortune (ed.), Canberra: National Library of Australia.

Chowning, A. (1969), 'Recent acculturation between tribes in Papua-New Guinea', *The Journal of Pacific History*, 4: 27–40.

—— (1978), 'Changes in West New Britain trading systems in the twentieth century', *Mankind*, 11: 296–307.

—— (1996), 'Relations among languages of West New Britain: an assessment of recent theories and evidence', in Ross, M.D. (ed.), *Studies in Languages of New Britain and New Ireland, vol. 1: Austronesian Languages of the North New Guinea Cluster in Northwestern New Britain*: 7–62, Pacific Linguistics,

Series C-135, Canberra: Department of Linguistics, Research School of Pacific Studies, Australian National University.

Connolly, R. and R. Anderson (1987), *First Contact*, New York: Viking.

Coombs, A.E. (1994), *Reinventing Africa: museums, material culture and the popular imagination*, New Haven and London: Yale University Press.

Coote, J., C. Knowles, N. Meister and A. Petch (1999), 'Computerizing Oceania: some Pacific projects at the Pitt Rivers Museum, University of Oxford, England', *Journal of Pacific Arts*, 19/20: 48–80.

Counts, D.E.A. and Counts, D. (1970), 'The *Vula* of Kaliai: a primitive currency with commercial use', *Oceania*, 41: 90–105.

Dark, P. (1979), 'The art of the peoples of West New Britain and their neighbours', in S. Mead (ed.), *Exploring the Visual Art of Oceania*: 72–83, Honolulu: University of Hawai'i Press.

—— (1996), '[Review of] Cousins, J. 1993 "The Pitt Rivers Museum: a souvenir guide"', *Journal of Pacific Arts*, Nos. 13/14: 129–31.

Dobres, M.A. (2000), *Technology and Social Agency*, Oxford: Blackwell.

Downs, I. (1986), *The Last Mountain: a life in Papua New Guinea*, St Lucia: University of Queensland Press.

Elkin, A.P. (1943), 'Anthropology and the peoples of the South-west Pacific', *Oceania,* 14: 1–19.

Errington, F. (1988), Review of Frederik Barth: *Cosmologies in the Making, Man,* 23: 766.

Feil, D. (1987), *The Evolution of Highland Papua New Guinea Societies*, Cambridge: Cambridge University Press.

Firth, S.G. (1973), 'German recruitment and employment of labourers in the west Pacific before the First World War', unpublished DPhil thesis, University of Oxford.

—— (1977), 'German firms in the Pacific Islands 1857–1914', in J.A. Moses and P.M. Kennedy (eds), *Germany in the Pacific and the Far East 1870–1914*: 3–25, Brisbane: University of Queensland Press.

—— (1986), *New Guinea under the Germans*, Port Moresby: Web Books.

Foster, R. (1995), *Social Reproduction and History in Melanesia*, Cambridge: Cambridge University Press.

Freedman, M.P. (1970), 'Social organization of a Siassi Island community', in T.G. Harding and B.J. Wallace (eds), *Cultures of the Pacific*: 159–79, New York: The Free Press.

Gammage, B. (1998), *The Sky Travellers: journeys in New Guinea 1938–1939*, Melbourne: Melbourne University Press.

Gell, A. (1998), *Art and Agency: an anthopological theory*, Oxford: Clarendon Press.

Gewertz, D. (1983), *Sepik River Societies: a historical ethnography of the Chambri and their neighbors*, New Haven: Yale University Press.

Godelier, M. (1986), *The Making of Great Men: male domination and power amongst the New Guinea Baruya*, Cambridge: Cambridge University Press.

Golson, J. (1977), 'No Room at the Top: agricultural intensification in the New Guinea Highlands', in J. Allen, J. Golson and R. Jones (eds), *Sunda and Sahul: prehistoric studies in Southeast Asia, Melanesia and Australia*: 601–38, London: Academic Press.

—— (1982), 'The Ipomean Revolution Revisited: society and the sweet potato in the upper Wahgi Valley', in A. Strathern (ed.), *Inequality in New Guinea Highland Societies*: 109–36, Cambridge: Cambridge University Press.

—— and D. Gardner (1990), 'Agriculture and sociopolitical organisation in New Guinea Highlands prehistory', *Annual Review of Anthropology*, 19: 395–417.

Goodale, J. (1995), *To Sing with Pigs is Human: the concept of person in Papua New Guinea*, Seattle: University of Washington Press.

—— with A. Chowing (1996), *The Two-Party Line: conversations in the field*, Lanham: Roman & Littlefield.

Gosden, C. (1994a). *Social Being and Time: an archaeological perspective*. Oxford: Blackwell.

—— (1994b), 'Understanding the settlement of Pacific islands in the Pleistocene', in M.A. Smith, M. Spriggs and B. Fankhauser (eds), *Sahul in Review*, Occasional Papers 23: 131–43, Department of Prehistory, Australian National University, Canberra.

—— (1999). *Archaeology and Anthropology: a changing relationship*, London: Routledge.

—— (2000), 'On his Todd: material culture and colonialism', in M. O'Hanlon and R. Welsch (eds), *Hunting the Gatherers*: 225–50, Oxford: Berghahn.

—— and Y. Marshall (1999), 'The cultural biography of objects', *World Archaeology*, 31: 169–78.

—— and C. Pavlides (1994), 'Are islands insular? Landscape vs. seascape in the case of the Arawe Islands, Papua New Guinea', *Archaeology in Oceania*, 29: 162–71.

—— and N. Robertson (1991), 'Models for Matenkupkum: interpreting a late Pleistocene site from southern New Ireland, Papua New Guinea', in J. Allen and C. Gosden (eds), *The Results of the Lapita Homeland Project*: 20–45, Occasional Papers 20, Department of Prehistory, ANU.

—— and J. Webb (1994), 'The creation of a Papua New Guinean landscape: archaeological and geomorphological evidence', *Journal of Field Archaeology*, 21: 29–51.

Gray, A.C. (1999), 'Trading contacts in the Bismarck Archipelago during the whaling era, 1799–1844', *Journal of Pacific History*, 34: 23–43.

Guinness, W.E. (1936), *Walkabout*, London: William Heinemann.

Haberle, S. (1994), 'Anthropogenic indicators in pollen diagrams: problems and prospects for late Quaternary palynology in New Guinea', in J. Hather (ed.), *Tropical Archaeobotany: applications and new developments*: 172–201, London: Routledge.

Hahl, A. (1980 [1937]), *Governor in New Guinea*, ed. and trans. by P. Sack and D. Clark, Canberrra: Australian National University Press.

Hannerz, U. (1996). *Transnational Connections: culture, people, places*, London: Routledge.

Harding, T.G. (1967), *The Voyagers of the Vitiaz Strait*, American Ethnological Society Monograph 44, Seattle: University of Washington Press.

Harrison, S. (1993), 'The commerce of cultures in Melanesia', *Man*, 28: 139–58.

Hempenstall, P.J. (1978), *Pacific Islanders under German rule: a study in the meaning of colonial resistance*, Canberra: Australian National University Press.

Herle, A. (1998), 'The life-histories of objects: collections of the Cambridge Anthropological Expedition to the Torres Strait', in Herle and Rouse (eds): 77–105.

—— and S. Rouse (eds) (1998), *Cambridge and the Torres Strait: centenary essays on the 1898 anthropological expedition*, Cambridge: Cambridge University Press.

Hinsley, C.M. (1981), *Savages and Scientists: the Smithsonian Institution and the development of american anthropology 1846–1910*, Washington D.C: Smithsonian Institution Press.

Hogbin, H.I. (1932), '[Review of] "Ethnology of Melanesia" by A.B. Lewis', *Oceania*, 3: 114–15.

Hoskins. J. (1998), *Biographical Objects: how things tell the story of people's lives*, London: Routledge.

James, W. and N.J. Allen (eds) (1998), *Marcel Mauss: a centenary Tribute*, New York and Oxford: Berghahn Books.

Jeanneret, A. (1969), 'Aperçu historique du Musée d'Ethnolographie de Bâle', *Etudes Asiatiques*, 23, 1–2: pp. 58–68.

Kaplan, M. (1990), 'Meaning, agency and colonial history: Navosavakadua and the *Tuka* movement in Fiji', *American Ethnologist*, 17: 3–22.

—— and J. D. Kelly (1994) 'Rethinking resistance: dialogics of "disaffection" in colonial Fiji', *American Ethnologist*, 21: 123–51.

Kaufmann, C. (1996), 'Felix Speiser: ethnologist', in Speiser, F. *Ethnology of Vanuatu: an early twentieth century study*: 411–15, Bathurst: Crawford House Press.

—— (2000), 'Felix Speiser's fletched arrow: a paradigm shift from physical anthropology to art styles', in M. O'Hanlon and R. Welsch (eds), *Hunting the Gatherers*: 189–219, Oxford: Berghahn.

Keller, C.M. and Keller, J.D. (1996), *Cognition and Tool Use: the blacksmith at work*, Cambridge: Cambridge University Press.

Knowles, C. (2000), 'Reverse trajectories: Beatrice Blackwood as collector and anthropologist', in M. O'Hanlon and R. Welsch (eds), *Hunting the Gatherers*: 251–71, Oxford: Berghahn.

——— C. Gosden and H. Leinert-Emmerlich (in press), 'German collectors in southwest New Britain 1884–1914', *Journal of Pacific Arts*.

Kopytoff, I. (1986), 'The cultural biography of things: commoditization as process', in A. Appadurai (ed.), *The Social Life of Things: commodities in cultural perspective*: 64–91, Cambridge: Cambridge University Press.

Kuchler, S. (1997), 'Sacrificial economy and its objects: rethinking colonial collecting in Oceania', *Journal of Material Culture*, 2: 39–60.

Lattas, A. (1998), *Cultures of Secrecy: inventing race in Bush Kaliai Cargo Cults*, Madison: University of Wisconsin Press.

Lawrence, P. (1964), *Road Belong Cargo: a study of the Cargo Movement in the southern Madang District, New Guinea*, Melbourne: Melbourne University Press.

——— and M.J. Meggitt (1972), 'Introduction', in P. Lawrence and M.J. Meggitt (eds), *Gods, Ghosts and Men in Melanesia*: 1–26. Melbourne: Oxford University Press.

Lemonnier, P. (ed.) (1993), *Technological Choice: transformation in material culture since the Neolithic*, London: Routledge.

Leroi-Gourhan, A. (1943), *Evolution et techniques: l'homme et la matière*, Paris: Albin Michel.

——— (1945), *Evolution et techniques: milieu et techniques*, Paris: Albin Michel.

Lewis, A.B. (1922), *New Guinea Masks*, Department of Anthropology Leaflet no. 4, Chicago: Field Museum of Natural History.

——— (1923), *The Use of Sago in New Guinea*, Department of Anthropology Leaflet no. 10, Chicago: Field Museum of Natural History.

——— (1924), *Use of Tobacco in New Guinea and Neighboring Regions*, Department of Anthropology Leaflet no. 17, Chicago: Field Museum of Natural History.

——— (1925), *Decorative Art of New Guinea: incised designs*, Anthropology Design Series no. 4, Chicago: Field Museum of Natural History.

——— (1931), *Carved and Painted Designs from New Guinea*, Anthropology Design Series no. 5, Chicago: Field Museum of Natural History.

——— (1932), *Ethnology of Melanesia*, Department of Anthropology Guide part 5, Chicago: Field Museum of Natural History.

——— (1988), 'New Britain notebook', (ed.) R.L. Welsch, *Field Museum of Natural History Bulletin*, 59: 1–15.

Lilley, I. (1986), *Prehistoric Exchange in the Vitiaz Strait, Papua New Guinea*, unpublished PhD thesis, Department of Prehistory, Research School of Pacific Studies, Australian National University, Canberra.

—— (1988), Prehistoric exchange across the Vitiaz Strait, *Current Anthropology*, 29: 513–16.

McCarthy, J. K. (1963), *Patrol into Yesterday: my New Guinea years*, Melbourne: F.W. Cheshire.

Mair, L. (1970), *Australia in New Guinea*, Melbourne: Melbourne University Press.

Malinowski, B. (1922), *Argonauts of the Western* Pacific, London: Routledge & Kegan Paul.

Mark, J. (1980), *Four Anthropologists: an American science in its early* years, New York: Science History Publications.

Maschio, T. (1994), *To Remember the Faces of the Dead: the plenitude of memory in southwestern New Britain*, Madison: University of Wisconsin Press.

Mauss, M. (1979), *Sociology and Psychology: essays of Marcel Mauss*, trans. B. Brewster, London: Routledge & Kegan Paul.

Mead, M. (1938), *The Mountain Arapesh 1: an importing culture*, New York: American Museum of Natural History.

—— (1963 [1930]). *Growing up in New Guinea*, Harmondsworth: Penguin.

—— (1972), *Blackberry Winter: my earlier years*, New York: Morrow.

Melanesian Mission Annual Report (1935).

Melanesian Mission Annual Report (1937).

Moseley, H.N. (1892), *Notes by a Naturalist: an account of observations made during the voyages of H.M.S. Challenger*, London: John Murray.

Mudimbe, V.Y. (1988), *The Invention of Africa: gnosis, philosophy and the order of knowledge*, Bloomington: Indiana University Press.

Neumann, K. (1992), *Not the Way it Really Was*, Pacific Islands Monograph Series, No. 10. Honolulu: University of Hawai'i Press.

Oakes, L. (1988), *The Collection of J. A. Todd from New Britain, Papua New Guinea*, unpublished report, Australian Museum, Sydney.

O'Hanlon, M. (1993), *Paradise: portraying the New Guinea Highlands*, London: British Museum Press.

—— (1999), '"Mostly harmless?": missionaries, administrators and material culture on the coast of British New Guinea', *Journal of the Royal Anthropological Institute*, 5: 377–98.

—— and R. Welsch (eds) (2000), *Hunting the Gatherers*, Oxford: Berghahn Bboks.

Ohnemus, S. (1998), *An Ethnology of the Admiralty Islands: the Alfred Bühler Collection, Museum der Kulturen, Basel*, Bathurst, Crawford House Publishing.

Pacific Islands Monthly, 1934 Sydney, NSW. November 22.

Parkinson, R. (1907), *Dreissig Jahre in der Südsee*, Stuttgart: Strecker & Schröder.

—— (1999 [1907]), *Thirty Years in the South Seas*, trans. J. Dennison, Bathurst: Crawford House Press.

Bibliography

Pavlides, C. (1988), *Trade and Exchange in the Arawe Islands, West New Britain, Papua New Guinea*, unpublished Honours thesis, Department of Archaeology, La Trobe University, Melbourne.

—— (1999), *The Story of Imlo: the organisation of flaked stone technologies from the Lowland Tropical rainforest of West New Britain, Papua New Guinea*, unpublished Thesis, La Trobe University, Bundoora.

—— and C. Gosden (1994), '35,000 year old sites in the rainforests of West New Britain, Papua New Guinea', *Antiquity*, 68: 604–10.

Penny, G. (1998), 'Municipal displays: civic self-promotion and the development of German ethnographic museums, 1870–1914', *Social Anthropology*, 6: 157–68.

Petch, A. (1998), '"Man as he was and man as he is": General Pitt Rivers's collections', *Journal of the History of Collections*, 10: 75–85.

Reche, O. (1954), *Nova Britannia*, II. *Ethnographie*: A. *Melanesian*, Band 4. Hamburg: Ludwig Appel.

Ross, M. (1988), *Proto Oceanic and the Austronesian Languages of Western Melanesia*, Pacific Linguistics, Series C- 98, Canberra: Department of Linguistics, Research School of Pacific Studies, Australian National University.

—— (1989), 'Early Oceanic linguistic prehistory', *Journal of Pacific History*, 24: 135–49.

Rowlands, M. (1998), 'The archaeology of colonialism', in K. Kristiansen and M. Rowlands, *Social Transformations in Archaeology: global and local perspectives*: 327–33, London: Routledge.

Rowley, C.D. (1958), *The Australians in German New Guinea*, Melbourne: Melbourne University Press.

Rydell, R.W. (1983), *All the World's a Fair: visions of empire at American international expositions*, Chicago: University of Chicago Press.

Sack, P and Clark, D. (eds) (1979), *German New Guinea: the annual reports*, Canberra: Australian National University Press.

Schieffelin, E.L. and R. Crittenden (1991), *Like People You See in a Dream: first contact in six Papuan societies*, Stanford: Stanford University Press.

Schildkrout, E. and C.A. Keim (eds) (1998), *The Scramble for Art in Central Africa*, Cambridge: Cambridge University Press.

Schindelbeck, M. (1997), 'The art of the Head-Hunters: collecting activity and recruitment in New Guinea at the beginning of the twentieth century', in H.J. Hiery and J.M. MacKenzie (eds), *European Impact and Pacific Influence*, London: Tauris Academic Studies.

Schlanger, N. (1998), 'The study of techniques as an ideological challenge: technology, nation and humanity in the work of Marcel Mauss', in W. James and N.J. Allen (eds), *Marcel Mauss: a centenary tribute*: 192–212 New York and Oxford: Berghahn Books.

Sillitoe, P. (1988), *Made in Niugini*, London: British Museum Press.

Simpson, C. (1954), *Adam with Arrows: inside New Guinea*, Sydney and London: Angus & Robertson.

Smith, A. (1991), *Mollusc of the Ancient Mariner: shell artefacts: typology, technology and Pacific prehistory*, unpublished Honours thesis, Department of Archaeology, La Trobe University, Melbourne.

Smith, W.D. (1991), *Politics and the Sciences of Culture in Germany 1840–1920*, Oxford: Oxford University Press.

Specht, J. (1999), 'The German Professor': Richard Parkinson In R. Parkinson *Thirty Years in the South Seas*: xv–xxxi, Bathurst: Crawford House Press.

—— (In press), 'Traders and collectors: Richard Parkinson and family in the Bismarck Archipelago, Papua New Guinea', *Pacific Arts*.

Speiser, F. (1923), *Ethnographische Materialien aus den Neuen Hebrides und den Banks-Inseln*, Berlin: C.W. Kreidel's Verlag.

—— (1934), 'Observations on the cultural history of New Caledonia and the New Hebrides', *Man*, 34: 71.

—— (1936), 'Über Kunststile in Melanesien', *Zeitschrift für Ethnologie*, 68: 304–69.

—— (1938), 'Melanesien und Indonesien', *Zeitschrift für Ethnologie*, 70: 463–481.

—— (1941), *Kunststile in der Südsee*, Führer durch das Museum für Völkerkunde, Basel: Museum für Völkerkunde.

—— (1945), *Neu-Britannien*, Führer durch das Museum für Völkerkunde, Basel: Museum für Völkerkunde.

—— (1945/6), 'Kulturgeschichtliche Betrachtungen über die Initiationen in der Südsee', *Bulletin der Schweizerischen Gesellschaft für Anthropologie und Ethnologie*, 22: 28–61.

—— (1946), *Versuch einer Siedlungsgeschichte der Südsee*, Denkschriften der Schweizerischen Naturforschenden Gesellschaft vol. 77, Abh. 1, Zurich: Fretz.

—— (1996), *Ethnology of Vanuatu: an early twentieth century study*, trans. D.Q. Stephenson, Bathurst: Crawford House Press.

Spriggs, M. (ed.) (1990), *Lapita Design, Form and Composition*, Occasional Papers in Prehistory no. 19, Canberra: Department of Prehistory, Research School of Pacific Studies, Australian National University.

Stocking, G. (1995), *After Tylor*, London: Athlone Press.

Strathern, A. (1971), 'Alienation of valuables', *Oceania*, 41: 261–72

—— (1982), 'Alienating the inalienable' (correspondence), *Man*, 17: 548–51.

—— (1984), *A Line of Power*, London: Tavistock Publications.

Strathern, M. (1988), *The Gender of the Gift*, Berkeley: University of California Press.

—— (1993), 'Entangled objects: detached metaphors', *Social Analysis*, 34: 88–98.

—— (1999), *Property, Substance and Effect: anthropological essays on persons and things*, London: Athlone Press.

Summerhayes, G. R. (2000), *Lapita Interaction*, Terra Australis 15. Canberra: ANH Publications and The Centre for Archaeological Research, The Australian National University.

—— J. R. Bird, R. Fullagar, C. Gosden, J. Specht and R. Torrence (1998), 'Application of PIXE-PIGME to archaeological analysis of changing patterns of obsidian use in West New Britain, Papua New Guinea', in S. Shackley (ed.) *Archaeological Obsidian Studies: method and theory*: 129–58, New York: Plenum Press.

Swadling, P. (1996), *Plumes from Paradise*, Boroko: Papua New Guinea National Museum.

—— (1997), 'Changing shorelines and cultural orientations in the Sepik-Ramu, Papua New Guinea: implications for Pacific prehistory', *World Archaeology*, 29: 1–14.

Terrell, J. and R. Welsch (1991), 'Trade networks, areal integration, and diversity along the north coast of New Guinea', *Asian Perspectives*, 29: 156–65.

Thilenius, G. (1927), *Ergebnisse der Südsee-Expedition, 1908–1910*, Hamburg: Friedrichsen & Co.

Thomas, N. (1991), *Entangled Objects: exchange, material culture and colonialism in the Pacific*, Cambridge, Mass.: Harvard University Press.

—— (1994), *Colonialism's Culture: anthropology, travel and government*, Oxford: Polity Press.

Thurston, W.R. (1992), 'Sociolinguistic typology and other factors effecting change in north-western New Britain, Papua New Guinea', in T. Dutton (ed.), *Culture Change, Language Change – case studies from Melanesia*: 123–39, Pacific Linguistics Series C-120, Canberra: Department of Linguistics, Research School of Pacific Studies, Australian National University.

Todd, J.A. (1934a), 'Report on research work in South West New Britain, Territory of New Guinea', *Oceania*, 5: 80–101.

—— (1934b), 'Report on research work in South West New Britain, Territory of New Guinea', *Oceania*, 5: 193–213.

—— (1935a), 'Glimpses into daily life of the natives of New Britain', *Mankind*, 1: 278–9.

—— (1935b), 'Redress of wrongs in South West New Britain', *Oceania*, 5: 401–42.

—— (1935c), 'Native offences and European law in South-West New Britain', *Oceania*, 5: 437–60.

Torrence, R. (1993), 'Ethnoarchaeology, museum collections and prehistoric exchange: obsidian-tipped artifacts from the Admiralty Islands', in *World Archaeology*, 24: 467–81.

—— (2000), 'Just another trader? an archaeological perspective on European barter with Admiralty Islanders, Papua New Guinea', in R. Torrence and A. Clark (eds), *The Archaeology of Difference: negotiating cross-cultural engagement in Oceania*: 104–41, London: Routledge.

Tylor, E.B. (1871), *Primitive Culture: researches into the development of mythology, philosophy, religion, language, art, and custom*, 2 vols, London: John Murray.

Wallerstein, I. (1974), *The Modern World System, I*. New York: Academic Press.

—— (1980), *The Modern World System, II*. New York: Academic Press.

Welsch, R.L. (1988), 'The A.B. Lewis Collection from Melanesia – 75 years later', *Field Museum of Natural History Bulletin*, 59: 10–23.

—— (1996), 'Collaborative regional anthropology in New Guinea: from the New Guinea Micro-Evolution Project to the A.B. Lewis Project and beyond', *Pacific Studies*, 19: 143–86.

—— (ed.) (1998), *An American Anthropologist in Melanesia: A.B. Lewis and the Joseph N. Field South Pacific Expedition 1909–1913 Vol. I and II*, Honolulu: University of Hawai'i Press.

—— (1999), 'Historical ethnology: the context and meaning of the A.B. Lewis collection', *Anthropos (St Augustin)*, 94: 447–65

—— J. Terrell and J.A. Nadolski (1992), 'Language and culture on the north coast of New Guinea, *American Anthropologist*, 94: 568–600.

Wiessner, P. and A. Tumu (1998), *Historical Vines: Enga networks of exchange, ritual and warfare in Papua New Guinea*, Bathurst: Crawford House Publishing.

Williams, F.E. (1976), 'The Vailala madness and the destruction of native ceremonies in the Gulf Division', in E. Schwimmer (ed.), *Francis Edgar Williams: 'The Vailala Madness' and other essays*: 331–84, St Lucia: University of Queensland Press.

Wright, M. (1966), *The Gentle Savage*, Melbourne: Landsdowne Press.

Zelenietz, M. (1980), *After the Despot: changing patterns of leadership and social control among the Kilenge, West New Britain Province, Papua New Guinea*, unpublished PhD thesis, McMaster University, Ontario.

—— and Grant, J. (1981), 'Kilenge *Narogo*: ceremonies, resources and prestige in a West New Britain society', *Oceania*, 51: 98–117.

—— and Grant, J. (1986), 'The problem with *Pisins*', parts I and II, *Oceania*, 56: 199–214, 264–74.

Index

Index

earrings, 64

enchainment organiques, 19, 22

Enga, 203–5

exchange, 21, 84, 146, 150, 153, 158, 161, 167, 168, 170, 173, 177, 178, 179, 180, 181, 182, 183, 184, 185, 186, 190, 192, 193, 194, 195, 196, 197, 199, 200, 201, 202, 203, 204, 205, 206, 209, 210
  ceremonial, 135, 196, 205, 206
  commercial, 196

expeditions *see* collecting

explorers, 51, 52

fighting, 90, 113, 121, 177

fire-plough, 64, 163

First World War, 93, 95, 110, 169, 177

Firth, Raymond, 129, 131

fishhooks, 194

fishing *see* nets

Forsayth, 38, 80, 86

Fortune, Reo, 107, 131

gardens, 7, 22, 36, 39, 171, 172, 173, 177, 186, 198

Gasmata, 30, 34, 40, 58, 106, 109–10, 115, 132, 134, 136, 146, 150

Gazelle Peninsula, 28, 30, 32, 33, 34, 38, 51, 75, 194

Gell, Alfred, 18, 23

gender, 15, 71, 129, 141, 170
  see also women, Owas

gifts, 185, 209
  see also exchange

Godeffroy und Sohn, 32

gold-lip shells, 45, 59, 64, 86, 89, 93–4, 113, 135, 150, 153, 157–9, 163, 169, 182–3
  production of, 94

government officials, 79–80, 153

guns, 32, 38

Haddon, Alfred Cort, 107, 116

Hahl, Governor Albert, 33, 34, 51, 79, 80, 93, 95, 106

hair ornaments, 116

Hamburger Südsee Expedition, 52, 81, 95, 112

Harding, Tom, 184

head binding, 1–5 *passim*, 88, 115, 119–20, 146, 154, 157, 162

see also barkcloth

head deformation, 116, 125, 139

headdress, 30, 86, 87

Heidegger, Martin 18

Hernsheim and Co., 93

Holmes, Colonel, W. H., 39, 76

informants, 11, 81, 83, 98, 105, 109, 116–18, 139, 150
  see also Aliwa, Magnin, Owas,

initiation, 30, 119, 125, 178–9, 181, 190, 203

Japanese, 93, 107

Joseph N. Field South Pacific Expedition, 78

Kaliai, 7, 30, 45, 178

Kandrian, 30, 43, 58, 60, 86–8, 115, 133, 134, 145, 146, 150, 177, 181, 182, 186, 190

Kaulong, 35, 89, 95, 150, 157, 181, 182, 185, 201

Kilenge, 36, 41, 44, 90, 178

kin, 36, 39, 45, 134, 150, 151, 179, 181

kinship, 21, 27, 41, 47, 110, 116, 210

knives, 34, 58–9, 89, 149–50, 153–54, 158, 163, 167, 171, 173,

Koch, Harold, 146, 185

Komine, Isokichi, 92–5 *passim*

Komine's collection, 90, 93, 97

land, 32, 36, 114, 134, 190
  alienation, 34, 43
  rights, 22, 35

language, 28, 31, 97, 105, 115–6, 210

Lapita, 198–200

lavalava, 14, 16, 17, 158

Leroi-Gourhan, A., 18

Lewis, Alfred, 53, 59, 119, 124, 137, 139, 163, 169, 173, 178, 181, 185, 197
  and big man, 84
  and colonial society, 47, 79–80, 107, 143
  collecting practice, 18, 60, 71, 86, 90, 92–93
  early career, 75–6
  fieldwork of, 9, 78–86
  publications of, 82, 96
  return from the field, 95, 162
  see also Chicago Field Museum, Schoede

Lewis' collection, 86–8, 94, 96–7, 154, 155, 170, 172, 176–7